THE GOSPEL OF MARK

The Gospel of Mark

Authorship and Place of Composition

GABRIEL NIETO ZAHÍNO

RESOURCE *Publications* • Eugene, Oregon

THE GOSPEL OF MARK
Authorship and Place of Composition

Resource Publications
An Imprint of Wipf and Stock Publishers
199 W. 8th Ave., Suite 3
Eugene, OR 97401

www.wipfandstock.com

PAPERBACK ISBN: 978-1-6667-6718-6
HARDCOVER ISBN: 978-1-6667-6719-3
EBOOK ISBN: 978-1-6667-6720-9

Copyeditor: Nathan Rhoads.

03/06/26

To my parents,
Carmen and Ángel María,
and to my brothers,
Aingeru, Iñaki, and Réda

Contents

Abbreviations

Ancient Works

1 Apol.	Justin, *First Apologia*
2 Apol.	Justin, *Second Apologia*
1 Clem.	1 Clement
2 Clem.	2 Clement
2 Bar.	2 Baruch
א	Codex Sinaiticus
A	Codex Alexandrinus
Acts Pet.	Acts of Peter
A.J.	Josephus, *Antiquitates Judaicae*
Alex.	Plutarch, *Alexander*
Ascen. Isa.	Ascension of Isaiah
B	Codex Vaticanus
Ben.	Seneca the Younger, *De Beneficiis*
BH	Biblical Hebrew
B.J.	Josephus, *Bellum Judaicum*
C	Codex Bezae Cantabrigiensis
C. Ap.	Josephus, *Contra Apionem*
Comm. Jo.	Origen, *Commentarii in evangelium Joannis*
Comm. Matt.	Origen, *Commentarium in evangelium Matthaei*
Const. ap.	Apostolic Constitutions
Dial.	Justin, *Dialogus cum Tryphone*
Eph.	Ignatius, *Ad Ephesios*
Geogr.	Strabo, *Geographia*

Gos. Thom.	Gospel of Thomas
Haer.	Irenaeus, *Adversus Haereses*
Herm. Sim.	Shepherd of Hermas, *Similitudes*
Hist. Eccl.	Eusebius, *Historia Ecclesiastica*
Hom. Jes. Nav.	Origen, *In Jesu Nave Homiliae xxvi*
LXX	Septuaginta
Mag. Rom.	Ioannes Lydus, *De Magistratibus Romanis*
Magn.	Ignatius, *Ad Magnesios*
Marc.	Tertullian, *Adversus Marcionem*
Mart. Pol.	Ignatius, *Martyrium Polycarpi*
MT	Masoretic Text
NT	New Testament
OT	Old Testament
Pan.	Epiphanius, *Panarion*
Phil.	Polycarp, *Ad Philippenses*
Phld.	Ignatius, *Ad Philadelphos*
Pol.	Ignatius, *Ad Polycarpum*
Praescr.	Tertullian, *De Praescriptione Haereticorum*
PT	Palestinian Talmud
Rom.	Ignatius, *Ad Romanos*
Scorp.	Tertullian, *Scorpiace*
Smyrn.	Ignatius, *Ad Smyrneos*
Strom.	Clement Alexandrinus, *Stromateis*
Syb. Or.	Sibylline Oracles
Trall.	Ignatius, *Ad Trallanos*
Vir. Ill.	Jerome, *De Viris Illustribus*

Modern

AJN	*American Journal of Numismatics*
AJSLL	*American Journal of Semitic Languages and Literatures*
Archaeo	*Archaeofauna*
BA	*Biblical Archaeologist*
BASOR	*Bulletin of the American Schools of Oriental Research*
Bib	*Biblica*
BTB	*Biblical Theology Bulletin*

CBQ	*Catholic Biblical Quaterly*
CCGG	*Cahiers du Centre Gustave Glotz*
CIG	*Corpus Inscriptionum Graecarum*
CIIP	*Corpus Inscriptionum Iudaeae/Palaestinae*
CIL	*Corpus Inscriptionum Latinarum*
CurBR	*Currents in Biblical Research*
EncJud	*Encyclopaedia Judaica*
Elec	*Electrum*
ExpTim	*Expository Times*
HTR	*Harvard Theological Review*
IG Rom	*Inscriptiones Graecae ad Res Romanas Pertinentes*
ILS	*Inscriptiones Latinae Selectae*
JBL	*Journal of Biblical Literature*
JETS	*Journal of the Evangelical Theological Society*
JHS	*Journal of Hellenistic Studies*
JJMJS	*Journal of the Jesus Movement in His Jewish Setting*
JJS	*Journal of Jewish Studies*
JNSL	*Journal of Northwest Semitic Languages*
JR	*Journal of Religion*
JRS	*Journal of Roman Studies*
JSJ	*Journal for the Study of Judaism in the Persian, Hellenistic and Roman Periods*
JSNT	*Journal for the Study of the New Testament*
JTS	*Journal of Theological Studies*
NA[28]	Nestle-Aland, *Novum Testamentum Graece*, 28th ed.
NEAEHL	*New Encyclopaedia of Archaeological Excavations in the Holy Land*
NJB	New Jerusalem Bible
NovT	*Novum Testamentum*
NRSV	New Revised Standard Version
NTS	*New Testament Studies*
NumC	*Numismatic Chronicle*
NV	*Nova Vulgata*
PAAJR	*Proceedings of the American Academy of Jewish Research*
PL	*Patrologiae Cursus Completus*: Series Latina
QC	*Qumran Chronicle*
RB	*Revue Biblique*

REB	Revised English Bible
RHR	*Revue de l'Histoire des Religions*
SBL	Society of Biblical Literature
SCI	*Scripta Classica Israelica*
SPLP	*Stellenbosch Papers in Linguistic Plus*
StPatr	Studia Patristica
TynBul	*Tyndale Bulletin*
VC	*Vigiliae Christianae*
WH	Westcott-Hort New Testament

Introduction

ANYONE WHO ATTEMPTS TO cross the field of gospel criticism, to delve into it, must be shielded from the outset of his noble purpose with two elemental virtues, endurance and humbleness. The former prevents the overestimating of the difficulties, pervasive as they are, whilst the latter hinders the cross into the not-less-perilous soil, into clinging to one's own conclusions as if they were the last word in a meager profitable material business whose nature, not rarely, is subjected to a moderate degree of interpretation. Barrages of criticism are awaiting newcomers into the field if their work ever surpasses the line of anonymity. Consequently, every position which pretends to remain cemented in truthfulness crossing this line must have worked with the sources of information reached in the water table until their extinction.

Primary sources, the foundational rock-level of the gospel field where the stern trees of good proposals are clinched, are four: grammar—embracing, no doubt, the gospel text under its final form and all its composition history; traditions; archaeology with her partners epigraphy and paleography; and last but not least ancient literature. Strongly conservative positions in any of the exegetical grounds and trends leave a waxing bias to avoid one (or more than one!) of the salad's ingredients, reason whereupon in the twenty-first century, when the enormous amount of available critical studies turn the dialogue and the inclusiveness in methodology inexcusable obligations, can be classified as comfortable exegesis, or sofa-exegesis. Though, be that as it may, whatever position is built at the expense of others, nothing prevents that fragments of the truth were contained in partial trends, so for the modest researcher will always be worthy to open the door to almost any claim of truth and its contraries.

In the present monograph, the reader will taste the full salad, not permitting him to abandon the symposium of commensals without being more, or highly if he resists the chewing of the second and third dishes, attuned with the second gospel traditions and the intricacies of its diagnostic material. Indeed, the modest size of the work, intended to be such from the beginning, is inversely proportional to its deepness and inclusiveness in the ground of criticism. Beyond that, of course, the result of any research can be outdone by a future work; I have striven to grant all time possible to the reader to access the primary source material, deleting superficial theorization, ligating myself to the provision of solid food whenever the sources entail a taking of position, and finally offering him the cornerstones of my study, which alongside the conclusions are the materials, neatly arranged in packs of information, well within the text body, well at the footer, to be useful in his own creations, be he a scholar, a preacher, or a student.

I must confess that the occasion for the monograph was fortuitous. Some four years back, I invested several summer afternoons to the gospel reports on the empty tomb (Matt 28:1–8; Mark 16:1–8; Luke 24:1–12; John 20:1–10). Setting aside the Pauline account of Jesus' apparitions in 1 Cor 15:3–7, a report which quite problematically for mythologists allows one also to trace Jesus' burial from AD 55 well into the 30s (1 Cor 15:4)—though it is fair to place the gospel tomb accounts around AD 70 onwards—I applied a minimalistic criticism, removing by means of the dragnet of plausibility all details not common to the four gospel reports: the presence of several women (reduced to Mary Magdalene in John), the angel or angels announcing Jesus was not in the sepulcher (displaced in John), the earthquake (absent in Mark, Luke, and John), the guard keeping the entrance (lacking in Mark, Luke, and John), the vision of the wrappings (exclusive to Luke and John), and finally the presence of Peter in the tomb (shared by Luke and John). Applying the scissors as if I were a judge to whom it had been commissioned the task to reach the surest degree of truthfulness from an insurmountable case, I decanted the primitive traditional nucleus of the empty tomb accounts, namely, the common features of the four narratives: that the tomb where Jesus' corpse was laid was found open and empty in the second day after his death by at least one woman who had accompanied Jesus. Beyond this line form criticism works well, but before we should take into account that the evangelists considered there was a datum preceding them. They felt free to adorn the datum, possibly aiming to bolster, clarify, or enlarge communitarian beliefs, but they didn't substitute it.

In that study, as it was expected, it was also palpable that Mark, Matthew, and Luke had more in common in the tomb accounts than John with any of the three (especially if for Luke are taken the verses 24:1–9), and that Matthew and Luke report stronger heavenly interventions than Mark: the earthquake and Roman guards falling to the ground as if dead for fright before the angel apparition of Matt 28:2–4, and the angels who announce a long Easter message to the terrified women inside the sepulcher of Luke 24:4–7. Whereas the common source—most likely written—to the three synoptic accounts, Matt 28:1–8, Mark 16:1–8, and Luke 24:1–9, must be accepted, it is also difficult to conceive the reason why Mark should have lessened the literary effect of the events in Matthew and Luke if he had use any of the two as base for his narration, whereas Matthew and Luke are more easily explained by the natural reinforcement of Mark. Thence, one probable solution to the synoptic empty tomb comparison is that Mark is the first version of the three, or the least edited, regarding their common tradition.

In the free academic environment, when the final proof of whatever question related to religious authority is lacking, the field is fertilized for controversy. I halted the draft of what was intended to be an article I never published in that point, achieving the general taste of incompleteness, the feeling that this draft of eight pages was of little help if it was not seasoned with the scrutiny of the Greek text and was not warmed with the flame enlivened with the bibliographical bellows. Then, I returned my mind again to the lessons at the theological school where I heard that the first gospel to be composed was, according to twentieth-century criticism, Mark, and it was some weeks thereafter, in that while, when I forged the purpose to undertake the theological specialization in the shortest of the canonical gospels. The path to get this point could have been any other, but was got by this precise way, informal, but original and independent.

The present monograph's objective is the discernment of the second gospel authorship and place of composition, the assumed (certainly not for all) first gospel to be written under its final form. Issues concerning date throughout the work, and especially in the first chapter, are fully supplied, but my aim has been to avoid the discussion on the second gospel date under its final form as such, thinking that in a possible sequel monograph questions related to the composition of Mark 13, the Marcan priority theory, the synoptic problem, and other diagnostic material on the date will be attended. The reader won't find a handicap in this since a fully discussed span for the second gospel from ca. AD 70 to AD 130 stems from the analysis of the sources linked to the traditional image of Mark the evangelist in the first chapter, and deep examination over the date of particular Marcan sections in the remaining chapters, 2–4, are provided as well when they are necessary to discern the authorship and place of composition. In other words, this monograph focuses on the second gospel authorship and place of composition under the assumption of a ca. AD 70–130 date.

The monograph's topics are well known in Marcan exegesis, though unusually treated so profoundly, circumstance that has led to the avoidance of weird or extreme exegetical positions, contingency which not infrequently requested a shift in the argumentation whenever the evidence made me a call as the research moved forward. The work, which examines only and all the foremost available Marcan diagnostic material up to the early III AD, has pretended the highest level of certainty, almost always leaving open the door to contrary claims though inviting potentially them to assume criticism in the very motion that the reader's demand for additional knowledge is satisfied.

Chapter 1 is perhaps, to date, the most complete critical survey of the Marcan tradition from I AD to early III AD,[1] exhaustively gleaned under genetic perspective. Traditional reports and extant manuscripts are the earliest surviving witnesses to Mark. Avoiding their discussion would result in the avoidance of the historical substratum. The Marcan tradition was built onto two ancillary axes which in our pages will struggle against external criticism, Mark the interpreter of Peter, and Rome for the composition place.

The second chapter contemplates Mark under the Semitic magnifying glass, the Petrine gospel imbued of vivid Galilean reports though crossed by some geographical inconsistencies, discarding preferably Galilean authorship. Yet, the full Marcan account of Semitic features, largely illustrated by the LXX, Hebrew, and Aramaic examples, proves Semitic provenance. I have hesitated whether to encompass the detail of the Semitic grammatical fundamentals analyzed in this chapter within the main text body or rather to leave them for the parallel criticism. After much pondering, I have decided to entrust the reader to the full concordance for the Semitic Mark at the footnotes and give thirty-one lucid examples in ten categories ordered into functional grammatical list form in the main text body.

Mark from the Latin gaze is the topic of chapter 3. Eleven Latin loans in nineteen occurrences plus one Latin semantic loan and another possible Latin-fashioned neologism disclose a Romanized author and a probable Romanized I AD target audience, though not Italian and preferably circumscribed to a post-AD 70 context. The third chapter includes one of the most seer examinations of the Marcan simple parataxis (paratactic *καί*) against Latin, Hellenistic, LXX, and NT authors in current criticism. Chapter 3 has further taken the pain to compile the chief Latin Marcan diagnostic material and put it under dialogue with the archaeological outcome.

Chapter 4 begins with the critical summary of the Marcan tradition arisen from external and internal criteria, including deeper progression in

1 Following the convention in Spanish, centuries are denoted by Roman numerals.

several points. Though dressed with theological coloring, the likely Caesarean or Jerosolimite-Caesarean source detected in Acts, checked against the NT, especially Mark, against its internal Semitic interference, and against archaeology endures criticism, acknowledges itself as historical in character and provides the matrix for the grammatical Semitic and Latin features of the second gospel as well as the trigger for the two fundamentals proposed to examine, authorship and place of composition.

Lastly, a small remark on the bibliography and the critical apparatus should be offered before leaving the reader alone with the work, hoped to be something like an executive's suitcase that will make his own for his private devotion to Scripture or for his future interventions in public. The bibliography has been adjusted to consistent cited sources. As a rule, for the NT, including Mark, I follow the Greek text of the Nestle-Aland 28th edition, and for the OT, the LXX Rahlfs' edition and the *Biblia Hebraica Leningradensia*, edited by A. Dotan. Throughout the main text of the monograph the reader will not find practically any secondary author, being that this is devoted as much as it has been possible to the biblical world, to early Christian accounts, and to Greek-Latin authors from the classical period. Since the reconstruction of the second gospel genesis requires interpretation, secondary criticism is inescapable and thus dully supplied, but always at the footnotes. This difference has been established on purpose, granting the ancient sources the honor position in the line of discussion, breaking the trend in gospel criticism where not seldom secondary ones turn into the first object of attention. I eagerly wish this doesn't result in detriment of the authors' reputation, always acknowledged in the critical apparatus and which are so-called secondary only in reference to the more ancient sources, and excluding Scripture, for the major part never in merit.

Unless the contrary is pointed out, all the translations of Greek, Latin, and Hebrew texts are by the author, tending expressly to literality, word by word whenever possible.

1

External Evidence

Tradition and Scripture

The Testimony of Papias Hierapolite (AD 110–140)

THE CERTAIN MOST PRIMITIVE witness to the tradition on the origin of the second gospel is Papias, bishop of Hierapolis, today Turkish Pamukkale. Irenaeus states around AD 180 that Papias composed one single work in five treatises which collected earlier material under the name *Interpretation of the Sayings of the Lord.*[1] Depending on this work, the second gospel was written by Mark, the interpreter of Peter (Μάρκος μὲν ἑρμηνευτὴς Πέτρου).[2] According to Eusebius, the extant transmitter of Papias on Mark, since Irenaeus was more interested in other aspects of Papias' work, the Phrygian bishop received this tradition from John the Presbyter, a follower of the apostles.[3] In the book of Acts, the presbyters or elders (πρεσβύτεροι) are companions of the apostles (11:30; 14:23; 15:2,4,6,22; 16:4; 20:17; 21:28), different from the brethren (ἀδελφοί) in that they assumed the leading position in the assemblies or early churches (6:3; 9:30; 11:1; 21:7; 28:14–15).

1. Λογίων κυριακῶν ἐξηγήσεως (Irenaeus, *Haer.* 5.33:4). Depending on Irenaeus: Eusebius, *Hist. Eccl.* 3.39:1; Jerome, *Vir. Ill.* 18. Λογίων can be variously rendered *Oracles, Sayings, Deeds.* Papias' work included chiliast prophecies of the earthly paradise at Jesus' second advent to which Irenaeus gave credit (*Haer.* 5.33:3), favoring the first rendering, *Oracles.* Notwithstanding, *Sayings* is here chosen in concordance to the accepted translation of λόγια in the Jesus gospel tradition to which Papias must also be referred (for the Papias fragments, Ehrman, *Apostolic Fathers*, 2:92–118).

2. Eusebius, *Hist. Eccl.* 3.39:15.

3. Eusebius, *Hist. Eccl.* 3.39:3–7.

In the II century AD, the term *elders* is intended to mean the generation which received the apostolic teaching and handed it down to the next one.[4] Therefore, according to Eusebius, Papias belonged to the third generation of believers, John the Presbyter to the second, and the apostles to the first. When compared one with another, *generation* is a term that comprises, anyway, elastic boundaries.

Eusebius settles Papias, Ignatius, and Polycarp after the death of Clement Romanus in the third year of Trajan's rule (AD 98–117), whence the earliest dating for Papias' testimony would be around AD 100.[5] Papias is said to have known the daughters of Philip, which should've been of young age when Paul visited the Evangelist in Caesarea before his imprisonment, AD 57/58 (Acts 21:8–10).[6] This would have occurred in the last part of their life, counting sixty years from their birth, at the end of the I century AD as the earliest, most preferably first decade of the II. Since the daughters of Philip represent indeed the next generation to the apostles, Papias must be set within the third. Irenaeus makes Papias companion of Polycarp, who was burned in AD 155, being an aged man. Irenaeus calls Papias himself πρεσβύτερος, but later on distinguishes the technical meaning of elder, calling Papias "ancient man" (ἀρχαῖος ἀνῆρ).[7]

Papias and Polycarp thus represent the generation before Irenaeus, and after Clement Romanus; in other words, the generation born in the second half of the I century, whose heyday falls in the first part of the II AD, and whose end in the second half of the same century. The first mention of the tradition on the origin of the second gospel must be fixed accordingly around AD 130, ten to twenty years up down:[8]

4. Eusebius, *Hist. Eccl.* 3.39:6: καὶ ὁ νῦν δὲ ἡμῖν δηλούμενος Παπίας τοὺς μὲν τῶν ἀποστόλων λόγους παρὰ τῶν αὐτοῖς παρηκολουθηκότων ὁμολογεῖ παρειληφέναι (but the one we are now dealing with, Papias, confesses that he received the words of the apostles from their followers).

5. Eusebius, *Hist. Eccl.* 3.34:1; 36:1–2.

6. Eusebius, *Hist. Eccl.* 3.39:9.

7. Irenaeus, *Haer.* 5.33:3–4.

8. Yarbrough, "Date of Papias," 186–90 fixed Papias' work from AD 95 to 110, adducing five reasons and dissapproving any other later date: (a) Papias is set by Eusebius necessarily before the twelfth year of Trajan (AD 109) that opens the book 4 of his *Hist. Eccl.*; (b) Eusebius confirms this date in his other work, *Chronicon*; (c) Irenaeus considered Papias even more ancient than Polycarp; (d) for Irenaeus, Papias was a witness to the late John the apostle; (e) Papias' work ignores the Gnostic upheaval in AD 130. The less arguable are reasons (a) and (b) but the remainder hold some flaws since Irenaeus' words ἀρχαῖος ἀνῆρ (*Haer.* 5.33:4) don't unequivocally imply Papias was older than Polycarp, Irenaeus confused John the author of Revelation, who Papias likely knew (see discussion below) with John the apostle, and the Gnostic raising in AD 130 can be challenged by Ignatius letters and 1 John 2:18–23; 4:2–3; 2 John 7–10. The precision of

> And the Presbyter used to say this: that Mark became Peter's interpreter, (and) as far as he remembered, accurately wrote, but not in order, the things said or done by the Lord. For he neither heard the Lord nor he followed him, but afterwards, as I was saying, (followed) Peter: who before the necessities performed the teachings, but not as making an ordered compilation of the sayings of the Lord, so in no respect Mark erred when he wrote some things as he recorded them. For one thing did with caution, that no one which he heard left behind or falsify anything in them. These things, then, are narrated by Papias about Mark. (Eusebius, *Hist. Eccl.* 3.39:15)[9]

A key point for the preliminary understanding of the underground circumstances implicit to the passage is that Peter apparently was not with Mark when he wrote the gospel, because the materials came from Mark's memory and not from direct inquiry to Peter. Peter is seen no more with Mark, and when Mark is composing the gospel he appears to be looking at other people. This key point is quite interesting since the next certain correlate for the tradition, Irenaeus, seems to keep the difference between the time of Peter and that for the composing of the gospel, whereas the third certain witness to the tradition, Clement Alexandrinus, received it in a slightly different version. Depending on Papias, the date for the second gospel would then have followed the company of Mark with Peter, whose death usually is ascribed to mid AD 60s, the occasion for Peter's martyrdom in Rome according to tradition, placing the making up of the second gospel in the span of the second generation of believers.

On the other hand, the exam of another utterance of Eusebius on Papias and Clement Alexandrinus suggests that, though the bishop of Hierapolis states he received the tradition on the second gospel from John the Elder, an earlier connection between Mark and Peter could be 1 Pet 5:13, where Mark, a faithful fellow of the epistle's author, is named in the farewell.[10] Indeed, the expression Μᾶρκος ὁ υἱός μου (Mark my son) in 1 Pet 5:13 denotes

---

AD 95–110 hence should be accepted with reservations, i.e., as the *terminus post quem* for his work, especially if Papias must be considered representant of the third Christian generation who survived Ignatius, who died before AD 120.

9. καὶ τοῦθ' ὁ πρεσβύτερος ἔλεγεν· Μάρκος μὲν ἑρμηνευτὴς Πέτρου γενόμενος, ὅσα ἐμνημόνευσεν, ἀκριβῶς ἔγραψεν, οὐ μέντοι τάξει, τὰ ὑπὸ τοῦ κυρίου ἢ λεχθέντα ἢ πραχθέντα. οὔτε γὰρ ἤκουσεν τοῦ κυρίου οὔτε παρηκολούθησεν αὐτῷ, ὕστερον δὲ, ὡς ἔφην, Πέτρῳ· ὃς πρὸς τὰς χρείας ἐποιεῖτο τὰς διδασκαλίας, ἀλλ' οὐχ ὥσπερ σύνταξιν τῶν κυριακῶν ποιούμενος λογίων, ὥστε οὐδὲν ἥμαρτεν Μάρκος, οὕτως ἔνια γράψας ὡς ἀπεμνημόνευσεν. ἑνὸς γὰρ ἐποιήσατο πρόνοιαν, τοῦ μηδὲν ὧν ἤκουσεν παραλιπεῖν ἢ ψεύσασθαί τι ἐν αὐτοῖς. ταῦτα μὲν οὖν ἱστόρηται τῷ Παπίᾳ περὶ τοῦ Μάρκοῦ.

10. Eusebius, *Hist. Eccl.* 2.15:1–2.

a close tie between Mark and the author of the epistle, believed to be Peter, who also wrote his name in the salutation (1 Pet 1:1). The epistle was soon canonically accepted and ascribed to Peter the apostle, who would have ordered Silvanus the work of writing the letter.[11] This Silvanus is mentioned in the farewell along with Mark (1 Pet 5:12) and could tally with Silvanus of 2 Cor 1:19; 1 Thess 1:1; and 2 Thess 1:1, identical to Silas as well, a partner of Paul in Acts 15:22, pushing to the stage more sources of information requiring an individualized study. Thus, the scrutiny will be turned henceforward to the chain of witnesses for the second gospel tradition under a genetic perspective, namely, from 1 Peter to Clement Alexandrinus.

1 Peter 5:13 (AD 85–90)

As it will be unfolded below, around AD 200 Clement Alexandrinus, possibly supported in Irenaeus and/or in 1 Pet 5:13, a verse of an epistle he amply knew, sanctioned the common tradition to Papias adding the detail of Rome as the place where Mark was with Peter and where Mark composed the gospel.[12] In this respect, 1 Pet 5:12–13 utters that Peter, Silvanus the secretary writing on behalf of Peter, and Mark are in Babylon, a symbolic name for Rome: *ἀσπάζεται ὑμᾶς ἡ ἐν Βαβυλῶνι συνεκλεκτὴ καὶ Μᾶρκος ὁ υἱός μου* (sends you greetings the co-chosen (church) in Babylon and Mark my son; v.13). Modern criticism, however, considers the passage heterogeneously and questions the assumption of Peter or Silvanus on his behalf as the authors of the letter and Rome as the composition place, making weak the vindication supported in 1 Pet 5:12–13 that Mark is with Peter in Rome when he writes the gospel.

On the other hand, the reports of Clement Alexandrinus are not always reliable. Before the report on Mark in relation with Peter and Rome, Eusebius, from whom Clement on Mark has come to us, makes him say Hebrews was a translation of Luke from a Semitic original of Paul, and that the gospels of Matthew and Luke were written before Mark, a view today forsaken.[13] In spite of this inconvenience, to support the fathers' tradition that links Mark, 1 Pet 5:13, and Rome, we can say 1 Peter has a clear Jewish flavor. In fact, its

11. Irenaeus, *Haer.* 4.9:2; 5.7:2//1 Pet 1:8; 4.16:5//1 Pet 2:16.

12. Eusebius, *Hist. Eccl.* 2.15:1–2; 6.14:6–7. For the employment of 1 Peter by Clement see the specific note in the subheading devoted to the Alexandrine.

13. Eusebius, *Hist. Eccl.* 6.14:2–5. The passage of Clement Alexandrinus in question, a piece of book 6 of the *Hypotyposeis* (Outlines), is independently unknown from *Hist. Eccl.* 2.15:2; 6.14:6–7. Many of the twenty-four surviving fragments from this lost work have indeed come down to us from Eusebius. See Stählin, *Fragmente*, xxviii–lii, 195–202.

author most probably is a Judeo-Christian, being that 1 Peter is one of the NT texts which uses the OT more in proportion to its length.[14]

In addition, there are points of contact with NT Petrine and Roman traditions. Before going deeper, it's fair to offer the full account of them. Since the NT Petrine tradition and the Roman Petrine tradition only can be throughout overlapped if they are uncritically put forward, it is preferable to present two dissimilar groups of parallels to 1 Peter. With NT Petrine tradition we can isolate: (a) one same OT quotation to the gospel of Mark (1 Pet 2:4,7//Ps 118:12//Mark 12:10); (b) one common theological idea to the speeches of Peter in Acts—Jesus at God's right hand sat over the heavenly powers (1 Pet 3:22//Acts 2:33), though perhaps better paralleled in Ephesians (1:20–21); and (c) the notion of Christ as supreme shepherd common to the fourth gospel (1 Pet 2:25; 5:4//John 21:15–23).[15] References to the crucifixion or sufferings of Jesus (1 Pet 2:21–24; 3:17–18; 4:1,13; 5:1) only in very broad terms parallel the gospels, where, contrarily to the bereft 1 Peter, umpteen geographical, temporal, and personal data are supplied.[16]

With early Roman tradition, 1 Peter parallels: (a) four clauses to Clement Romanus' epistle (AD 95–98), the first in the header: 1 Pet 1:2: *χάρις ὑμῖν καὶ εἰρήνη πληθυνθείη* (grace and peace for you (may) be increased) //1 Clem. *Prae.*: *χάρις ὑμῖν καὶ εἰρήνη ἀπὸ παντοκράτορος θεοῦ διὰ Ἰησοῦ Χριστοῦ πληθυνθείη* (grace and peace for you (may) be increased from the Almighty God by Jesus Christ); 1 Pet 2:9: *τοῦ ἐκ σκότους ὑμᾶς καλέσαντος εἰς τὸ θαυμαστὸν αὐτοῦ φῶς* (who having called you out of darkness to his marvelous light)//1 Clem. 59.2: *δι' οὗ ἐκάλεσεν ἡμᾶς ἀπὸ σκότους εἰς φῶς* (by whom called us from darkness to light);[17] 1 Pet 4:8: *ὅτι ἀγάπη καλύπτει πλῆθος ἁμαρτιῶν* (because love covers a multitude of sins)//1 Clem. 49.5: *αγάπη καλύπτει πλῆθος ἁμαρτιῶν* (love covers a multitude of sins); 1 Pet 5:5: *ὑποτάγητε πρεσβυτέροις* (be subjected to (the) presbyters)//1 Clem. 57.1:

14. The author of 1 Peter rests on the LXX rather than in the MT. He largely surpasses two tens of direct alluded or quoted OT verses, not dissembling preference for Isaiah, Psalms, and Proverbs: 1 Pet 1:16//Lev 19:2; 1:24–25//Isa 40:6–8; 2:3//Ps 34:9; 2:6–8//Ps 118:22; Isa 8:14; 28:16; 2:9//Exod 19:5–6; Isa 43:20; 2:10//Hos 1:6,9,25; 2:11// Ps 39:13; 2:22//Isa 53:9; 2:24–25//Isa 53:5–6,12; 3:10–12//Prov 34:13–17; 3:14//Isa 8:12; 4:14//Isa 11:2; 4:18//Prov 11:31; 5:5//Prov 3:34.

15. Meade, *Pseudonymity and Canon*, 189–90 collects some more parallels to the discourses of Peter, but too general to be consistent: 1 Pet 1:19; 2:22–23; 3:18//Acts 3:13.26; 4:27.30. On the other hand, Meade's reading (pp. 177, 185, 189) of 1 Pet 5:1,4 from the Transfiguration (Mark 9:2–3), having projected it before into 2 Pet 1:16–18, is far-fetched.

16. It's enough here to issue the second gospel. Temporal data: Mark 15:1,25,33–34,42; geographical: Mark 15:16,22,46; personal: Mark 15:1,2,7,16,21,27,39,40,43.

17. Acts 26:18: *ἐπιστρέψαι ἀπὸ σκότους εἰς φῶς* (to turn from darkness to light).

ὑποτάγητε τοῖς πρεσβυτέροις (be subjected to the presbyters); (b) one idea partaken by Clement Romanus: 1 Pet 1:19: τιμίῳ αἵματι . . . Χριστοῦ (with the precious blood . . . of Christ)//1 Clem. 7.4: τὸ αἷμα τοῦ Χριστοῦ . . . τίμιον τῷ πατρὶ αὐτοῦ (the blood of Christ . . . precious for his Father); and (c) one shared OT quotation with James and Clement Romanus: 1 Pet 5:5//Prov 3:34//Jas 4:6//1 Clem. 30.2.[18]

Alongside with its Petrine and Roman connection, 1 Peter shows some notorious inconsistencies as to be matched without commentary to the Galilean apostle, no less in the field of authorship than in the Pauline orientation. First, against the expression παρεπιδήμοις διαςπορᾶς (to the exiles of the Diaspora) in 1 Pet 1:1, the letter seems addressed to Christians who had been pagans and not to Jews or Judeo-Christians as it is shown by 1 Pet 1:14; 2:9–12 and especially 4:3–4, where the past and present environment of the recipients visibly is a heathen one.[19] Certainly, according to Acts 10:1–48 Peter opened the gospel to converts coming from heathenism in Caesarea on the Sea, but Paul, writing to the churches in Galatia, one of the Christian communities addressed in 1 Pet 1:1, presents Peter entrusted with the gospel to the circumcised and he to the pagans (Gal 1:2; 2:7–9). Beyond the already-reported common OT locus (1 Pet 2:4,7//Ps 118:12// Mark 12:10), 1 Peter has but remote evidence of connection with Mark's gospel, the residence in Rome is at odds with the care for distant Anatolian communities to which almost nothing biographical beyond the salutation of the letter units Peter (1 Pet 1:1), and no reference of Jesus' life out of the common tradition (1 Pet 2:4,21–25; 3:18,22; 4:1,13) puts 1 Pet 1:1; 5:12–13 under suspicion of pseudepigraphy.[20]

18. I find, in sum, three NT Petrine parallels plus six Roman parallels: 1 Pet 2:4,7// Ps 118:12//Mark 12:10; 3:22//Acts 2:33//Eph 1:20–21; 5:4//John 21:15–23; 1:2//1 Clem. *Prae.*; 1:19//1 Clem. 7.4; 2:9//1 Clem. 59.2; 4:8//1 Clem. 49.5; 5:5/1 Clem. 57.1; 5:5// Prov 3:34//Jas 4:6//1 Clem. 30.2.

19. 1 Pet 1:1: Πέτρος ἀπόστολος Ἰησοῦ Χριστοῦ ἐκλεκτοῖς παρεπιδήμοις διαςπορᾶς. (Peter apostle of Jesus Christ to the chosen exiles of the Dispersion). A similar formula is restated in Jas 1:1: Ἰάκωβος θεοῦ καὶ κυρίου Ἰησοῦ Χριστοῦ δοῦλος ταῖς δώδεκα φυλαῖς ταῖς ἐν τῇ διάσπορᾷ χαίρειν (James servant of God and Jesus Christ to the twelve tribes in the Dispersion, greetings). On the header 1 Pet 1:2–3 see further below.

20. The reasons to refute direct Petrine authorship in 1 Peter as well as those for pseudonymity have been collected, leaving few leeway for contrary radical assertions: (a) the letter is Pauline in its conception, but not indicating direct dependence; (b) absence of any reference to Paul in 1 Pet 5:13, where it would be expected if Peter really was in Rome in the middle 60s, the required date if the Petrine authorship is accepted; (c) the areas to which the letter is addressed are more associated with Paul (Acts 16:6–8; 18:2–3; Rom 16:3) than with Peter, but even in that case not to the extent of the early date proposed by Petrine tradition; (d) there is no mention of 1 Peter in the early Canon Muratori (lines 39–69); (e) lack of tension between Christians and Jews; (f) Israel is

Furthermore, 1 Pet 1:10–12 sets the author's *Sitz im Leben* at soon in the second generation of believers, particularly 1 Pet 1:12 where it would be more appropriate to appeal for personal authority rather than to the OT. If the sender really was Peter, more originality by means of biographical references either to the man Jesus or to Peter himself would be expected, as we see in the Petrine speeches of Acts. In 1 Peter, Jesus never is mentioned alone, only as Christ (1:11,19; 2:21; 3:15–16,18; 4:1; 5:1,10,14), Jesus Christ (1:1,3,7,13; 2:5; 3:21), and Lord (1:3; 3:15; less clear 2:13), whilst in Acts Peter exposes variety of historical titles, Jesus alone (2:32,36; 3:20; 5:30), the man Jesus (2:22–23), Jesus the Nazorean (2:22), Jesus Christ the Nazorean (3:6; 4:10), Jesus of Nazareth (10:38), besides the usual NT Christological titles Lord (10:36; 11:17; 15:11) and Jesus Christ (2:38; 9:34; 10:36; 11:17), being additionally remarkable the absence in 1 Peter of the title servant of God (παῖς θεοῦ; Acts 3:13,26; 4:27,30).

It is like if the faith would have come to the author of 1 Peter from the word of the OT that he (through the Pauline mission) has understood fulfilled in Jesus (1 Pet 1:23–25; 2:6–8; 3:1). Despite the appeal to the vital witness of Jesus (1 Pet 5:1), the epistle doesn't seem the testimony of one who has known Jesus for years in the flesh. The author of 1 Peter seems more a preacher, built over Scripture knowledge, thoroughly acquainted with late Pauline theology in his worry for the disturbances the new faith could inflict to social order (1 Pet 2:13–17//Rom 13:1–7; 1 Pet 2:18//Eph 6:5//Col 3:22//1 Tim 6:1–2; 1 Pet 3:1–7//Eph 5:22–33//Col 3:18–19//1 Tim 2:9–12; 1 Pet 3:8–9//Rom 12:14–21), and instructed in themes more common to the Matthean tradition than to the Marcan (1 Pet 1:15–16//Matt 5:48; 1 Pet 2:4//Matt 21:42; 1 Pet 2:12//Matt 5:16; 1 Pet 4:13–14//Matt 5:11–12; 1 Pet 5:7//Matt 6:25).[21]

---

not directly mentioned, though the LXX flavor of the letter; (g) however, in Hellenistic Antiquity and even rabbinic circles there existed the advice that students should attribute their ideas to the master who originated the doctrine and not to themselves; (h) a "therapeutic lie" for the greater good of the hearers was tolerated in ancient Christianity when doctrine was orthodox and condemned when it was heterodox; (i) the Greek level of the epistle seems incompatible with Simon Peter, Galilean fisherman; (j) Silvanus could master that level (2 Cor 1:19; 1 Thess 1:1; 2 Thess 1:1), but his absence in the salutation 1 Pet 1:1 is striking if he was not a cosender and only a transmitter of the epistle (1 Pet 5:12); (k) the mention of Rome as Babylon seems an usage favored by the Jewish national disaster in AD 70; (l) the absence of clear mention of 1 Peter in Clement Romanus and Ignatius is more than surprising (Achtemeier, *1 Peter*, 39–50, 348–56).

21. Of these five 1 Peter quotations, two cover themes common to the Q tradition and as such are echoed also in Luke: 1 Pet 4:13–14//Matt 5:11–12//Luke 6:22–23; 1 Pet 5:7//Matt 6:25//Luke 12:22. The other three are out of Q: 1 Pet 1:15 is echoed solely in Matt 5:48; 1 Pet 2:4 parallels Matt 21:42//Mark 12:10//Luke 20:17; and 1 Pet 2:12 only Matt 5:16. Despite these five 1 Peter verses certainly borrow from themes common to

Since the author preferably relies on the OT and alludes to Pauline epistles, to the extent that he even copied the Pauline introductory clause (1 Pet 1:3//2 Cor 1:3; Eph 1:3; Col 1:3,5), and there is no biographical hint to episodes or direct quoting of Jesus, the author's background betrays heavy dependence on Scripture, not on direct witness.[22] The author of 1 Peter would thus be a Judeo-Christian of the second or early third generation who wrote for Christians coming from paganism in Minor Asia. Criticism vindicates AD 80 for the composition of 1 Peter because the community is a presbyterian college (1 Pet 5:1–5), not yet the monarchical episcopate of the Pastorals established in the first decade of the II century AD. This is perfectly at home with the lack of reference to bloody martyrdom, that would put Trajan's persecution in AD 112–14 against Bithynian Christians, the last of the communities addressed in the salutation (1 Pet 1:1), after the time for the epistle's composition.

On the contrary, the disturbed state of affairs in 1 Pet 1:7; 2:12,15,17; 3:16–17; 4:4,12–16,19; and 5:9–10 more resembles the apostasy that occurred some twenty-five years before among Bithynian Christians according to the letter of Pliny the Younger.[23] The concurrence of the current salutation

---

the Matthean tradition, the equivalence rests on one or two words each and in four instances we have OT loci at back, and of these four, in three the common OT source (here underlined) is evident (1 Pet 1:15–16//Matt 5:48//Lev 11:44; 1 Pet 2:4//Matt 21:42//Ps 118:22–23//Isa 28:16; 1 Pet 4:13–14//Matt 5:11–12; Ps 1:1; 89:51–52; 1 Pet 5:7//Matt 6:25//Ps 55:23).

22. 1 Pet 1:2b–3a: *χάρις ὑμῖν καὶ εἰρήνη πληθυνθείη. Ἐὐλογητὸς ὁ θεὸς καὶ πατὴρ τοῦ κυρίου ἡμῶν Ἰησοῦ Χριστοῦ* (grace and peace for you (may) be increased. Blessed (be) the God and Father of our Lord Jesus Christ). The introductory formula *χάρις ὑμῖν καὶ εἰρήνη ἀπὸ θεοῦ πατρὸς ἡμῶν καὶ κυρίου Ἰησοῦ Χριστοῦ* (grace and peace to you from God our Father and the Lord Jesus Christ), usually followed by a praise, thanksgiving, or blessing to God we nuanced find in 1 Pet 1:2–3 (and in 2 Pet 1:2) must be considered general and totally Pauline (Rom 1:7–8; 1 Cor 1:3–4; 2 Cor 1:2–3; Gal 1:3; Eph 1:2–3; Phil 1:2–3; Col 1:2–3; 1 Thess 1:1–2; 2 Thess 1:2–3; Titus 1:4; Phlm 3–4). The headers 1 Tim 1:2; 2 Tim 1:2–3; 2 John 3 combine *χάρις* (grace), *εἰρήνη* (peace) and *ἔλεος* (mercy). Jude 2: *ἔλεος ὑμῖν καὶ εἰρήνη καὶ ἀγάπη πληθυνθείη* (mercy and peace and love for you (may) be increased).

23. Pliny the Younger, *Epistulae* 10.96; Tuñí and Alegre, *Cartas Católicas*, 327–50; Achtemeier, *1 Peter*, 48–49. Meade, *Pseudonymity and Canon*, 164 deems too informal the persecution in 1 Peter to stem from policy, preferring popular reaction to the Christian lifestyle, which could be dated anytime. However, spontaneous persecution is not expected to persist for long and 1 Pet 4:12,14 implies some sort of permanency, though persecution is not aggressive enough for martyrdom and the sender expects final reconciliation (1 Pet 3:16; 4:19; 5:10). Even if, almost all the historical features of the letter are general in character likely to reach broader fan of potential recipients, the inclusion of the persecution motif in the epistle's purpose (1 Pet 5:12) implies, too, something more than spontaneous persecution in the mind of the sender (1 Pet 3:15–16). 1 Pet 4:14 reveals the Christians are well identified in the pagan environment: *εἰ ὀνειδίζεσθε ἐν ὀνόματι Χριστοῦ, μακάριοι* (if you are reviled for the name of Christ, blessed (you

ἀσπάζεται ὑμᾶς (greets you) with συνεκλεκτή (co-chosen) in 1 Pet 5:13 seems, indeed, akin to the NT Asian tradition, if put alongside with the final farewell of 2 John 13: Ἀσπάζεταί σε τὰ τέκνα τῆς ἀδελφῆς σου τῆς ἐκλεκτῆς (greets you the children of your chosen (church) sister).[24] Even more, the other NT occurrences of Babylon for Rome approach 1 Peter to a later date and to the Asian tradition, for Revelation calls the imperial power and the city of Rome *sensu stricto* Βαβυλὼν ἡ μεγάλη (the great Babylon; 14:8; 16:19; 17:5,18; 21:2,10,21).

Outside the NT, occurrences of Babylon for Rome belong all to the post-AD 70 period: 2 Ezra 3:1–2,28,31 (= 4 Ezra in Vulgate Appendix); 2 Bar. 11.1–2; and Sib. Or. 5.207. It has been argued that Babylon in the book of Daniel has become an eschatological symbol making possible the early date of 1 Pet 5:13.[25] But the argument, slowly explored, shows inconsistency. Though Daniel embodies some metaphors which see the power of Babylon breaking and being transformed into other earthly realms (2:31–45; 5:5,24–28; 7:1–12), Babylon itself is never intended to mean another city. The extant proofs, four certain post-AD 70 (4 Ezra; 2 Baruch; Revelation; Sibylline Oracles) against one possible pre-AD 70 (1 Pet 5:13), bow the balance to the later date of 1 Pet 5:13.[26] Whereas the early date for 1 Pet 5:13 is nourished with the effort to deny 1 Peter's pseudonymity, the Jewish War against Rome (AD 66–70) makes the identification with Babylon straightforward: Rome destroyed the temple of Jerusalem in AD 70, as Babylon did, enslaved several thousands of Jews, as Babylon did, and deported them, as Babylon did (2 Kgs 24:10—25:17).[27]

---

are); cf. Matt 5:11; Luke 6:22). The situation is later and different from the Ephesian mob persecution of Paul (Acts 19:23–41), where the Christians were not still clearly perceived by pagans as different from Jews.

24. The occurrence of ἐκλεκτή in 2 John 13 forms a fully suggestive chiasmus with the entering 2 John 1: Ὁ πρεσβύτερος ἐκλεκτῇ κυρίᾳ καὶ τοῖς τέκνοις αὐτῆς (The Elder to the chosen Lady and to their children).

25. Meade, *Pseudonymity and Canon*, 165 alleges Dan 1:1–8; 3:8–12 and 6:2–24, but the references seem misassigned. Verses quoting Babylon in Dan are: 1:1; 2:12,14,18,24,48–49; 3:1,12,30; 4:6,29–30; 5:7; 7:1; Sus 1,5; Bel 3 (Babylonians), 6 (Babylonians), 34–36. At every verse only Babylon in Chaldea is in mind. On 1 Pet 5:13 see further discussion below, in Eusebius on Clement Alexandrinus.

26. *Pace* Brown and Meier, *Antioch and Rome*, 128–33, who accepted the pseudonymous character of 1 Pet 5:13 but who somewhat tendentiously defended (see the surfaced exegetical leanings in 176–83) Rome (Babylon) and Peter as real data of the early Roman tradition.

27. Josephus, *A.J.* 10.98–101 gives 13,900 deported to Babylon in the VI century BC (some 13,800 in 598 BC and less than 100 in 587 BC). 2 Kgs 24:14 has 10,000, and 24:16 has 7,000; Jer 52:28–30 takes 4,600 in total (3,023 in 598 BC, 832 in 587 BC, and 745 in 582 BC). *B.J.* 5.420 gives 97,000 Jews carried captive in AD 66–70, an inflated figure though still an eloquent sample of the national disaster.

Following Clement Romanus, the earliest quotations of 1 Peter appear in the letter that the bishop of Smyrna, Polycarp, sent to the Philippians somewhen between AD 120 and 155, not far from Papias or from the addressees of 1 Peter, whereas Ignatius to the Romans (before AD 120) and especially Canon Muratori (AD 150–200), the expected locus if 1 Peter really belonged to the fabric of the early Roman church, ignore it.[28] The earliest available criticism for 1 Peter, therefore, places the epistle with moderated precision around AD 85–90, preferably in Anatolia, though Rome in the same date in full view of the link with 1 Clement cannot be driven out.

John Mark, the Partner of the Apostles in Acts

The link between the apostolic pillars and Mark, the traditional author of the second gospel, has further development in Peter's acts and in Paul's acts and letters, where John Mark, the partner of Paul and Barnabas' relative, is quoted (Acts 12:12,25; 13:5,13; 15:37–39; Col 4:10; Phlm 24; 2 Tim 4:11). Despite the later date for 1 Peter, nothing uncontroversially proves this John Mark intendedly differs from the Mark that has been put into relation with Peter in 1 Pet 5:13 or from the alleged author of the second gospel according to Papias, being interesting to depict who was this Mark of the apostolic era. In the Jewish Passover of AD 44, Herod Agrippa I (AD 41–44), friend of the emperor Gaius (AD 37–41), beheaded James the Great and jailed Peter with the purpose of killing him after the feast, but Peter miraculously fled during the night. Forthwith, Peter took refuge in the house of Mary, the mother of John, whose other name was Mark, where some fervent believers were praying for Peter's release (Acts 12:1–12). This means that Mark's mother, most likely a Judeo-Christian, owned a house in Jerusalem where Mark could have lived or lodged and where Peter fled.

In accordance with Acts 11:19–26, the Antiochian church was founded by Hellenistic Christians of Jewish origin escaping from Jerusalem after Stephen's martyrdom in AD 33, prior to James' and Peter's persecution. In Antioch the disciples of Jesus were called Christians for the first time, a term (χριστιανός/χριστιανοί) used in Acts 11:26; 26:28; 1 Pet 4:16; and in Ignatius out of the NT for the first time.[29] If we consider the chronology of Acts,

28. Consistent quotations: Polycarp, *Phil.* 1.3//1 Pet 1:8; 2.1//1 Pet 1,13,21; 2.2//1 Pet 3:9; 8.1//1 Pet 2:22,24; 10.2//1 Pet 2:12. *Phil.* 5.3 parallels equally 1 Pet 2:11 and Gal 5:17. It's difficult to say which one follows: the use of πνεῦμα (spirit) instead of ψυχή (soul) points better to Gal 5:17, but the verb στρατεύεται (war) to 1 Pet 2:11. Canon Muratori mentions all the NT except for Hebrews, James, and the two of Peter (lines 2–69; Tregelles, *Earliest Catalogue*, 29). For the date of Muratori, see below.

29. Ignatius, *Magn.* 10.1.3 (two times); *Rom.* 3.3; *Phld.* 6.1. Until the IV century

the term began to designate the followers of Jesus before Agrippa's death in AD 44 (12:20–23).[30] The chief heads of the Antiochian church were then five people: Barnabas, Simon, Lucius from Cyrene, Manaen, foster-brother of Herod Antipas, and Paul (Acts 13:1). From this town departed the first mission of Barnabas and Paul, taking this John Mark as assistant (ὑπηρέτης) and embarking for Cyprus (Acts 13:4–5). Leaving Cyprus, they crossed northwards to Perga in Minor Asia, but here Mark decided to return to Jerusalem (Acts 13:13).

When Barnabas and Paul accomplished the mission, some Judaean brothers attached to circumcision came to Antioch demanding the Law of Moses to be saved. The subject was a major risk for all the work done so Paul and Barnabas went up to Jerusalem in AD 50 to discuss the matter with the church's columns, James the Just, John of Zebedee, and Peter (Acts 15:1–21; Gal 2:9). The council determined not to foist the Jewish Law upon the new converts who entered the Christian faith.[31] Barnabas and Paul were sent back with Silas and Judas, delivering the decision to the church in Antioch (Acts 15:22–30). Here, Barnabas and Paul set up the second visit to the communities of the first journey (Acts 15:36). Barnabas aimed to take Mark, but Paul preferred to dispense with him because Mark had not completed the first journey and left them at Perga (Acts 15:37–38). The disagreement increased. Barnabas severed from Paul, took Mark and crossed to Cyprus. Paul and Silas traveled overland to Cilicia (Acts 15:39–41).

The terms of the friction are unknown and the reason Acts adduces for Mark's withdrawal of the first journey could be the only one in dispute. The

AD, the terms χριστιανός and χριστιανισμός out of the NT belong to the Levant in this order: Ignatius (ca. AD 120, cited loci), *Mart. Pol.* 10.1 (ca. AD 160), Clement Alexandrinus, *Strom.* 7.1.3 (ca. AD 200). See discussion in Norelli, "Χριστιανισμός e Χριστιανός," 177–85.

30. Josephus, *A.J.* 19.343–51.

31. The break at Antioch with the Judeo-Christians of Jerusalem attached to circumcision after AD 50 fits better than the 40s with the innovation of the name for the converts to the new faith. From Ignatius, *Magn.* 10.1.3 and *Phld.* 6.1, Norelli, "Χριστιανισμός e Χριστιανός," 177–85, assumes a similar context for the term that came to differentiate Christians from Jews, but in the Antioch of the early II century AD. As appointed by him, to understand the origin of the term one must consider the incompatibility of the two ways of life mentioned in Ignatius, one according to Judaism (κατὰ ἰουδαισμόν) and one according to Christianism (κατὰ χριστιανισμόν), but there is no serious reason to demur the chronology of Acts/Galatians for the term since they were written before Ignatius. Christians would have first differentiated the believers not attached to circumcision and to Jewish food laws, whence the subsequent general difference respect Judaism. This second development of the term would have arrived not before the second or third generation, when the Judeo-Christians and their Gentile-Christian converts (claiming Peter and/or James) cessed to be the central party in the Antiochian church.

shared context of Acts, Galatians, and James, nevertheless, indicates that the problem of Pauline communities with Judeo-Christians who persisted in the Jewish Law continued after the council and had a sequel between Peter, Barnabas, and Paul in Antioch (Gal 2:1–14; Jas 2:14–26). The council accepted salvation without circumcision; howbeit, Barnabas and Mark could have still preferred a moderated speech, at least when they joined Christians of Jewish origin who could be disturbed by Paul's revolutionary ideas (Rom 2:25–29; 9:8; 1 Cor 7: 17–19; 12:12–13; Gal 5:2–6,14,18; 6:15; Col 3:11). Even so, a sign of permanent hostility in the divorce is avoidable. Mark and Barnabas went to Cyprus, where they had been in the first mission along with Paul, and Paul and Silas to Cilicia. Cilicia was on the inland track to Derbe and Lystra, part of the first journey too (Acts 14:6–22; 16:1).

Mark in the Epistles of Paul

Again, Mark is mentioned in Col 4:10–14; Phlm 24; and 2 Tim 4:11. The final greetings in Colossians differentiate two Christian parties, one coming from Judaism in which Jesus, who is called Justus, Mark, and Aristarchus are included, and another group of Christians, Luke the physician, Demas, and likely Epaphras, who had been Gentiles. Col 4:10 states Mark is the cousin of Barnabas (Μάρκος ὁ ἀνεψιὸς Βαρναβᾶ). This fact possibly shows that Mary the mother of Mark was kindred with Barnabas, but not necessarily. The date of Colossians among scholars is not clear. Paul hints two times he is in prison (4:10,18), but the conditions are soft enough to send letters, dispatch delegates, and organize the community in the distance. Mark and Aristarchus remain with him, and Mark seems to envisage a visit to the Colossians (4:10). If we accept Colossians' authenticity, and that this Mark is the same person as John Mark, our protagonist would thus have found the occasion to be reconciled with Paul after the missionary break of Acts 13:13 and 15:37–40.

The letter to the Colossians could be ascribed either to the period of Paul in Rome in AD 61–63 (Acts 28:16), to his previous detention in Caesarea in 58–60, or to the worse attested incarceration in Ephesus around AD 54–55 (Acts 19:28–31). A Jewish plot to kill him in Caesarea makes at first illogical the epistolary work for the profit of the communities (Acts 23:12–15,23–24; 24:1–9). This major threat for his life should have occurred during the first months, but the imprisonment in Caesarea lasted for two years (διετίας δὲ πληρωθείσης; Acts 24:27), was not appalling, and according to Acts, Felix allowed Paul to receive visits (24:23). But if Paul were not writing Colossians from Caesarea, and the Roman background is preferred,

Mark should be in the imperial capital accompanying Paul, as the reading of Col 4:10 in its first contact apparently accepts. Hence, the presence of John Mark in Rome in the early 60s before the traditional date for Peter's death would not be inconsistent, though to be firm Colossians' place of composition must be cleared out.

At this point, it is interesting exploring Caesarea on account of another fact. According to Acts 9:36–43 Peter preached on the way to the coastal plain, in Lydda and then in Joppa. Afterwards Peter converted Cornelius in Caesarea, centurion of the Italian company who became Christian with all his household (Acts 10:1–48). Caesarea was the largest port for Palestine. It was rebuilt by Herod the Great (37–34 BC) and maintained shipping with Rome, Minor Asia, West Syria, and Cyprus to the north and with Joppa, Gaza, and Alexandria southwards.[32] It also was the Roman garrison for Palestine, with population half Gentile, half Jewish, a situation that fairly fits Cornelius, the charitable soldier who feared the Jewish God even though remaining Gentile (Acts 10:2–4).[33]

It is not remotely improbable that the small community of Caesarea claimed Peter, and that the first Christians embarking from Caesarea called upon his apostolic authority when they needed to justify the origin of their faith. But regardless that the same is not stated about Rome, it is also reported that Peter stayed in Caesarea for a time (Acts 10:48), wherefrom Petrine converts and Peter himself (though in another occasion) could have embarked to the imperial capital. Against it stands that Peter in Rome is not

32. Josephus, in *A.J.* 15.331–39 and *B.J.* 1.408–15, describes the construction of Caesarea by Herod in twelve years over the previous city of Strato's tower in the northern coast of the Sharon plain, some miles southwards from the skirts of Mount Carmel. Herod added a haven to the shore to avert the waves so the big ships could anchor, a maneuver not possible in other ports like Joppa or Dora. Herod also built a circus for chariot racing which could hold 7,000 spectators, a palace, a temple to Rome and Augustus, storehouses in the line of port, a network of streets in the city center, and some other buildings. The heavy slog needed materials and most probably the settlement of the workforce. From Archelaus on, Herod's son's banishment in AD 6, Caesarea became the see of the governor for Roman Judaea. Archaeology has revealed big amounts of pozzolana, a special concrete of Italian origin, as well as kurkar, a local sedimentary rock employed in the harbor construction. The port was one of the greatest hydraulic works of the time, but the underwater welding with the mother rock was not perfect and the waves and tectonic energy broke the main quay and was never repaired. From the II century AD onwards, the unrepaired quays and the filling with sea sand forced the big ships to anchor outside the main port, but this was not an impediment for trade and the enlargement of the town, which surpassed 3,300 hectares (8,000 acres) at its maximum extent (*NEAEHL* 5:1658–76; Govaars, Spiro and White, *Joint Expedition to Caesarea*, 1).

33. Josephus, *A.J.* 18.55–59; 20.116.176.182; *B.J.* 2.332; Avi Yonah and Gibson, "Caesarea," 332–34.

unquestionably recorded until Irenaeus in the second half of the II century (*Haer.* 3.1), although it is fair too to bring that the first mention of his death outside the NT is given by a Roman bishop, Clement, in the end of the I century (1 Clem. 5.4), a tradition supported by Ignatius of Antioch, who, in his martyrdom's anteroom two or three decades later, says he doesn't give instructions to the Roman Christians like Peter and Paul did (*Rom.* 4.3). The possibility that Peter met John Mark in Rome, in accord to 1 Pet 5:13, finds certainly in this set of traditional reports, one of its best supporters.[34]

The gaze at Scripture can be more refined. The occurrence of Mark in Philemon includes the group of Paul's fellows in Col 4:10–14, Mark, Aristarchus, Epaphras, Demas, Luke, Timothy, and Onesimus (10,23–24). It doesn't supply extra information dealing with the tie of Peter and Mark, but constitutes an indirect proof of Colossians' authenticity where Mark accompanies Paul in his captivity. In this line, Paul commands Timothy in his second letter to take Mark and hasten to Rome, where Paul is prisoner, because Mark is useful for the ministry (1:8,16–17; 2:9; 4:9,11). Howbeit, the opinion on the authenticity of 2 Timothy is divided. Some scholars consider it should form part of a homogeneous group of deutero-Pauline writings with 1 Timothy and Titus. Indeed, common features to the Pastorals separate them from the main corpus of Pauline epistles, especially an insistence in moral duties and in the qualities for ministry.[35]

From 1 Tim 2:9 onwards and in the most part of Titus, the moralizing speech to the third singular is dominant, but likely the name of the apparent recipient is a device to speak authoritatively to a third plural the author doesn't know personally. The hypothesis arises because if Timothy and Titus have been trustworthy enough for Paul to found churches and establish their episcopal structure, the heavy amount of commands and advisements of how they must carry out the task and the rude change between the personal

34. For Clement's and Ignatius' statements see discussion below.

35. Sánchez Bosch, *Escritos Paulinos*, 454–62 balancedly considers the Pastoral Letters not original but belonging to the Pauline sphere where details of the life of Paul could be well known. He summarizes the alleged non-Pauline character of the Pastoral Letters in three main subjects: (a) Christology: absence of the cross theology, lack of the title ὁ υἱὸς τοῦ θεοῦ (the Son of God), and no mention of the resurrection; (b) soteriology: absence of the justification by faith and on the contrary, insistence in the need to do good deeds, an outstanding non-Pauline feature; (c) ecclesiology: presence of hierarchical structure and absence of charismatic gifts. Considering the mention of the Ephesians Phygelus, Hermogenes, and Onesiphorus in 2 Tim 1:15, and the occurrence of Alexander in 2 Tim 4:14 (Acts 19:33; see also Hymenaeus and Philetus—the second otherwise unknown—in 2 Tim 2:17 and Hymenaeus and Alexander in 1 Tim 1:20), Sánchez Bosch points to an Ephesian origin of the Pastorals, or to a Roman from the occurrence of Prisca and Aquila in 2 Tim 4:19,21 and Rom 16:3, Eubulus, Pudens, Linus, and Claudia.

speech and the advisements seem to be out of place (1 Tim 1:18—2:13; Titus 1:5–9). In both epistles, and undeniably in Titus 2:2–10; 3:1–14, the speech is unfolded from the position of authority. The author dictates how bishops, presbyters, and deacons must be, as if he was addressing communities differently organized than the structure he considers right and that he represents. The language is vertical and the author doesn't halt in the situation of the apparent main addressee, except in the first part of 1 Timothy (1:1–20), that attending to this argument could be originally Pauline.

In Titus the author impolitely speaks of the Jewish or Judeo-Christian Cretans (Titus 1:10–16; 3:9–11). One can think in the harsh expression against the circumcision party of the Pauline epistle to Philippians (3:2): *βλέπετε τοὺς κύνας, βλέπετε τοὺς κακοὺς ἐργάτας, βλέπετε τὴν κατατομήν* (beware of the dogs, beware of the evil workers, beware of the mutilation). Another link of Titus with Philippians is the formal greeting to the *ἐπισκόποις καὶ διακόνοις* of the community in Phil 1:1. Yet, we have critics to Judaism in late writings like Revelation (2:9; 3:9) and especially Ignatius of Antioch, whose insistence on the figure of the bishop and contrarily to the ephemeral Philippians' references more closely recalls Titus. Furthermore, the geographical position of Crete reinforces the link of Ignatius and Titus, because in spite of the distance to the west the island could be under the Antiochian sphere of influence.[36]

There are indeed several hints more of lateness in Titus and 1 Timothy. One is brought by Titus 1:5–6 and 1 Tim 3:3–4 because the presbyters are there not recent converts, but old enough to have children who have

36. Ignatius, ca. AD 120, is the first non-biblical Christian and Antioch the first town where the hierarchical structure bishop-deacon appears within an anti-Semitic milieu as a sign of the separation between the Christians of Gentile origin, who take the leadership of the church, and the Judeo-Christians, who are invited to reprove forth Judaism (Zetterholm, *Christianity in Antioch*, 203–11). The insistency in the episcopal structure in Ignatius' letters to the churches of Minor Asia in his way to Rome is unceasing, giving the impression that he is speaking to churches where another organization coming from the foundational Pauline stage exists along the emergence of the episcopal structure (*Eph.* 1.1; 2.1–2; 4.1; 5.1–3; 6.1; *Magn.* 2; 3.1; 7.1; 13.1–2; 15; *Trall.* 1.1; 2.1–2; 3.1; 7.1; 12.1; 13.2, etc.). For instance, in the famous passage of *Smyrn.* 8.1–2, where Ignatius states that the unique valid Eucharist is the one presided by the bishop and in *Phld.* 4.1, where he advises to frequent only one Eucharist, Ignatius supposes the existence of other practices in the communities he is admonishing. The rejection of Ignatius to Judaism in *Magn.* 8.1; 9.1; 10.1–3, and *Phld.* 6.1; 8.2, and his insistence upon the episcopal structure to keep the order and the unity against the heresies, permit to date 1 Timothy and Titus as post-Pauline letters, in the 80s or 90s, or perhaps with more security around the end of the I century AD, when the first extra-biblical mention of the bishop as successor of the apostles appears in 1 Clem. 44.1. Indeed, the stylistic resemblance between sections of Ignatius, *Pol.* and 1 Timothy and Titus suggests a not very early date and approaches the authorship of the two latter to the Antiochian church.

been raised Christian. The second is the worry about social stability. Slaves obeying masters in every respect in 1 Tim 6:1–2 and Titus 2:9–10, women perfectly submissive to husbands in 1 Tim 2:9–10 and Titus 2:3–5 (which hardly could enjoy the freedom for ministry we see in Rom 16:1–15 and Phil 4:2–3), and social subjection to authorities avoiding quarreling in 1 Tim 2:1,8; Titus 3:1–2 don't see the first stage of Christianity, where the conflict was a necessary step in the consolidation of religious identity, conflict Paul was forced to face but that he also set off many times (1 Cor 3:1–4,18; 4:12–13; 5:1–11; 6:1–11; 2 Cor 1:8–9; 4:8–10; 7:11–12; 10:10–11; 11:3–4,13,19–33; 12:20; Gal 1:6–9; 2:4–5,11–14; 3:28; Phil 3:2; 1 Thess 2:2).[37] First Timothy and Titus contemplate the state of affairs depicted less markedly in Col 3:18—4:1 and 1 Pet 2:18—3:7, making it logical to ascribe them to the late second or third generation, when the tension derived from the need to break with the forefathers' tradition and environmental influences has passed away and has been shifted into inner concern for stability within local communities, better organized and entirely Christianized (1 Tim 4:14—5:22).

The hierarchical ministry in 1 Tim 3:1–12 and Titus 1:5–9 with the bishop at the head and the deacons below preferably points to the third generation of believers. It is subtle there to see the itinerant Paul and one is tempted to date them later. A secure dating attempt can be between the apostolic succession mentioned in Clement to the Corinthians towards the

37. 1 Cor 14:34–35 forbids women to speak in the Christian assemblies. The language and style is very akin to 1 Tim 2:11–13, raising the possibility of interpolation because in 1 Cor 11:2–16, where the question on women is treated more in extent it is assumed they pray and prophecy, the latter function most likely publicly (11:5–6,13). In any event, interpolation seems a reality in the Pauline circuit. Rom 16:1 reports one Phoebe, our sister, who is deacon of the church in Cenchreae (Φοίβην τὴν ἀδελφὴν ἡμῶν, οὖσαν καὶ διάκονον τῆς ἐκκλησίας τῆς ἐν Κεγχρεαῖς), and who has become patroness of many and of Paul himself (προστάτις πολλῶν ἐγενήθη καὶ ἐμοῦ αὐτοῦ). Notice that Cenchreae was the port of Corinth and the town next to it. The datum very rarely subscribes the female prohibition to speak in the assembly of 1 Cor 14:34–35, assuming this woman was well-off enough to help Paul and others with her goods, in whom one is led to see the enriched Roman female citizen perhaps widowed in youth (see Acts 16:13–15). Besides, Rom 16:3–15 gives the names of four women prominent for their hard work in the Lord without reference to husband, father, or son: Mary, Tryphaena, Tryphosa, and Persys. In last place, Phil 4:2–3 appeals to two known evangelizer women, Euodia and Syntyche. Cotter, "Women's Authority," 350–72, supported in ancient literary evidence, reached for all these reasons the conclusion that women held in the position of authority in the Pauline epistles were female members of Romanized society enjoying greater freedom than women under Greek conventions, especially in domestic churches. We can infer from her clever approach that the situation under 1 Timothy and Titus is typically Hellenistic, and that either Paul is adapting his mind to different contexts or, preferably, we are before interpolators or different authors. The widows indeed envisage larger freedom in 1 Cor 7:39–40 than in 1 Tim 5:14–16.

end of the I century, and the clear episcopate structure in Ignatius *Ad Smyrneos* in the first quarter of the II AD at the latest.[38] On the contrary, 2 Timothy can be ascribed to Paul's Roman captivity in the 60s, where he could have met John Mark. It doesn't mention the episcopate and the biographical references are copious (1:3–5,15–18; 3:10–11; 4:9–17,19–21). Anyhow, 2 Tim 2:22—4:5 recalls 1 Timothy and Titus, but even if 2 Timothy is not ascribed to Paul but to 1 Timothy and Titus, it is compelling to see that its author grasped that Mark should be someone important and retained the notice of Paul's captivity in Rome (1:8,16–17).

The mentions of Mark in Col 4:10; 2 Tim 4:11; and Phlm 24 cannot be blindly overlapped. Colossians and Philemon see the same situation in Paul's companions, but 2 Timothy responds to different stage. In Col 4:10–14 Mark and Demas are with Paul the prisoner, but in 2 Tim 1:17 and 4:10–11 Paul is prisoner in Rome without Mark and Demas, who forsook (ἐγκατέλιπεν) Paul. Assuming Pauline authorship, Demas' defection alone means 2 Timothy is later than Colossians. On the other hand, the characters in Phlm 23–24 play the same role of Col 4:10–14: Aristarchus, Epaphras, Mark, and Demas accompanying Paul the prisoner. Moreover, the slave Onesimus, who has been co-prisoner with Paul (Phlm 10), is sent in Phlm 11–17 to his master Philemon, whilst in Col 4:8–9 the same person is being sent with Tychicus to Colossae. Colossians is thus earlier than 2 Timothy but coetaneous with Philemon, which reports the same roles for Paul' companions, except for Tychicus, who is not mentioned in Philemon.

Second Timothy 4:12 sees Tychicus in Ephesus sent by Paul. Tychicus' stay in Ephesus could have occurred when he was on the way with Onesimus to Colossae, or on the way back. Paul in Phil 2:19 informs that he hopes to send Timothy soon to Philippi. In 2 Tim 4:11 Timothy is asked to take Mark to Paul, who is prisoner in Rome depending on 1:16–17 and 2:9. In addition, it is said in 2 Tim 4:13 that Timothy should pass by Troas before, which like Philippi is in the northern Aegean, though in the Anatolian shore and not in Macedonia. This implies Timothy in his second epistle is seen in the northern Aegean, possibly in Philippi, and that Mark, commissioned to go to Paul with Timothy, is also there.

The cross-reference Col 4:8–11; Phil 2:19; 2 Tim 2:9; 4:10–13; and Phlm 23–24 shows startling consistency, despite not being fully errorless. First, their compatibility is not very surprising considering they are not dated and, except 2 Timothy, bad localized, so some maneuver would

38. 1 Clem. 42.1; Ignatius, *Smyrn.* 8.1. For the composition of the Pastorals, Sánchez Bosch, *Escritos Paulinos*, 460–61 boldly claims the year AD 85 at the latest, ten years before Clement, in whose Roman community Bosch considers well established the hierarchical structure.

result in compatibility among them if the same characters presented diverse roles. Second, from the coordinates of the speaker, 2 Tim 4:20–21 seems dispatched not from Rome as 1:17 affirms but from somewhere in the Aegean basin, and the same is applicable to 4:10–11.[39] Thirdly, one additional major problem is that Timothy is co-sender with Paul in Phlm 1:1 and Col 1:1 so the instruction to Timothy of Tychicus' whereabouts in 2 Tim 4:12 is superfluous, unless a second mission of Tychicus to Ephesus is admitted respect which Timothy was ignorant. And in fourth place, the uncomfortable verse for radical Paulinists, Col 4:16, commands the Colossians to exchange their letter with another of Paul to the Laodiceans (perhaps our Epistle to the Ephesians), a deed which justifies the re-edition of both by inspired deutero-Pauline authors that could have also included transfer of information from Phlm 23–24 into Col 4:8–11: *καὶ ὅταν ἀναγνωσθῇ παρ' ὑμῖν ἡ ἐπιστολή, ποιήσατε ἵνα καὶ ἐν τῇ Λαοδικέων ἐκκλησίᾳ ἀναγνωσθῇ, καὶ τὴν ἐκ Λαοδικείας ἵνα καὶ ὑμεῖς ἀναγνῶτε* (and when the letter is read among you, have it read in the church of the Laodiceans, and read that of Laodicea).[40] All in all, it remains a possibility that Mark left Paul in the stage when Demas deserted and Tychicus was sent to Colossae by way of Ephesus, and that some time later Paul in Rome asked Mark through Timothy to return to him from the northern Aegean basin, possibly from Philippi.[41]

39. The situation of Paul in 2 Tim 4:10–13,20 is despairing: Demas has deserted to Thessalonica, Crescens has gone to Galatia, Titus to Dalmatia, Tychicus has been sent to Ephesus, Timothy is ordered to Troas, Erastus remained in Corinth, and Trophimus is left ill in Miletus, but all the scene is rare from the Roman position of 1:17. Acts 27:5 reports Paul traveling from Caesarea to Rome called in Myra, port in southern Lycia, from where the suffering Trophimus could have been dispatched to Miletus. Timothy had to leave Paul before, in Sidon (Acts 27:3) or in Caesarea (Acts 23:2). Otherwise, Timothy would have known the situation of Trophimus in 2 Tim 4:20 and the news are out of the case. ℵ read Gaul (Γαλλίαν) instead of Galatia in 2 Tim 4:10, perhaps from 1:17.

40. Important witnesses in this sense don't bring the receivers' demonym in Eph 1:1: P^{46}, ℵ, B, etc. $P^{4}6$ has the Pauline corpus less 2 Thess and the Pastorals. Dated AD 100–150 (Comfort and Barrett, *Earliest New Testament Manuscripts*, 1:183–88), the Fayumite $P^{4}6$ includes Colossians within the corpus, therefore very early, but it also has Hebrews after Romans, usually deemed inauthentic. Colossae, Laodicea, and Hierapolis were three close cities in southern Phrygia. See last note of the monograph for their geographical connection to Ephesus.

41. Abbott, *Ephesians and Colossians*, xxx already saw Tychicus in Eph 6:21 and Col 4:7–9 collated with Phlm 13 as the proof that the three epistles were written at once. In Eph 6:22 and Col 4:8 Tychicus is said to have been sent by Paul to the addressees of the epistles with the same expression (ἔπεμψα πρὸς ὑμᾶς). Authenticity accepted, the letters of Colossians, Philemon, and Ephesians had to be part of the same mission in the hands of Tychicus. Anyhow, Ephesians could be a deutero-Pauline product of Colossians despite that for Abbott, *Ephesians and Colossians*, xxiii the thirty-nine parallels listed between Ephesians and Colosisans—in my opinion too coolly rejected—would not be impediment to accept its originality. More on Colossians is discussed at footnotes in chapter 4.

The NT Tradition of Peter in the Roman West

Acts and Paul's epistles, from which most of the data on John Mark is taken, ignore Peter in Rome. Excluding 1 Pet 5:13, the westernmost spot where Peter can be placed relying on the NT is Corinth. 1 Cor 1:11–15 and 3:3–4,21–22 denounce divisions apropos apostolic paternity. In Corinth, some said they belonged to Paul, others to Apollos, and others to Cephas (Peter). This mention of Cephas along with Paul and Apollos implies the possibility of traveling to Corinth before AD 57. Corinth could be a stopover on the way to Rome and could be connected with Caesarea and Seleucia Pieria, the port for Antioch on the Orontes. Acts and Galatians record Peter in Caesarea and Antioch and nothing prevents the mission to Corinth (Acts 10:1–48; Gal 2:11). Notwithstanding, the possibility of converts traveling west from Caesarea, Antioch, or the same Jerusalem claiming Peter's authority must be considered. Asia Minor and Roman Jews visited Jerusalem during the feasts and were among the three thousand first converts that heard Peter's preaching already in AD 33, as we read in Acts (2:5–41; 28:21).

1 Cor 3:3–8 restates the dispute over the apostolic paternity of the Corinthians and doesn't mention Cephas, but only Paul and Apollos, and neither does Acts in the account of Apollos' ministry (18:24—19:1). Paul excluding Peter in 1 Cor 3:6 is meaningful: ἐγὼ ἐφύτευσα, Ἀπολλῶς ἐπότισεν, ἀλλ' ὁ θεὸς ηὔξανεν (I planted, Apollos watered, but God made grow). The possibility that Peter evangelized Corinth cannot be denied, but turns weak taking into account that in Rom 15:20 and 2 Cor 10:15–16 Paul says he evangelized places where no other apostle had been before. Paul to the Romans was written from Corinth during his second journey, possibly in the winter of AD 55/56, standing out a community already founded that Paul longs to meet (15:23–24). In the final salutations of Christians accompanying Paul from Corinth, Peter is unrecorded (16:21–23), and neither is he within the Roman church in the same letter (16:3–15). It could be that Peter, as tradition defends, was later in Rome in the 60s, but this contradicts the suggestion of Col 4:10 that Mark is with Paul in Rome in AD 63/64 and doesn't mention Peter. The fourth gospel, usually ascribed to Minor Asia, attests the martyrdom of Peter, but doesn't report the place where it occurred (John 21:18–19).[42]

42. Irenaeus, *Haer.* 3.3:4 reports that Paul founded the church of Ephesus, and that John afterwards remained there with the believers until times of Trajan (AD 98–117) (Ἰωάννου δὲ παραμείναντος αὐτοῖς μέχρι τῶν Τραϊανοῦ χρόνων). If the long life of John according to *Haer.* 3.3:4 really explains the rumor on the life lasting forever of the loved disciple in John 21:20–23, we could have a proof of the Ephesian origin of the second ending of the fourth gospel (John 21), and of Peter's primacy (John 21:15–17) and martyrdom (John 21:18–19) under Ephesian tradition around the last decade of the I

The Death of Peter in 1 Clement 5.4 (AD 95–98)

One of the temptations of any person who seeks the truth in ancient sources is to find corroboration to one's own initial position when more than one reading in the sources is possible. This handicap assaults every conquest in research of the far past and even in the most scrupulous of the studies it is never thoroughly expunged. Clement of Rome to the Corinthians (5.4) at the end of the I AD and Ignatius to the Romans (4.3) in the first quarter of the next century endorse the Roman death of Peter. Worth noticing is that, despite that both suggest the fact, neither of these apostolic fathers reports directly Peter's death in Rome, being difficult though possible to take out from the mind what later tradition will say about Peter when we approach these two ancient sources to check them against their own contexts before than from later ones.

Actually, if we assume the task to erase the mind and read Clement's famed epistle not from later authorities but ignoring what was to be written in future, it is hard to see there an unquestionable mention of Peter's death in Rome. Certainly, Clement in first place mentions the exemplar lives and deaths of Peter and Paul (1 Clem. 5.2–7), and secondly addresses the Corinthians with the example of contemporaneous Roman martyrs (1 Clem. 6.1–3) to encourage them in their actual difficulties and to call them to repentance (1 Clem. 7.1–5). But that Clement uses rhetorical language seems suggested by 1 Clem. 4.9 where Joseph is said to have been persecuted to death (Ἰωσὴφ μέχρι θανάτου διωχθῆναι), something the very Clement knew it didn't occur in material sense, as it was already remarked in the recent past.[43] Clement attaches the death of Peter and Paul with the Roman martyrs and in a second motion these last with the Corinthians, but which relation is implied in the first link is not fully discernible, being difficult to assess the overall terms used for the death of Peter and determine if they unite it to a distant fact or rather they are an expression that conceals real connection with martyrdom:

---

century AD. *Haer.* 3.3:3 reports that Polycarp (d. AD 155)—bishop of Smyrna, fifty-six kilometers from Ephesus—had been instructed by the apostles and had socialized with many who had seen the Lord (*καὶ Πολύκαρπος δὲ οὐ μόνον ὑπὸ ἀποστόλων μαθητευθεὶς καὶ συναναστραφεὶς πολλοῖς τοῖς τὸν Κύριον ἑωρακόσιν*). *Haer.* 3.3:4 mentions a less credible report, that some men heard from Polycarp that John the apostle was going to have a bath in Ephesus (*καὶ εἰσὶν οἱ ἀκηκοότες αὐτοῦ ὅτι Ἰωάννης ὁ τοῦ Κυρίου μαθητὴς ἐν τῇ Ἐφέσῳ πορευθεὶς λούσασθαι*), where he met Cerinth the heresiarch, whom John rebuked. In favor of the Asia Minor origin of the Johannine tradition, it is worth noting that Polycarp, *Phil.* 7.1 quotes 1 John 4:2–3 and 2 John 7, although not the fourth gospel.

43. Hare, *Jewish Persecution*, 40. See Gen 37:25–28; 39:7–20.

> Let us take the noble examples of our generation. Because of jealousy and envy the great and most righteous pillars were persecuted and fought until death. Let us take before our eyes the good apostles. Peter, who by unrighteous jealousy endured not one nor two but many labors, and having in this way borne witness went to the owed place of glory. Because of jealousy and strife Paul showed a prize of patient endurance, having carried seven times chains, banishing, stoning, became preacher in the east and in the west, (and) received the noble fame for his faith; having taught justice to the whole world he came to the edge of the occident: and having borne witness before the rulers, so he departed from the world and went to a holy place, having become the greatest model of endurance. (1 Clem. 5.1b–7)[44]

As we see, the passage affirms that the columns of the church, understood to be Peter and Paul for what follows, were persecuted for jealousy and envy (*διὰ ζῆλον καὶ φθόνον . . . ἐδιώχθησαν*) and contended until death (*ἕως θανάτου ἤθλησαν*; 1 Clem. 5.2). The key verse for Peter, next to the next clause, is 1 Clem. 5.4, where it is reported that because of jealousy and envy after enduring not one nor two but many hardships (*διὰ ζῆλον ἄδικον οὐκ ἕνα οὐδὲ δύο, ἀλλὰ πλείονας ὑπήνεγκεν πόνους*) Peter died, but mentioning no geographical reference. The direct object *πόνους* admits several renderings: pains, sufferings, fatigues, labors, toils, difficulties, hardships. Attending solely to this clause, the choice for pains or sufferings would strengthen the reading in favor of Peter's bloody death. But the remaining usages of *πόνος* in the document, 1 Clem. 16.3 (toil), 16.4 (toil), and with more clarity 16.12 (burden), advise leaning towards psychological connotations.[45]

44. *Λάβωμεν τῆς γενεᾶς ἡμῶν τὰ γενναῖα ὑποδείγματα. Διὰ ζῆλον καὶ φθόνον οἱ μέγιστοι καὶ δικαιότατοι στύλοι ἐδιώχθησαν καὶ ἕως θανάτου ἤθλησαν. Λάβωμεν πρὸ ὀφθαλμῶν ἡμῶν τοὺς ἀγαθοὺς ἀποστόλους. Πέτρον, ὃς διὰ ζῆλον ἄδικον οὐκ ἕνα οὐδὲ δύο, ἀλλὰ πλείονας ὑπήνεγκεν πόνους, καὶ οὕτω μαρτυρήσας ἐπορεύθη εἰς τὸν ὀφειλόμενον τόπον τῆς δόξης. Διὰ ζῆλον καὶ ἔριν Παῦλος ὑπομονῆς βραβεῖον ὑπέδειξεν, ἑπτάκις δεσμὰ φορέσας, φυγαδευθείς, λιθαςθείς, κήρυξ γενόμενος ἔν τε τῇ ἀνατολῇ καὶ ἐν τῇ δύσει, τὸ γενναῖον τῆς πίστεως αὐτοῦ κλέος ἔλαβεν, δικαιοσύνην διδάξας ὅλον τὸν κόσμον καὶ ἐπὶ τὸ τέρμα τῆς δύσεως ἐλθών· καὶ μαρτυρήσας ἐπὶ τῶν ἡγουμένων, οὕτως ἀπηλλάγη τοῦ κόσμοῦ καὶ εἰς τὸν ἅγιον τόπον ἐπορεύθη, ὑπομονῆς γενόμενος μέγιστος ὑπογραμμός.*

45. 1 Clem. 16.3–14 is a quoting of Isa 53:1–12, the Fourth Servant Song. 1 Clem. 16.12 (= LXX Isa 53:10b–11a): *καὶ κύριος βούλεται ἀφελεῖν ἀπὸ τοῦ πόνου τῆς ψυχῆς αὐτοῦ* (and the Lord wanted to remove the burden from his soul). The psychological tone of *πόνος* is stressed in the Fourth Song by the opposition to the term *πληγή* (wound, bruise, blow) in Isa 53:4 and 53:10–11. The MT word for *πόνος* in Isa 53:11 is clearly psychological, עָמָל (toil, labor), the tone read by the NRSV (anguish). In Isa 53:4 the trio *εἶναι ἐν πόνῳ* stands for נָגוּעַ (being smitten with disease or stricken; NRSV has stricken). In the NT *πόνος* is found in Col 4:13 (labor); Rev 16:10 (pain); 16:11 (pain); and 21:4 (pain).

The contrast in grade indeed between the notice on Peter and the notice on the Roman martyrs, despite their connection in the narrative order, is served because the Roman bishop chooses stronger expressions in 1 Clem. 6.1–2, especially the terms *βασάνοις* (torments) and *αἰκίσματα δεινά* (terrible grievances), reinforced by *παθόντες* (suffering) and *παθοῦσαι* (suffered), cognates of the verb *πάσχω* (suffer).[46] The expression *ἕως θανάτου ἤθλησαν* in 1 Clem. 5.2 and *οὕτω μαρτυρήσας ἐπορεύθη εἰς τὸν ὀφειλόμενον τόπον τῆς δόξης* (having in this way borne witness went to the owed place of glory) in 1 Clem. 5.4 suggest the martyrdom of Peter, but, seen from the lack of defined physical pains in the wording in the case of Peter, turn general and though martyrdom always remains possible they don't account for any kind of death.

It should be noted that *διὰ φθόνον* (because of envy) occurs during the trial of Jesus, in Mark 15:10. Here the narrator states Pilate knew it was on account of envy of the chief priests that Jesus had been delivered up (*ἐγίνωσκεν γὰρ ὅτι διὰ φθόνον παραδεδώκεισαν αὐτὸν οἱ ἀρχιερεῖς*). In 1 Clem. 3.1—4.13, the section which serves Clement to introduce the subject of jealousy and envy (*ζῆλος* alone occurs six times and *ζῆλος* combined with *φθόνος* three), several righteous who suffered envious persecution are listed: Abel, Jacob, Joseph, Moses, Aaron, Miriam, and David. It would have been the perfect occasion to make a conclusion alluding to Jesus' death caused by envy of the chief priests if Clement had known the Marcan tradition, but the text goes on to Peter and Paul. This makes the parallel of Mark 15:10 with 1 Clem. 5.4 fortuitous.

The reading implying a cruel death for Peter can even be rebutted from 1 Clem. 5.5–7, the sentences on Paul. There, sixty-one words devoted to Paul alone against twenty-three to Peter denote a more complete picture of Paul against Peter in 1 Clem. 5.4, but even in this case the account for Paul's martyrdom is not totally apprehensible. 1 Clem. 5.5–6 matches 5.4 and says because of envy and strife (*διὰ ζῆλον καὶ ἔριν*) Paul endured three hardships

46. *Τούτοις τοῖς ἀνδράσιν ὁσίως πολιτευσαμένοις συνηθροίσθη πολὺ πλῆθος ἐκλεκτῶν, οἵτινες πολλαῖς αἰκίαις καὶ βασάνοις, διὰ ζῆλος παθόντες, ὑπόδειγμα κάλλιστον ἐγένοντο ἐν ἡμῖν. Διὰ ζῆλος διωχθεῖσαι γυναῖκες, Δαναΐδες καὶ Δίρκαι, αἰκίσματα δεινὰ καὶ ἀνόσια παθοῦσαι, ἐπὶ τὸν τῆς πίστεως βέβαιον δρόμον κατήντησαν καὶ ἔλαβον γέρας γενναῖον αἱ ἀσθενεῖς τῷ σώματι* (To these holy men were gathered great multitude of the elect, who suffering because of jealousy many grievances and torments, became the best example among us. Because of jealousy women were persecuted, Danaids and Dircae, suffered terrible and impious grievances, reached the firm race of the faith and the weak in the body got the noble homage; 1 Clem. 6.1–2). Though in this case some cognates of *πάσχω* are also employed in the NT with psychological connotations (Rom 8:18; 2 Cor 1:6; Gal 5:24, etc.), other cognates of the same root are indeed favorite for physical sufferings. See for instance Matt 17:15; Mark 5:26; 8:31; 1 Pet 1:11; 4:1; 5:1; Heb 2:9.

before dying: ἑπτάκις δεσμά (seven times chains), φυγαδευθείς (banishing), and λιθαςθείς (stoning). This is striking because if Clement is referring to Paul's martyrdom in Rome, two of them, chains and stoning, fall in the common tradition (2 Cor 11:23–25), and the third one, φυγαδευθείς, points to the commutation of the capital punishment, in tune with Paul's relaxed captivity in Rome according to Acts 28:16–31.[47] In Italian coordinates, ἐπὶ τὸ τέρμα τῆς δύσεως ἐλθών (came to the edge of the occident) in 1 Clem. 5.7 suggests indeed Paul died further to the west, making a wink to the announced trip to Spain (Rom 15:24–28).[48]

47. Marguerat, *First Christian Historian*, 205–30 defends the denouement of Paul in Acts 28:30–31, eluding his death, as a rhetorical silence. Marguerat reasons convincingly: Acts 23:11; 25:11–12,25; 26:32; 27:23–24; and 28:19 manifest the author of Acts displaying a deliberated end whose motif is the appeal of Paul to the emperor and his travel to Rome. The death of Paul is announced (Acts 20:25,38) and the author knows it (21:11), but chooses a planned suspension of the audience to the emperor, displacing the final attention of the reader to Paul's missionary activity in Rome (28:30–31) and leaving the reader the task to fulfill the gap with what had been previously told (Marguerat, *First Christian Historian*, 206–16). The martyr death of Paul is compatible with such a literary strategy. However, the innocence of Paul in terms of Roman justice is defended in Acts 23:29 (the tribune of Jerusalem); 26:30–32 (Festus the prefect and Agrippa II); and 28:18 (Paul himself). Indeed, we must admit the open end of Acts 28:30–31 accepts a less heroic death of Paul according to Christian standards.

48. A point I share with Tregelles, *Earliest Catalogue*, 41. Ζῆλος and φθόνος appear in the list of evil deeds of Gal 5:20, and ζῆλος and ἔρις in the lists of Rom 13:13 and 1 Tim 6:4–5. Clement possibly is reading 1 Cor 3:3 (ζῆλον καὶ ἔριν) when he goes on to Paul in 1 Clem. 5.5–6. We know he knew 1 Corinthians from memory: 24.1//1 Cor 15:20; 34.8//1 Cor 2:9; 37.3; 41.1//1 Cor 15:23; 37.5//1 Cor 12:14–26; 47.1–3//1 Cor 1:12; 49.5//1 Cor 13:4–7. The motif of the ζῆλος, φθόνος, and ἔρις serves the vertebral motif of 1 Clem., but equally is one of the main themes of Paul to Corinthians (1:10–12; 3:1–9; also Phil 1:15). Expectedly, Clement admonishes the Corinthians returning to 1 Corinthians. The references to this Pauline motif are manifold: 1 Clem. 3.2: ζῆλος, φθόνος, ἔρις (referred to the Corinthians); 4.7: ζῆλος, φθόνος (Abel); 4.8.9.10.11.12: ζῆλος (Jacob; Joseph; Moses; Aaron, and Miriam; Dathan and Abiram); 4.13: ζῆλος, φθόνος (David); 5.2: ζῆλος, φθόνος (pillars of the present time; for what comes Peter and Paul, or Peter, Paul, and the Roman martyrs); 5.4: ζῆλος (Peter); 5.5: ζῆλος, ἔρις (Paul); 6.1.2: ζῆλος (Roman martyrs; Danaids, Dircae); 6.3: ζῆλος (wifes; it can be referred to persecuted Roman women or for what follows to a general situation out of Italy); 6.4: ζῆλος, ἔρις (great cities and nations); 9.1: ζῆλος, ἔρις (Corinthians); 14.1–2: ζῆλοι, ἔρις (Corinthian leaders); 39.7: ζῆλος (the foolish; Job 5:2); 44.1: ἔρις (episcopate); 45.4: ζῆλος (persecutors); 54.2: ἔρις (Corinthians). Brown and Meier, *Antioch and Rome*, 122–27 failed to acknowledge the dependence of the motif ζῆλος καὶ ἔρις on Pauline epistles, even if for Clement the motif concurred to describe Paul's martyrdom to the Corinthians.

The Synoptic Tradition in Clement, Ad Corinthios (AD 95–98)

Some clustered synoptic sayings in 1 Clem. 13.2 and 46.8 launch the question of whether the Roman Christian community was in possession of the second gospel. If it was, there are several reasons to decline the early datation of these materials, and to fix them as part of the epistle between AD 95 and 98.[49] 1 Clem. 13.2 holds seven apothegms of Jesus: Ἐλεᾶτε, ἵνα ἐλεηθῆτε· ἀφίετε, ἵνα ἀφεθῇ ὑμῖν· ὡς ποιεῖτε, οὕτω ποιηθήσεται ὑμῖν· ὡς δίδοτε, οὕτως δοθήσεται ὑμῖν· ὡς κρίνετε, οὕτως κριθήσεσθε· ὡς χρηστεύεσθε, οὕτως χρηστευθήσεται ὑμῖν· ᾧ μέτρῳ μετρεῖτε ἐν αὐτῷ μετρηθήσεται ὑμῖν ([1] Be merciful, to be shown mercy; [2] forgive, for you be forgiven; [3] as you do, so shall be done to you; [4] like you give, so will be given to you; [5] as you judge, so will you be judged; [6] as you use, so will be used with you; [7] with the measure you measure, with it you will be measured).

The most exact parallel to 1 Clem. 13.2 is Luke 6:36–38. It has seven maxims too, five coincident (1//1; 2//4; 4//5; 5//2; 7//7): Γίνεσθε οἰκτίρμονες καθὼς καὶ ὁ πατὴρ ὑμῶν οἰκτίρμων ἐστίν. Καὶ μὴ κρίνετε, καὶ οὐ μὴ κριθῆτε· καὶ μὴ καταδικάζετε, καὶ οὐ μὴ καταδικασθῆτε. ἀπολύετε, καὶ ἀπολυθήσεσθε· δίδοτε, καὶ δοθήσεται ὑμῖν· μέτρον καλὸν πεπιεσμένον σεσαλευμένον ὑπερεκχυννόμενον δώσουσιν εἰς τὸν κόλπον ὑμῶν· ᾧ γὰρ μέτρῳ μετρεῖτε ἀντιμετρηθήσεται ὑμῖν ([1] Become merciful like your Father is merciful; [2] And don't judge, and you won't be judged; [3] and don't condemn, and you won't be condemned; [4] forgive, and you will be forgiven; [5] give, and it will be given to you; [6] a good pressed down, shook measure to your lap will they give you; [7] with the measure you measure you will be measured in return).

We find in Matthew a clear parallel to the formers: Μὴ κρίνετε, ἵνα μὴ κριθῆτε . . . ἐν ᾧ γὰρ μέτρῳ μετρεῖτε μετρηθήσεται ὑμῖν (Matt 7:1–2 to 5//2 and 7//7); and some indirect entailing developed forms: Matt 6:12,14 to 2//4; 7:7 to 4//5; with less confidence: Matt 5:7,48 to 1//1. The mutual dependence of 1 Clem. 13.2 and Mark is hard to demonstrate. Mark has one direct parallel: ἐν ᾧ μέτρῳ μετρεῖτε μετρηθήσεται ὑμῖν καὶ προστεθήσεται ὑμῖν (Mark 4:24 to 7//7); and two far indirect: Mark 4:25 to 4//5, repeated in Matt 25:29 and Luke 19:26; and Mark 11:25 to 2//4.

49. 1 Clem. 1.1 mentions sudden misfortunes suffered by the Roman community. Ayán, *Clemente de Roma*, 25–26 gives three reasons to refuse the Neronian date and to affix the misfortunes to the persecution during the last years of Domitian (AD 81–96): (a) there has been time enough for a second succession of bishops (42.4; 44.2–3); (b) the church of Corinth is called ἀρχαῖα, ancient, namely, going back to the origins (47.6); (c) the Roman messengers delivering the epistle have conducted virtuous life from childhood to the old age (63.3).

1 Clem. 46.8 is a compound of οὐαὶ τῷ ἀνθρώπῳ ἐκείνῳ· καλὸν ἦν αὐτῷ, εἰ οὐκ ἐγεννήθη (woe to that man: better is for him, if he had not been born; Matt 26:24; Mark 14:21 lacking ἦν; Luke 22:22 lacking from καλόν onwards) and the warning on scandal: ἢ ἕνα τῶν ἐκλεκτῶν μου σκανδαλίσαι· κρεῖττον ἦν αὐτῷ περιτεθῆναι μύλον, καὶ καταποντισθῆναι εἰς τὴν θάλασσαν, ἢ ἕνα τῶν ἐκλεκτῶν μου διαστρέψαι (than cause one of my chosen to sin: it was better for him to be tied to a millstone, and be thrown to the sea, than lead astray one of my chosen; Matt 18:6; Mark 9:42; Luke 17:1–2; only matching Matthew καταποντισθῆναι). Finally, we have one last parallel from a common OT quotation in 1 Clem. 15.2, whose first part is more akin to Mark than to the Septuagint or Matthew. Itemized, this last interesting parallel will be easier to grasp.

1 Clem. 15.2: Λέγει γάρ που· οὗτος ὁ λαὸς τοῖς χείλεσίν με τιμᾷ, ἡ δὲ καρδία αὐτῶν πόρρω ἄπεστιν ἀπ' ἐμοῦ (for He says somewhere: this people with the lips honors me, but their heart far is away from me). Isa 29:13 has: ὁ λαὸς οὗτος τοῖς χείλεσίν αὐτῶν τιμῶσιν με, ἡ δὲ καρδία αὐτῶν πόρρω ἀπέχει ἀπ' ἐμοῦ (the people this with their lips honor me, but their heart far is apart from me). Matt 15:8: ὁ λαὸς οὗτος τοῖς χείλεσίν με τιμᾷ, ἡ δὲ καρδία αὐτῶν πόρρω ἀπέχει ἀπ' ἐμοῦ (the people this with the lips honors me, but their heart far is apart from me). Mark 7:6: οὗτος ὁ λαὸς τοῖς χείλεσίν με τιμᾷ, ἡ δὲ καρδία αὐτῶν πόρρω ἀπέχει ἀπ' ἐμοῦ (this people with the lips honors me, but their heart far is apart from me).[50]

As it stands, the first part of 1 Clem. 15.2, wherein the demonstrative (οὗτος) precedes the subject (λαός) and where the verb is singular (τιμᾷ), only appears traced in Mark. Unhappily, the second verb of 1 Clem. 15.2, ἄπεστιν (is far or away), differs grammatically from Mark, who partners Matthew ensuing the synonym ἀπέχει (is far or apart) of Isaiah. The latter, besides, has an additional genitive (αὐτῶν) in the first part, which has been dropped in the rest. With this complexity at sight, it would be biased to stress the possibility of a Marcan reading in 1 Clem. The introductory formula in 1 Clem. 15.2, λέγει γάρ που (for He says somewhere), outside this occasion is employed by Clement always in OT quotations (21.2//Prov 20:27; 26.2//Ps 28:7; 28.2//Ps 139:7–8; 42.5//LXX Isa 60:17), but by contrast he mentions the words of the Lord Jesus (τῶν λόγων τοῦ κυρίου Ἰησοῦ) when he brings in the already-studied synoptic tradition (13.1–2//Luke 6:36–38; 46.7–8//Matt 18:6; 26:24; Mark 9:42; 14:21; Luke 17:1–2; 22:22).

50. See that in translation level the emphatic expression πόρρω ἀπέχει ἀπό (far is apart from) is redundant, and so NRSV renders freely the second part of the quotation: *but their hearts are far from me* (verb and subject in plural and adverb deleted). I am indebted to Black, *Mark*, 80 for a second look at the parallel 1 Clem. 15.2//Mark 7:6, though its peer review lowers in this case the force of his intuition.

The decades-later document 2 Clem. 3.5 indeed accredits the OT source, agreeing with 1 Clem. 15.2 in the second part, but with Matt 15:8 in the first part. 2 Clem. 3.5, it will be granted, empowers the hypothesis that for single quotations with multiple attestations in early Christian literature, oral tradition or manuscripts where the quotations were handed down or copied nuanced and mingled with diverse and selected scriptural materials must be the common source: λέγει δὲ καὶ ἐν τῷ Ἡσαΐα· ὁ λαὸς οὗτος τοῖς χείλεσίν με τιμᾷ, ἡ δὲ καρδία αὐτῶν πόρρω ἄπεστιν ἀπ' ἐμοῦ.[51]

The Letters of Ignatius (AD 107–120)

Ignatius to the Romans 4.1–3 appears a little surer than Clement to attest Peter's death in Rome and linearly read strengthens the Christian tradition of Peter. Ignatius, foreseeing his end in the circus, tells the Romans that he doesn't do like Peter and Paul, giving commands to the Romans. Ignatius' words weigh more than Clement's to assign the death of Peter to Rome, but again the direct statement of Peter's martyrdom, nor of Peter's death, is not reported. Hence, Ignatius' testimony needs external material to be determinant, entering once more the field of interpretation: οὐχ ὡς Πέτρος καὶ Παῦλος διατάσσομαι ὑμῖν. ἐκεῖνοι ἀπόστολοι, ἐγὼ κατάκριτος· ἐκεῖνοι ἐλεύθεροι, ἐγὼ δὲ μέχρι νῦν δοῦλος. ἀλλ̓ ἐὰν πάθω, ἀπελεύθερος γενήσομαι Ἰησοῦ Χριστοῦ καὶ ἀναστήσομαι ἐν αὐτῷ ἐλεύθερος. νῦν μανθάνω δεδεμένος μηδὲν ἐπιθυμεῖν (I don't give instructions to you like Peter and Paul. They apostles, me condemned; they free, but I a servant until now. But if I suffer, I will be freedman of Jesus Christ and I will rise free in him. Now, a prisoner, I learn to desire nothing; *Rom.* 4.3). Without underestimating Peter's link to the Roman community—to which we will return—it must be pointed that greater solicitude deserves Ignatius as early witness to the gospel tradition.

Excluding more ambiguous reports, the seven letters bring some twenty-five Matthean quotations/allusions (see note), one independent Lucan tradition *(Smyrn.* 3.3//Luke 24:9), and three apparent traditions from the fourth gospel (*Rom.* 7.2//John 4:10,14; *Phld.* 7.1//John 3:8; 9.1//John 10:7,9).[52] Lacking again our gospel great fortune, only one veiled reference

51. 1 Clem. 13.1: μεμνημένοι τῶν λόγων τοῦ κυρίου Ἰησοῦ (having remembered the words of the Lord Jesus); 46.7: Μνήσθητε τῶν λόγων Ἰησοῦ τοῦ Κυρίου ἡμῶν (Let be remembered the words of Jesus our Lord). Λέγει γάρ που (for He/the Scripture says somewhere), quoting the OT: 21.2; 26.2; Λέγει γάρ που τὸ γραφεῖον (for says somewhere the Writing): 28.2; οὕτως γάρ που λέγει ἡ γραφή: 42.5 (for thus says somewhere the Scripture).

52. I will precise and complete the list of Smit, "Ignatius and Matthew," 266. Unquestionably Matthean: Ignatius, *Eph.* 5.2 (Matt 18:19); 6.1 (Matt 21:33); 14.2 (Matt 7:20; 12:33); 19.1–2 (Matt 1:18,23; 2:2); *Phld.* 6.1 (Matt 23:27*); Smyrn.* 1.1 (Matt 1:18,23); 1.1

to Mark appears in Ignatius, usually overlooked in the reckonings: τοὺς περὶ Πέτρον (to those around Peter; *Smyrn.* 3.2),[53] which at all lights parallels Mark 16:8b in the shorter ending, τοῖς περὶ τὸν Πέτρον (to those around Peter). The shorter ending was adhered to the second gospel in its final composition stage. Comprising two scant sentences (Mark 16:8b–c), it is missing in the best majuscules, ℵ, B, D, A, etc.[54] Therefore, in the case we were before true dependence, it is not clear if Ignatius took it from Mark or a common source, more than the inverse.

Canon Muratori (AD 150–200)

Another report on Peter's death is Canon Muratori lines 34–39, datable to AD 150–200 if authenticity is accepted. In line with a short comment on the Lucan authorship of the book of Acts, the Latin fragment, seemingly utters it is normal the absence of Peter's martyrdom and the travel of Paul to Spain from that book since Luke only wrote what he was an eyewitness to: *Acta aute omniu apostolorum sub uno libro scripta sunt Lucas obtime theofile comprindit quia sub praesentia eius singula gerebantur sicute et semote passione Petri euidenter declarat Sed profectione pauli ad urbes ad spania proficescentis* (But all the acts of the apostles are written in a second book. Luke to optimum Theophilus gathered what under his presence solely carried on, just as he clearly declares by (setting) Peter's passion aside but (also) by the departure of Paul traveling from the city to Spain; lines 34–39).[55]

(Matt 3:15); 6.1 (Matt 19:12); *Pol.* 2.2 (Matt 10:16). Possibly Matthean: *Magn.* 9.1 (Matt 23:8); *Rom.* 6.1 (Matt 4:8); 6.1 (Matt 24:8; 13:8); *Phld.* 2.2 (Matt 7:15); 3.1 (Matt 13:24; 15:13). Indiscernible common tradition, but more likely Matthean: *Eph.* 5.2 (Matt 24:5; Mark 13:5; Luke 21:8); 11.1 (Matt 3:7// Luke 3:7); 16.1 (Matt 24:5; Mark 13:5; Luke 21:8); 17.1 (Matt 26:27; Mark 14:3); *Rom.* 9.3 (Matt 10:40–41; Mark 9:37); *Smyrn.* 6.1 (Matt 24:5; Mark 13:5; Luke 21:8); *Pol.* 1.3 (Matt 24:32; 25:13; Mark 13:35). Doubtfully Matthean: *Trall.* 8.2 (Matt 5:23); *Smyrn.* 5.2 (Matt 16:26); 10.1 (Matt 10:40); *Pol.* 1.3 (Matt 8:17); 2.1 (Matt 5:46).

53. The above five Matthean borrowings in Ignatius less clearly parallel Mark and should accordingly be attributed to a Matthean or proto-Matthean source: *Trall.* 8.2// Matt 5:23//Mark 11:25; *Smyrn.* 10.1//Matt 10:40//Mark 9:41; 5.2//Matt 16:26//Mark 8:36–37; *Eph.* 6.1//Matt 21:33//Mark 12:1; 17.1//Matt 26:7//Mark 14:3. As for the third gospel, see Bellinzoni, "Luke in the Apostolic Fathers," 57–58. To the mentioned above, I find only one extra Lucan parallel in Ignatius: *Pol.* 2.1, where χάρις σοι οὐκ ἔστιν (no merit is for you) matches better Luke 6:32 than Matt 5:46. Of the remaining three possible, Matthew better parallels Ignatius in two: *Eph.* 6.1//Matt 21:33//Luke 12:42; 14.2// Matt 7:20//Luke 6:44. The exception is *Eph.* 11.1//Matt 3:5//Luke 3:7, but it is normal to be attracted by Matthew.

54. NA[28] 174.

55. The text is corrupted: *sicute* must be *sicuti*, meaning as well as; *semote* seems the

The author of Muratori is here most probably referring to the second part of Acts, narrated in the first plural (15:36—28:31), and, as it was custom in the early church, adjusting the whole book to what for him was the secure datum received from tradition. What is important for the setting of the Petrine tradition is that the author of Muratori considers Peter's martyrdom and Paul's travel to Spain major events, but lacking the book of Acts remembrance of them—if Luke had been an eyewitness of the events he reports, it would be expected for him to make some kind of reference to these events. The last consideration vouchsafes for prudence when a Roman reading for the martyrdom of Peter is pretended in Muratori, i.e., that its author had it in mind when he mentioned Peter's death.[56] Indeed, the sources for the knowledge of the two reported facts, the fourth gospel (John 21:18–19) and Paul to the Romans (15:24–28), are included in the list of writings in the power of the fragment's author (l.9–16,44–46,53). In consequence, and in spite of the possible candidature of the canon for the period AD 150–200, we cannot be confident that its author is backing the possible early independent Roman tradition concerning Peter's death around AD 64–67, or whether he represents an early receptor of the tradition attested in John 21.

The answer for the date and provenance of the Latin fragment discovered by Muratori in the Ambrosian library comes from the second folio, where the author states: *Pastorem uero nuperrin et temporibus nostris in urbe Roma Herma conscripsit sedente cathedra urbis romae aeclesiae Pio eps frater eius* (the Shepherd indeed Hermas wrote in our times in the city of Rome, being sat in the cathedra of the church of the city of Rome Pius the bishop his brother; lines 73–77). Hence, Pius I, said to be brother or Hermas, gives the earliest possible date for the work as AD 141–54. Very remarkable in the document, in the case that claims of detractors are vanquished and as we said first the II AD date and Roman authenticity accepted for Muratori, is the attestation of all the works later accepted in the NT canon except 1–2 Peter, James, and Hebrews (lines 1–60).[57]

---

feminine *semota*, aside, determining *passione*, that would be *passionis*, but requiring a verb absent in the text (set, put, omit, etc.); *ad* is the preposition of ablative, *ab* (from); *profectione* is no doubt *profectionis*, the genitive of *profectio*, departure; *proficescentis* may be the genitive participle of the verb *profiscor*, i.e., *proficescendi,* of the traveling. Contrast with emended text in Schnabel, "State of Research," 237.

56. Tregelles, *Earliest Catalogue*, 40 was of that opinion.

57. The questionable existence of a canon in the early Roman church for some scholars has led to an attack on the II AD date (Hahneman, "Muratorian Fragment," 405–15; summary of the critics in Rothschild, "Muratorian Roman Fake," 71–74). Together with other objections, the heaviest arguments to drive Muratori away from the II century are the lack of other lists of NT writings before the IV century (refuted by Ferguson, "Canon Muratori," 677–81), and the improbability that Hermas was brother

We have material proof in the Fayum, mid-northern Egypt, that Hebrews was joined in P⁴6 to the Pauline corpus by the early to middle II AD.[58] Though this single papyrus is not determinant, I am inclined to see in P⁴6 the confirmation of Muratori's western fabric from Hebrews' absence in it and the possibility of the composition of Hebrews in Egypt or perhaps not far from the Aegean, where most of the Pauline corpus should have been promptly gathered attending to the concentration of cities related to the Pauline mission. However, 1 Clem. 36.1–5 parallels Heb 1:3–13 in such a way that dependence in one of the parts must be accepted, not staying in minor degree of importance the consideration that Heb 13:24 affirms to be writing from Italy (ἀπὸ τῆς Ἰταλίας), interpreted to be Paul by the compiler of P[46], who placed Hebrews between Romans and 1 Corinthians, and suggested by Heb 13:23 proper, which calls Timothy our brother (τὸν ἀδελφὸν ἡμῶν Τιμόθεον). As for the gospels, the third and fourth are named in Muratori (*tertio euangelii*—see discussion below; line 2; *quarti euangeliorum*; line 9), attributed to Luke and John, and discussed (lines 2–33). Regrettably, the first and second gospels' names were mutilated during the text's transmission and they have not been preserved. Even so, it can be easily deduced that they were Matthew and Mark.

The understanding of Muratori's abrupt beginning, *quibus tamen interfuit et ita posuit*, demands interpretation: "with whom, however, he was, and so he put it" (i.e., he put it in writing; line 1). But from the barbarized Latin expression in what follows forthwith, line 2, *tertio euangelii librum secundo Lucan* (the third gospel is the book according to Luke; tertio

---

of Pius and thence the impossibility to accept the relation of Pius with the timeline of the canon's compiler (refuted by Schnabel, "State of Research," 244–53; summary of the discussion in Rothschild, "Muratorian Roman Fake," 55–69). As to the stronger ones, it should be noted that a discernment of writings in the mid-II AD church is consistent with the statement in Irenaeus that heretics of the period, Marcionites and Valentinians (mentioned in Muratori, lines 81–92), added or removed gospels to the already established four canonicals around AD 180 (*Haer.* 3.11:8–9). On the other hand, the refusal of the kinship Hermas-Pius doesn't prove by itself the author didn't write in times of Pius since in the early church some pseudo-origins of Christian items were in circulation. Last but not least, the accusations against the II AD date tours around the picaresque intention of a IV-century writing dressed in a II-century shape to legitimize particular views of the posterior NT canon. To have been the case, wider distribution should be expected. On the contrary, the fragment's poverty and the inexistence of undeniable falsification claim for its authenticity limited to local use.

58. Comfort and Barrett, *Earliest NT Manuscripts*, 1:183. The Pauline corpus of Marcion, extreme Paulinist active in Rome in AD 130–140, was of ten epistles. It can be obtained from Tertullian, *Marc.* 5: Gal, 1–2 Cor, Rom, 1–2 Thess, Eph, Col, Phil, Phlm. It didn't include Hebrews, but for determining Hebrews' cradle it is not very significant because if Hebrews were a western epistle, Marcion would have expunged it for its Judaean flavor anyway.

= tertium; secundo = secundum), it seems clear that line 1 of the extant fragment is related to the second evangelist. This accepted, we can posit the author of Muratori found some excusable inconvenience in the second evangelist, and if this is correct too, it is not far from being reasonable to see here an early reception of Papias, who according to Eusebius excuses Mark from not being Jesus' ocular witness and of being unsystematic in the manner that he compiled what he remembered of Peter's testimony, a passage over which we will later fall (Eusebius, *Hist. Eccl.* 3.39:15).

The Memoirs of the Apostles in Justin Martyr (AD 139–165)

Justin Martyr brings some most valuable reports. He is the undeniable first author out of the NT to apply the term *gospel/gospels* to a written document. A passage from the First Apology, whose original edition dates from AD 139 and was addressed to the emperor Antoninus Pius, refers to the gospels as written texts Justin calls *Memoirs of the Apostles*: Οἱ γὰρ ἀπόστολοι ἐν τοῖς γενομένοις ὑπ' αὐτῶν ἀπομνημονεύματα, ἃ καλεῖται Εὐαγγέλια (for the Apostles in the Memoirs yielded by them, which are called Gospels; 66.12–14).[59] Unfortunately, only two more occurrences of the written gospel/gospels appear in Justin (*Dial.* 10.12–13; 100.7). This strikingly collides with Justin's one hundred quotations/allusions to the canonical gospels, largely outnumbering the earlier fathers.[60] In defiance of the evolution which implies the jump from the oral gospel (1 Cor 9:14,28; 15:1; 2 Cor

59. The exact date for the original *1 Apol.*, possibly much more contracted and later edited until its current extension by Justin, drops from the exordium's imperial titles: Αὐτοκράτορι Τίτῳ Αἰλίῳ Ἀδριανῷ Ἀντονίνῳ Εὐσεβεί Σεβαστῷ Καίσαρι, καὶ Οὐηρισσίμῳ υἱῷ φιλσόφῳ, καὶ Λουκίῳ φιλοσόφῳ Καίσαρος φύσει υἱῷ καὶ Εὐσεβοῦς εἰσποιήτῳ (To the Autocrator (= Self-Ruler) Titus Aelius Adrianus Antoninus Pius Emperor Caesar, and to the son Verissimus Philosopher, and to Lucius Philosopher natural son of Caesar and adopted of Pius). The complete name of the second authority, Verissimos the Philosopher, was Marcus Annius Verus (the later emperor Marcus Aurelius, AD 161–180), adopted as Lucius by Antoninus, who in the ascension to power didn't have male descendants. M. Verus, here Verissimus, received the participation in the title of Caesar in AD 140. Hence, we are just at the beginning of Antoninus' reign, AD 139. The reference in *1 Apol.* 46.2–3 to the birth of Christ 150 years before Justin was writing (πρὸ ἐτῶν ἑκατὸν πεντήκοντα) must be seen as a round number (see commentary in Trollope, *Apologia Prima*, 15–17, 99). Indeed, the adverb νῦν (now, at the present) when Justin speaks of Bar Kokhba's revolt, the Second Jewish War (AD 132–35), points to a most recent event (*1 Apol.* 31.22–23).

60. See index in Falls, *Justin*, 482. Citations in Justin habitually seem interwoven from memory. He feels a preference for Matthew with seventy-five quotations/allusions. Then comes Luke with twenty-five, Mark with six (see below), and John four.

2:12; 8:18; Gal 2:2; Eph 6:19; 1 Thess 2:4) to gospel documents, three usages alone of *εὐαγγέλιον/εὐαγγέλια* for one hundred occurrences denote Justin's reluctance for the free employment of the term.[61]

Two chief reasons are given to explain the fact: (a) for the Platonist Justin, only the Logos-Jesus is the spoken Word of God which fits alone the vital implications of the term, whereas the written gospels did not yet have independent authority;[62] (b) Justin shunned the term *gospel/gospels* because the Marcionite heretics had misappropriated it.[63] But, in view that Justin was the first sure extant author to apply the term *gospel* to a document, a third reason can be hypothesized if Justin is set within the general stream of the first half of II-century Christianity: the usual term for sacred documents was still the Jewish expression *ἡ γραφή/αἱ γραφαί* (the Scripture/Scriptures), which referred to the OT literature (Rom 1:2; 4:3; 1 Cor 15:3; Gal 3:22; 4:30; 2 Tim 3:16), while the written gospels were still on the way to reach the same level of authority.[64] Indeed, the third reason can be deemed a generalization of the first but including the second as well in the sense that heretics could only appeal for the greater authority of some writings against others if the NT canon was not yet established. At any rate, to solve the enigma, the discussion will focus the expression *Memoirs of the Apostles* (*ἀπομνημονεύματα τῶν ἀποστόλων*), which Justin preferably employs instead of *gospel/gospels*.

Justin has eleven usages of it in total (*1 Apol.* 66.13; 67.8; *Dial.* 101.24; 103.47; 104.10; 105.9.31.34; 106.11.19; 107.2). From all these, special heed must be given to the second occurrence in the *First Apology* of the expression *Memoirs of the Apostles*. It offers the precious early church detail concerning the reading of the gospels during the public assemblies along with the Jewish Scriptures: *καὶ τῇ τοῦ Ἡλίου λεγομένῃ ἡμέρᾳ πάντων κατὰ πόλεις ἢ ἀγροὺς μενόντων ἐπὶ τὸ αὐτὸ συνέλευσις γίνεται, καὶ τὰ ἀπομνημονεύματα τῶν ἀποστόλων ἢ τὰ συγγράμματα τῶν προφητῶν ἀναγινώσκεται, μέχρις ἐγχωρεῖ*

61. In the Pauline corpus, the oral character of the gospel manifests its author and object as God. The main expressions are εὐαγγέλιον τοῦ θεοῦ (gospel of God; Rom 15:16; 2 Cor 11:7; 1 Thess 2:8), and ε. τοῦ Χριστοῦ (g. of Christ; Rom 15:19; 1 Cor 9:12; 2 Cor 9:13; 10:14; Gal 1:7; Phil 1:27; 1 Thess 3:2). Incidentally: ε. τοῦ υἱοῦ τοῦ θεοῦ (g. of the Son of God; Rom 1:9); ε. τοῦ κυρίου ἡμῶν Ἰησοῦ (g. of our Lord Jesus; 2 Thess 1:8); ε. τῆς δόξης τοῦ μακαρίου θεοῦ (g. of the glory of the blessed God; 1 Tim 1:11); ε. τῆς δόξης τοῦ Χριστοῦ (g. of the glory of Christ; 2 Cor 4:4). For a complete account of εὐαγγέλιον in the NT see Thayer, *Lexicon of the New Testament*, 257.

62. Piper, "Gospel according to Justin," 162–66; a variant Cosgrove, "Justin Martyr," 221–25.

63. Cosgrove, "Justin Martyr," 224.

64. More occurrences of ἡ γραφή/αἱ γραφαί: Matt 21:42; 26:54; Mark 12:10; 14:49; Luke 24:27; John 5:39; 7:38; 10:35; Acts 8:32,35; 17:2,11; 18:24,28; Jas 2:8; 1 Pet 2:6; 2 Pet 1:20.

(and in the day called of the Sun, all from the cities or remaining in the fields come into the same meeting, and the Memoirs of the Apostles or the writings of the Prophets are read, as far as is allowed; *1 Apol.* 67.11–14).[65]

The lecture of the Memoirs side by side with the Jewish prophets in the Sunday service strongly suggests that in the mid II century the gospels were on the course of being considered, if not already, inspired literature. Patently, the advantage to read the gospels in the Christian meeting was to prove the fulfillment of the OT prophecies in Jesus (Rom 1:2; 16:26; 1 Cor 15:3; John 5:39; Acts 8:32–35; 18:28), and to present the community examples or teachings worth to imitate likewise.[66] Notwithstanding, in this stage the OT was possibly still considered sacred Scripture in a higher degree for its more ancient trajectory, for the fact that Jesus has since the dawn of Christianity been presented as the promised Messiah, because the oral gospel was yet a supreme spiritual event and less a group of documents, and lastly because the early discernment we see in Muratori about which Christian writings must be taken as canonical and which must not, was not yet universally accepted. This group of factors would coherently explain why earlier fathers to Justin, Clement Romanus, Ignatius, and Polycarp, don't yet refer to the gospels as written documents.[67]

In connection with this, another remarkable feature in Justin is the less-defined expression *Memoirs of the Apostles* compared to the lack of

65. According to Pliny the Younger, *Epistulae* 10.96 to Trajan (AD 98–117), the Christians of Bithynia ca. AD 110, north Anatolia, were used to meet at a fixed day before the daybreak (*quod essent soliti stato die ante lucem convenire*), most probably on Sunday. Even so, the observance of the Sabbath by the Anatolian Judeo-Christians survived the beginning of the II century AD. Ignatius; *Magn.* 9.1: *μηκέτι σαββατίζοντες, ἀλλὰ κατὰ κυριακήν* (no longer keeping the Sabbath, but according to the Lord's day).

66. *1 Apol.* 31–42 and 48–56 examines the OT searching prototypes of Christ. The *Dialogue* exploits so wearily the topic that the fictitious character of the conversation with Trypho the Jew is exposed, being by extension superfluous to itemize all the references: 32–34; 36–43; 58–92, etc. In *Dial.* 1.15–17 Trypho presents himself a refugee of the Second Jewish War (AD 132–35) living in Corinth, what would mark a date close to AD 140. The encounter with Justin could have occurred in Ephesus, if we accept Eusebius, *Hist. Eccl.* 4.18:6, but the work as it stands is fictitious in character. Trypho is endlessly adapted to the narrative purpose of the author in the manner of Socratic dialectics, something unconceivable in real conversation.

67. Certainly, τῷ εὐαγγελίῳ in Ignatius, *Smyrn.* 7.2 seems referred to a written document, though its written character is not directly reported and thus is subjected to interpretation. It may be true that Ignatius worked with written sources whence he borrows gospel quotations/allusions, but the claim of Hill, "Ignatius," 271–83 that all the eight usages of the term *gospel* in Ignatius (*Phld.* 5.1–2, three times; 8.2; 9.1–2, two times; *Smyrn.* 5.1; 7.2) respond to document sources loses fuel when the usages are put alongside the oral/spiritual gospel of Paul (see Foster, "Ignatius and the Gospels," 82–87, 105–6 and note above).

the evangelists' names proper. To the contrary, the contemporary Canon Muratori mentions the third and four evangelists, Luke and John, leaving the second position in the ladder of authority to the remaining NT canon (except Hebrews, James, 1 and 2 Peter). Fatefully or not, we saw that the head list is mutilated, lacking the names of the first and second evangelists. Hadn't Justin yet received the four gospel tradition attested in Muratori and Irenaeus, or was he intending to wedge a new expression? In my opinion, the first answer is more reasonable. The undisputable works of Justin, *First* and *Second Apology*, and *Dialogue with Trypho*, touch in extension too many themes of the Christian tradition, too much to consider Justin was aware of the four evangelists and averted from getting apologetic benefit. Hence, the expression *ἀπομνημονεύματα τῶν ἀποστόλων* would be a terminus medium between the four gospels after their anonym stage of composition during the late I-century and the II-century AD tradition of the four evangelists.

Curiously, one of six Marcan citations in Justin would be presenting the second extant attribution of the second gospel to Peter.[68] The earliest possible echo to Papias on Mark and Peter among the fathers of the II century would be, therefore, Justin's *Dialogus cum Tryphone* 106.16–19 quoting Mark 3:16–17 and referring to the second gospel with the intermediate term *Memoirs of Peter*. Howbeit, the obliqueness of the text sinks it into dispute. It runs as follows: *Καὶ τὸ εἰπεῖν μετωνομακέσαι αὐτὸν Πέτρον ἕνα τῶν ἀποστόλων καὶ γεγράφθαι ἐν τοῖς ἀπομνημονεύμασιν αὐτοῦ γεγενημένον καὶ τοῦτο, μετὰ τοῦ καὶ ἄλλους δύο ἀδελφούς, υἱοὺς Σεβαδαίου ὄντας, μετωνομακέσαι ὀνόματι τοῦ Βοανεργὲς, ὅ ἐστιν υἱοὶ βροντῆς* (and what is said that He changed the name to Peter, one of the Apostles, it is written in the Memoirs of him (that) this happened, and that afterwards to another two brothers, being sons of Zebedee, changed the name to Boanerges, which is sons of the thunder).

Just like the reader can observe, the genitive *αὐτοῦ* (his) in the expression *ἐν τοῖς ἀπομνημονεύμασιν αὐτοῦ* can be either directed to Jesus or Peter, i.e., in the Memoirs of Jesus or Peter. In favor of the second option, i.e., Memoirs of Peter, we have in first position that the expression *ὀνόματι Βοανεργὲς, ὅ ἐστιν υἱοὶ βροντῆς* belongs to Mark's gospel; secondly, that the former third personal pronoun in the expression *μετωνομακέσαι αὐτὸν Πέτρον* is referred to Peter (literally: changed him Peter the name); and in third place, that the expression *ἀπομνημονεύματα* (Memoirs) positively seems borrowed from a common tradition to Papias on Mark because for the bishop of Hierapolis, Mark didn't heard the Lord (*οὔτε γὰρ ἤκουσε τοῦ Κυρίου*), nor did he follow him (*οὔτε παρηκολούθησεν αὐτῷ*), but wrote as far as he remembered from

68. See detailed discussion below.

Peter (ὅσα ἐμνημόνευσεν), or as he remembered them (ὡς ἀπεμνημόνευσεν).[69] It is conceivable, therefore, that Justin leans on a tradition Papias knew before him when he calls the gospel documents Memoirs of the Apostles or that in the best of cases he even could discriminate the second gospel provenance as Petrine document before it acquired its definitive name, i.e., Gospel of Mark.[70] It sounds cogent. Albeit, Xenophon composed the work Ἀπομνημονεύματα, Memoirs (of Socrates) in the first half of the IV century BC, best known for its Latin title *Memorabilia*. It is doubtful if Justin got the notion of ἀπομνημονεύματα from it, but since Justin had been a Platonist (*Dial.* 1–7), the possibility of a borrowing from Xenophon cannot be fully disdained.[71]

In addition, the grammar of chapter 106 sheds some objections to the assumption that Justin is by force acknowledging the existence of a gospel comprising memories attributed to Peter and not better to the apostles in general or to Jesus. First is the fact that among the six occurrences of the genitive αὐτοῦ in chapter 106 of the *Dialogue*, five are unquestionably attributed to God/Jesus.[72] Moreover, amongst the remaining thirteen occurrences of the third singular pronoun, one nominative αὐτός (he), nine accusatives αὐτόν (him), and three datives αὐτῷ (to him), solely the already mentioned αὐτόν in line 16 represents, semantically, other substantive than God/Jesus (Peter).[73] Lastly, in line 29 we even have the full expression ἐν τοῖς ἀπομνημονεύμασιν τῶν ἀποστόλων αὐτοῦ (in the Memories of his Apostles),

69. Eusebius, *Hist. Eccl.* 3.39:15.

70. Heard, "Papias," 122–26.

71. Heard, "Papias," 125 feels skeptical with the possibility. More favorable is Fialová, "Memoirs of the Apostles," 169.

72. *Dial.* 100.16–18: πατέρα αὐτοῦ (his father; line 1); τῶν ἀδελφῶν αὐτοῦ (his brothers; line 5); πεισθῆναι ὑπ' αὐτοῦ (being persuaded by him; line 7); μετενόησαν ἐπὶ τῷ ἀφίστασθαι αὐτοῦ (they repented of the refusal of him; line 9); ἐν τοῖς ἀπομνημονεύμασιν αὐτοῦ (in the Memories of him; line 17); ἐν τοῖς ἀπομνημονεύμασιν τῶν ἀποστόλων αὐτοῦ (in the Memories of the Apostles of him; line 29).

73. *Pace* Fialová, "Memoirs of the Apostles," 173, who follows Heard, "Papias," 126, the resting thirteen occurrences of the third singular personal pronoun in chapter 106 only give one possible use for substantives other than God/Jesus: μετωνομακέναι αὐτόν (i.e., Peter; line 16). Leaving the six above genitives apart, we have one nominative (ἀνατέλλειν αὐτός, he is risen; line 17); nine accusatives (ἀνήγειρεν αὐτόν, they stood him up; line 2; μετὰ τὸ ἀναστῆσαι αὐτόν, after resurrecting him; line 6; ταῦτα αὐτὸν δεῖ παθεῖν, these things he must suffer; line 8; αἰνέσατε αὐτόν, praised him; line 14; δοξάσατε αὐτόν, glorified him; line 15; φοβηθήτωσαν αὐτόν, he was feared; line 15; μετωνομακέναι αὐτόν, changed him the name; line 16; ἦν τοῦ αὐτόν, was him; line 20; γεννηθῆναι αὐτόν, he was born; line 28), and three datives (παρέχειν αὐτῷ, grant to him; line 2; ἀνατολὴ ὄνομα αὐτῷ, the east (is) name for him; line 27; προσεκύνησαν αὐτῷ, they worshiped him; lines 30–31).

where αὐτοῦ unmistakably refers to Jesus. Following the more frequent plural Memoirs of the Apostles in Justin, ten uses for one singular, from line 29, it becomes reasonable to correct ἀπομνημονεύμασιν αὐτοῦ in line 17 by ἀπομνημονεύμασιν αὐτῶν, i.e., Memoirs of him, Peter, for Memoirs of them, the Apostles, or if the singular genitive αὐτοῦ in line 17 is maintained ascribe it to Jesus. Let the reader judge.

The remaining references in Justin to the second gospel are four in five occurrences: (1) *1 Apol.* 16.22–23: ἐξ ὅλης τῆς καρδίας σοῦ, καὶ ἐξ ὅλης τῆς ἰσχύος σου (from all your heart, and from all your strength)//Mark 12:30; (2) *1 Apol.* 16.24–25: Καὶ προσελθόντος αὐτῷ τινος, καὶ εἰπόντος, Διδάςκαλε ἀγαθὲ, ἀπεκρίνατο λέγων· Οὐδεὶς ἀγαθὸς, εἰ μὴ μόνος ὁ θεὸς (And approached someone to him, and saying, good Teacher, he answered saying: None is good, but God alone)//Mark 10:18; (3) *1 Apol.* 45.15–16, which overlaps the longer ending of Mark: τοῦ λόγου τοῦ ἰσχυροῦ, ὃν ἀπὸ Ἰερουσαλὴν οἱ ἀπόστολοι αὐτοῦ ἐξελθόντες πανταχοῦ ἐκήρυξαν (the mighty word, which his apostles departing from Jerusalem proclaimed everywhere)//Mark 16:20;[74] (4–5) *Dial.* 76.41–43; 100.16–18: Δεῖ τὸν υἱὸν τοῦ ἀνθρώπου πολλὰ παθεῖν, καὶ ἀποδοκιμασθῆναι ὑπὸ τῶν γραμματέων καὶ φαρισαίων, καὶ σταυρωθῆναι, καὶ τῇ τρίτῃ ἡμέρᾳ ἀναστῆναι (the Son of Man must suffer a lot, and be rejected by the scribes and Pharisees, and rise in the third day)//Mark 8:31.[75]

1 Apol. 16.22–23 and 16.24–25 offer two Marcan parallels, one following another. What sort of source Justin is quoting is not entirely clear. *1 Apol.* 16.22–23 appear to be taken from a shortened Mark 12:30 since τῆς ἰσχύος σου doesn't agree with the source, LXX Deut 6:5, which bears a synonym (τῆς δυνάμεώς σου; from your power/strength), nor with Matt 22:37 (lacks parallel word) or with the best attested form in Luke 10:27 (τῇ ἰσχύϊ σου; with your strength).[76] But *1 Apol.* 16.22–23 is clearly introduced by 16.20 μεγίςτη ἐντολή (greatest commandment), which resembles more Matt

74. *1 Apol.* 45.15–16, and more loosely 39.8–9 and *Dial.* 53.35–36 parallel Mark 16:20: ἐκεῖνοι δὲ ἐξελθόντες ἐκήρυξαν πανταχοῦ, τοῦ κυρίου συνεργοῦντος καὶ τὸν λόγον (but departing they proclaimed everywhere, cooperating the Lord and confirming the word). Metzger, *Greek New Testament*, 122–26 was of the opinion that *1 Apol.* 45.15–16 is not a true Marcan parallel. See further discussion on the matter in the assessment ending chapter 1.

75. *Dial.* 100.16–18: the same saying but alternating τῶν φαρισαίων καὶ γραμματέων. For the adverbial rendering of πολλά, see section on Semitisms. Otherwise πολλά means *many things.*

76. NA[2]8 228: the eldest witness to the dative τῇ ἰσχύϊ σου (with your force) is P[75], middle-II to early-III AD papyrus (Comfort, *Earliest NT Manuscripts* 2, 11–15). Other strong witnesses for the most ancient reading are: D and א.

22:36,38 ἐντολὴ μεγάλη (great commandment) than Mark 12:28 ἐντολὴ πρώτη (first commandment) and Luke 10:27 (lacks parallel expression).[77]

Out of doubt, the sources for the full reading of *1 Apol.* 16.20–23 form a conundrum: Μεγίςτη ἐντολή ἐστι, κύριον τὸν θεόν σου προσκυνήσεις, καὶ αὐτῷ μόνῳ λατρεύσεις ἐξ ὅλῆς τῆς καρδίας σοῦ, καὶ ἐξ ὅλῆς τῆς ἰσχύος σου (the greatest commandment is, (the) Lord your God shall worship, and Him alone you shall serve from all your heart, and from all your strength). Justin chain of quotations is apparently a sandwich framed with Matt 22:36 + LXX Deut 6:13 (or Deut 10:20) + Mark 12:30. Interestingly, the eastern reading in Codex Alexandrinus (A) for Deut 6:13 and 10:20 and at least one minuscule have προσκυνήσεις (you will worship) instead of the more attested φοβηθήσῃ (you will fear) from B and א.[78] As for *1 Apol.* 16.24–25, Διδάςκαλε ἀγαθέ and Οὐδεὶς ἀγαθός, εἰ μὴ μόνος ὁ θεός is closely similar to Mark 10:17 (διδάςκαλε ἀγαθέ; good teacher) and Mark 10:18 (Οὐδεὶς ἀγαθός, εἰ μὴ εἷς ὁ θεός; no one is good, but one, God) or Luke 18:18–19, where the same combination with εἷς (one) instead of μόνος (alone) is found.

It is impossible Justin is here conflating three sources. The more understandable answer to the conundrum is that Justin is paraphrasing from memory, or perhaps using a manuscript wherein the sayings doesn't equate the synoptic gospels in the case that he were literally reproducing one single written source. Peering at *Dial.* 100.16–18, one is led to the same conclusion, diluting the certainty to be before a Marcan reading: the first part is common to the synoptics but the reading φαρισαίων in the second one doesn't belong to them. Further, τῇ τρίτῃ ἡμέρᾳ (in the third day) doesn't appear in Mark 8:31 (μετὰ τρεῖς ἡμέρας; after three days) but in Matt 16:21 and Luke 9:22, and ἀναστήναι (rise) is seen in Mark 8:31 but not in Matt 16:21 and Luke 9:22 (ἐγερθῆναι; be raised).[79]

77. μεγάλη in Matt 22:36,38 should be understood as *greatest* because the Semitic adjective expected in Jesus would lack comparison degree.

78. Rahlfs, *Septuaginta*, 1:298; NA[28] 228. Codex A (V AD) also gives τῆς ἰσχύος σου for Luke 10:27. This codex presents the earliest form of the byzantine text for the gospels, less valuable to debug the original reading when it stands alone for the earliest variant, but yet says something about late eastern readings. This is not the case with A Luke 9:22 ἀναστήναι, commented in next note, attested also in D.

79. NA[28] 220. Codex A Luke 9:22 has τῇ τρίτῃ ἡμέρᾳ ἀναστήναι, the verb corroborated by the Bezaean, who has μετὰ τρεῖς ἡμέρας ἀναστήναι (after three days rise) also for Matt 16:21 and Mark 8:31. Defenders of the *Textus Receptus* will tend to assent the original reading in A, because Erasmus, the typesetter of the *Receptus*, relied on the Byzantine or Majority text-type for the NT.

Secunda Clementis (ca. AD 150)

The so-called Second Epistle of Clement to the Corinthians survives in three manuscripts, the eldest of which for the Greek text is the uncial Codex Alexandrinus (A), dated acceptably in the V century AD. In Codex A 2 Clem. is appended to 1 Clem., a deed that can say something about its place of composition or major employment. The epistle—chapters 19–20 reveal it was devised more as a homily than as letter—enters the domain of the great part of early Christian literature and its date is a disputed issue.[80] The author writes, apparently, from a harbor in which athletes disembark (καταπλέω) seeking fortune (2 Clem. 7.1–3).[81] The image of the harbor and the association of 2 Clem. with 1 Clem. in A bring to mind Rome and Corinth. According to Eusebius, 1 Clem. oftentimes was read by bishop Dionysius in Corinth (ca. AD 170) along with the letter of the Roman bishop Soter (AD 168–74), and it has been pointed out that, in fact, Soter could be the author of the so-called 2 Clem.[82] Against the Roman ascendance of 2 Clem. works the survival of the document beyond A only in medieval eastern manuscripts, H, and S, and some more indications that will be given below.[83]

On the question of date, some pointers heedfully assessed affix 2 Clem. to the temporal backdrop partaken by Justin. Noticeable from this viewpoint is that gospel is here, like in Justin, written authority. In 2 Clem. 2.4 the saying elsewhere found in Matt 9:13//Mark 2:17//Luke 5:32 is called ἡ γραφή (the Scripture), enabling the identification of the written character of the expression ἐν τῷ εὐαγγελίῳ (in the gospel) before quoting Luke 16:10–12 in 2 Clem. 8.5. The author of 2 Clem. ostensibly has before him the last edition of Matthew or Luke, or perhaps more accurately some sort of Q manuscript inasmuch as he basically borrows sayings, not episodes of Jesus' life, and for the main reason because some of the sayings are unknown to the canonical gospels or furnished by 2 Clem. mingled with apocryphal material.[84]

80. For the question of genre and structure, see Vermer, *Second Clement*, 17–28.

81. I take this insight from Donfried, "Theology of Second Clement," 499. 2 Clem. 7 speaks in such a manner that the audience seems familiar with the experience of athletes disembarking for the games. The crucial word καταπλέω is found twice in this chapter and once in Luke 8:26 in all I–II AD Christian literature (Vermer, *Second Clement*, 13–15).

82. Eusebius, *Hist. Eccl.* 4.23:11. The opinion returns back until von Harnack (d. 1930).

83. Beyond A, 2 Clem. has come down to the present in Codex Hierosolymitanus dated in 1056, housed in Jerusalem but found in Istanbul in 1873 (designed thus H, H^{54} according to catalog, or C), and in S, Syriac ms written by a monk from Edessa, today southeastern Turkey, from 1169 (Ehrman, *Apostolic Fathers*, 1:161–62).

84. Canonical sayings: 2 Clem. 3.2//Matt 10:32//Luke 12:8; 3.4//Mark 12:30; 4.2//

A level of ambiguity in the notion of written gospels cannot, certainly, be expunged from 2 Clem. It will be observed that when the author invokes the general authority of sacred writings in 14.2 he brings the phrase τὰ βιβλία καὶ οἱ ἀπόστολοι (the Books and the Apostles), denoting seemingly with *apostles* all Christian Scripture. Justin (ἀπομνημονεύματα τῶν ἀποστόλων) and Muratori (*neque inter profetas . . . neque inter apostolos*; nor among the Prophets . . . nor among the Apostles; lines 79–80) recall similar labels for the Christian Scriptures, a reason wherefore the date around AD 150 can be conjectured.[85] Chapter 14 in 2 Clem. is interesting for another question. It subscribes the ecclesiological notion of Christ's body (Eph 1:22–23; 4:12,15–16; 5:23,29–30; Col 1:18), standing startlingly next to Ephesians and Colossians like the exclusive loci for the Pauline σῶμα Χριστοῦ applied to the church in early Christian literature.[86] It should be also noted that in 2 Clem. the Pauline concept dresses Gnostic winks (14.1–3), regardless of the graveness and general orthodoxy of the remaining chapters (one exception is 2 Clem. 12.2 paralleling Gos. Thom. 22).[87]

Matt 7:21; 6.1//Matt 6:24//Luke 16:13; 6.2//Matt 16:26//Mark 8:36//Luke 9:25; 8.5// Luke 16:10–12; 9.10//Matt 12:50; 13.4//Luke 6,32,35. Between canonical and apocryphal composition: 2 Clem. 4.5//Ps 6:9//Matt 7:23; 25:12; 5.2–4//Matt 10:16,28//Luke 10:3; 12:4–5. Unknown provenance: 2 Clem. 13.9. Reminiscences to Jesus' sayings: 2 Clem. 11.3//Mark 4:28; 15.4//Acts 20:35.

85. The origin, shortly after 1 Clem., around AD 100 has also been proposed over the assumption that 2 Clem. was a response to the Corinthian community from the presbyters which would have been removed by rebellious elements some years before according to 1 Clem. 57.6 and 44.1–6 (Donfried, "Theology of Second Clement," 499; *Setting of Second Clement*, 1–15). Nevertheless, 2 Clem.'s first concern is not the reintegration of the presbyters, but leaves still broad space to the theory insofar as the document could be a rhetorical appeal to obedience. Anyhow, the theory doesn't settle perfectly 2 Clem. within the Levantine transmission of the text, but success in explaining the early association to 1 Clem. in Corinth.

86. The reading of 2 Clem. 14 points to certain but no more than oblique dependence in Ephesians or/and Colossians (Kelhoffer, "2 Clement 14," 383–407).

87. The teachings of 2 Clem., perhaps more than the author himself, betrays platonic background. Even so, the entire equilibrium of 2 Clem., its prevalence of orthodox resource to Scripture, the defense of virtuous deeds where if the author were a Gnostic it should be expected secret knowledge (4.3; 5.1; 8.1–6; 9.2; 10.1; 11.6; 12.3; 14.1), and the insistency in chastity but not falling in marriage condemnation (7.6; 8.4–6; 9.3; 13.5; 15.1) will prevent from overestimating its pro-heterodox major expressions: (1) 3.1; 20.5: τὸν πατέρα τῆς ἀληθείας (the Father of truth); (2) 9.5: Jesus as pre-existing πνεῦμα; (3) 12.2: ὅταν ἔσται τὰ δύο ἕν, καὶ τὸ ἔξω ὡς τὸ ἔσω. καὶ τὸ ἄρσεν μετὰ τῆς θηλείας, οὔτε ἄρσεν οὔτε θῆλυ (when the two things will be one, and the outside like the inside. And the male with the female, nor male neither female); (4) 14.1: ἐσόμεθα ἐκ τῆς ἐκκλησίας τῆς πρώτης, τῆς πνευματικῆς (we will be of the first church, the spiritual); (5) 14.1: ἀπὸ τῆς ἐκκλησίας τῆς ζωῆς εἶναι (be of the church of the life); (6) 14.2: ἦν γὰρ πνευματική (for she was spiritual); (7) 14.3: ἡ ἐκκλησία δὲ πνευματικὴ οὖσα (but being the church

For our case, the provenance of Secunda Clementis and its use yield diagnostic criteria for assessing 1 Peter and Mark. The foregoing analytical style will be maintained affording first the Marcan shadings and then the Petrine. Discounted synoptic parallels which in grammatical grounds belong to Matthean or Lucan sources, the Marcan coloring of 2 Clem. occurs in the next three spots: (a) 3.4 paraphrases the OT in a way resembling more Mark 12:30 than LXX Deut 6:5; Matt 22:37; and Luke 10:27: *ἀλλὰ ἐξ ὅλης καρδίας καὶ ἐξ ὅλης τῆς διανοίας* (but from all heart and from all the mind);[88] (b) 7.6 (restated in 17.5) quotes Isa 66:24, only used by Mark 9:48 among the canonical gospels; (c) 11.3, one homemade parable recalling the growing seed of Mark 4:28: *λάβετε ἄμπελον· πρῶτον μὲν φυλλοροεῖ, εἶτα βλαστὸς γίνεται, μετὰ ταῦτα ὄμφαξ, εἶτα σταφυλὴ παρεστηκυῖα* (take the vine: first it springs the leaves, then it comes a bud, after these things an unripe grape, then a dense bunch).

After squeezing 2 Clem., the Petrine reminiscences reckon nine instances:[89] (a) 1.1: Jesus Christ is called *κριτοῦ ζώντων καὶ νεκρῶν* (judge of living and dead)//1 Pet 4:5, but see also Acts 10:42; 2 Tim 4:1; (b) 1.2: *ὅσα ὑπέμεινεν Ἰησοῦς Χριστὸς παθεῖν ἕνεκα ἡμῶν* (how much suffering endured Jesus Christ for our sake)//1 Pet 1:11; 2:11; 4:1,13; 5:1; (c) 5.1: the present life as *παροικία* (exile)//1 Pet 1:17; 2:11; (d) 5.2–4: dialogue of Jesus with Peter framed with canonical (Matt 10:16,28; Luke 10:3; 12:4–5) and apocryphal material; (e) 11.2: expression on popular skepticism in God's coming//2 Pet 3:4;[90] (f) 16.4: *ἀγάπη δὲ καλύπτει πλῆθος ἁμαρτιῶν* (but love covers a multitude of sins)//1 Pet 4:8; (g) again 16.4: *προσευχὴ δὲ ἐκ καλῆς συνειδήσεως* (but prayer from a good conscience)//1 Pet 3:21: *συνειδήσεως ἀγαθῆς ἐπερώτημα* (an appeal from a good conscience); (h) again 16.4: *μακάριος πᾶς ὁ εὑρεθεὶς ἐν τούτοις πλήρης* (blessed every one who is found full in these things), and 19.3: *μακάριοι οἱ τοῦτοις ὑπακούοντες τοῖς προστάγμασιν* (blessed the ones obedient to these commandments)//Matt 5:3–11//Luke 6:20–22//1 Pet 3:14; 4:13; (i)

---

spiritual); (8) 14.3: *ἡ γὰρ σὰρξ αὕτη ἀντίτυπος ἐστιν τοῦ πνεύματος* (for this flesh is the antitype of the spirit); (9) 14.3: *τηρήσατε τὴν σάρκα, ἵνα τοῦ πνεύματος μεταλάβητε* (keep the flesh that you may receive the Spirit).

88. LXX Deut 6:5: *ἐξ ὅλης τῆς καρδίας* lacking *τῆς διανοίας*; Matt 22:37: *ἐν ὅλῃ τῇ καρδίᾳ . . . ἐν ὅλῃ τῇ διανοίᾳ*; Mark 12:30: *ἐξ ὅλης τῆς καρδίας . . . ἐξ ὅλης τῆς διανοίας*; Luke 10:27 seems a conflation with Matthew: *ἐξ ὅλης τῆς καρδίας . . . ἐν ὅλῃ τῇ διανοίᾳ* (from all the heart . . . with all the mind).

89. Vermer, *Second Clement*, 49–153 is recommendable for his lucid approach to 2 Clem., without which I would have been oblivious to some of the Marcan and Petrine parallels.

90. The unbelief in God's coming was, from yore, a topic in Israel: Isa 5:19; Jer 17:15; Ezek 12:22.

17.3.5 mention the πρεσβύτεροι (elders) as church admonishers and leaders but lacking reference to the bishop//1 Pet 5:1.

As we see, the Marcan and Petrine material in 2 Clem. is abundant, though partly it can be warranted by indirect borrowing. The conspicuous blessings in 2 Clem. 16.4 and 19.3 are in view OT fabric (Ps 1:1; 32:1; 65:4, etc.), perhaps Matthean, or it will be granted in the best of cases, more inspired from a Q source than lendings of 1 Peter. Some more parallels, the use of Deut 6:5 in 2 Clem. 3.4, or the notion of Jesus as judge of living and dead in 1.1, can be reduced likewise. Even so, especially remarkable is the parable of the vine in 2 Clem. 11.3 for its close likeness with Mark 4:28, and two consecutive 1 Peter's parallels in 16.4, the former appearing also in 1 Clem. 49.5.

The parallel cast between 1 Clem. 49.5; 2 Clem. 16.4; and 1 Pet 4:8 (love covers a multitude of sins) added to the survival of 2 Clem. annexed to 1 Clem., and to the fact that the letter of Bishop Soter was read alongside 1 Clem. by Dionysius in Corinth (if the hypothesis of a Roman hand behind 2 Clem. is accepted), contribute to the Roman ascription of Secunda Clementis, all of which enforces the Roman candidature of the second gospel insofar Marcan coloring in 2 Clem. is palpable accompanied there with Clementine and Petrine connections. Furthermore, the concern of 1 Pet 3:1–7; Eph 5:22–24; and Col 3:18 for setting a fence around women's ornament and independence, the seafaring context of 2 Clem. 7.1–3, the heterogeneous audience (men and women) hearing the homily in 2 Clem. 19.1 and 20.2, and the permissive sexual demeanor sieved through the insistence of 2 Clem. 7.6; 8.4–6; 9.3; 13.5; 15.1; and 18.2 in chastity denote a Hellenized or Romanized urban environment against rural scenery or smaller settlements where family relations are by rule more solid and sexual deviations less strong.

But if it were the case, if 2 Clem. were a Roman document, its absence in L, Belgian ms of Clementine writings from the XI century with a Latin translation of 1 Clem. going back to the II–III centuries, would be as incomprehensible as the lack of 1 Peter in Muratori if it were not pseudonymous.[91]

91. The editor of L's *princeps* found proven the II–III AD date in the next textual arguments (Morin, *Clementis Romani*, viii–xiv): (a) use of the Scripture and of Latin in a rustic way similar to the Vetus Latina anterior to the Vulgate (some twenty-five barbarisms underscored: *surrectionem diei*; *bestiae enim silvestrae*, etc.); (b) some Hebraisms have come to the Latin through a Greek scribe; (c) agreement in passages of Scripture with the Syriac version based in western translations; (d) accordance with quotations of 1 Clem. in Clement Alexandrinus (early III AD) when the two disagree from A 1 Clem. (IV–V AD). I find to be proven beyond doubt the early date pointed out by the editor in the last argument alone, namely: (1) L 1 Clem.1.10: *et in legitimis Dei ambulabatis* (and walked in the customs of God—Latin *legitimi*—); *Strom.* 4.17: καὶ ἐν τοῖς νομίμοις τοῦ

The verdict on 2 Clem. is, despite everything said, baffling, but if the problem of pseudonymity is taken seriously, we must surrender to Hellenistic provenance. The great part of Secunda Clementis' recognized witnesses are eastern: Eusebius, Apostolic Canons, Severus of Antioch, and Photius; but whereas in the IV AD Eusebius, who had larger knowledge of church tradition in the west, vetoed the authenticity of 2 Clem. (*Hist. Eccl.* 3.38:4), the Syrian document Const. ap. 8.47:85 in the same century considered it sacred Scripture, recognizing its eastern production and circulation, as did in the V AD its appending in Codex Alexandrinus.[92] The homily's subsistence in eastern mss beyond A and the common saying in 2 Clem. 12.2 to Gosp. Thom. 22 and *Stromateis* 3.12 stress further, in this sense, the eastern part of the Roman Empire.[93]

θεοῦ ἐπορεύεσθε (and walked in the customs of God); A 1 Clem. 1.3: καὶ ἐν τοῖς νόμοις τοῦ θεοῦ ἐπορεύεσθε (and walked in the laws of God—Latin *leges*—); (2) L 1 Clem. 28.6 on Ps 138:7: *Ubi fugiam?* (Where shall I flee?); *Strom.* 4.22: ποῦ φύγω; (Where shall I flee?); A 1 Clem. 18.3: ποῦ ἀφήξω; (Where shall I depart?); (3) L 1 Clem. 38.17: *non tantum uerbis* (not only with words); *Strom.* 4.17: μὴ λόγοις μόνον (not only with words); A 1 Clem. 38.2: μὴ ἐν λόγοις (not with words); (4) L 1 Clem. 46.5: *peruerteret* (pervert); Clement Alexandrinus (variant pointed in the *editio princeps* with no locus adduced, but according to Ehrman, *Apostolic Fathers*, 1:119 the Alexandrine has διαστρέψαι, *pervert*); A 1 Clem. 46.8: σκανδαλίσαι (scandalize); (5) L 1 Clem. 48.8: *justiciam* (to righteousness, *ad* missing in the ms but added by the editor); *Strom.* 1.7: ἐν δικαιοσύνῃ (in righteousness; sense requiring the article ἡ, to the righteousness); A 1 Clem. 48.4: ἡ ἐν δικαιοσύνῃ (to the righteousness); (6) L 1 Clem. 48.8: *pudicus operibus* (*virtuous* in deeds, since *castam*, Latin word for the Greek ἁγνή, is employed elsewhere in the same paragraph); *Strom.* 1.7: γοργὸς ἐν ἔργοις (vehement in deeds); A 1 Clem. 48.1: ἁγνὸς ἐν ἔργοις (chaste in deeds); (7) L 1 Clem. 51.16–17: *propter quasdam incursiones contrarii* (by some incursions of the Adversary); *Strom.* 4.18: διά τινας παρεμπτώσεις τοῦ ἀντικειμένου (by some incursions of the Adversary); A 1 Clem. 51.1: διά τινος τῶν τοῦ ἀντικεμένου (by some of those of the Adversary).

92. Varner, *Second Clement*, 8–11 points to indirect reminiscences to the language of 2 Clem. in Irenaeus, *Haer.* 3.3:3: *qui ignem praeparaverit diabolo et angelis ejus* (who has prepared fire for the devil and his angels; Greek text not extant), but the passages of 2 Clem. 7.6; 16.3; 17.5 don't speak of the devil, and Irenaeus is hence more reminiscent of Rev 20:10.

93. 2 Clem. 12.2: ὅταν ἔσται τὰ δύο ἕν, καὶ τὸ ἔξω ὡς τὸ ἔσω, καὶ τὸ ἄρσεν μετὰ τῆς θηλείας, οὔτε ἄρσεν οὔτε θῆλυ (when the two shall be one, and the outward like the inward, and the male with the female, is neither male nor female). Clement Alexandrinus assigns the saying to the gospel of the Egyptians. *Strom.* 3.12–13: καὶ ὅταν γένηται τὰ δύο ἕν καὶ τὸ ἄρρεν μετὰ τῆς θηλείας οὔτε ἄρρεν οὔτε θῆλυ. Πρῶτον μὲ οὖν ἐν τοῖς παραδεδομένοις ἡμῖν τέτταρσιν εὐαγγελίοις οὐκ ἔχομεν τὸ ρητόν, ἀλλ' ἐν τῷ κατ' Αἰγυπτίους (and when the two things become one and the male with the female nor male neither female. First then, in the four gospels handed to us we don't have the thing, but in that according to the Egyptians). The original Greek logion of the Coptic Gosp. Thom. 22 could be of AD 140, but holds a more developed guise in respect to the Alexandrine and 2 Clem. I take here the translation of the first editors (Guillamount et al., *Thomas*, 16–18): "when you make the two one, and when you make the inner as the

The Τρόπαιον of Peter in Rome (AD 160–200)

One step strengthening the possible authentic Roman tradition of Peter's martyrdom is to link Muratori's reference in line 37 to Peter's passion—but which, as it has been commented similarly to Clement Romanus and (in a lesser degree to) Ignatius, is too ambiguous by itself to support without objection the Roman reading, with the sure datable references for Peter's death in Rome. Strengthening the possibility of Peter's martyrdom in Rome hardens 1 Pet 5:13 against critics and, like a game of marbles, drives the Mark-Peter-Rome relation and derivatively the Roman ascendancy of the second gospel into the goal of historicity.

Favorable winds blow here, because these secure sources for dating Peter's death belong with certainty to the second half of the II AD, the conservative date proposed for Muratori. The Roman trophies (τὰ τρόπαια) of Peter and Paul were reported by Gaius the Roman presbyter writing against Proclus, leader of the Montanists, and their martyrdom in Rome by the epistle of Dionysius of Corinth to the Romans.[94] The two are excerpts in Eusebius, no longer extant independently, overlapping Dionysius' bishopric Soter of Rome (AD 168–74) in the second half of the II AD and Gaius that of Zephyrinus (AD 199–217) in the cross to the III AD.[95] More accurately, the excerpts must be set between Justin (AD 139–65), who acquainted with Roman affairs and who used available data in his apologetics silences Peter's martyrdom and tomb in Rome, and Irenaeus (AD 180–190) when the tradition already was spread.[96]

---

outer and the outer as the inner and the above as the below, and when you make the male and the female into a single one, so that the male will not be male and the female (not) be female, when you make eyes in the place of an eye, and a hand in the place of a hand," etc.

94. Eusebius, *Hist. Eccl.* 2.25:5–7.

95. Eusebius, *Hist. Eccl.* 4.19:1.

96. Irenaeus, *Haer.* 3.1:1. Early III AD sources for Peter's death in Rome are Tertullian (AD 197–222), who finds the occasion for his martyrdom under Nero (*Praescr.* 36.1; *Scorp.* 15.3), and the Acts of Peter (33–41). Before the martyrdom of Peter, this apocryphal presents the fanciful struggle of Simon Magus with Peter in Rome (Acts Pet. 4–32) and wants to continue but in Roman territory the canonical account of Simon the Magician, already related to Peter by Acts 8:9–25 in Samaritan context (Acts Pet. 4.4–6). Justin (*1 Apol.* 26.1–22; 56.7–18) and Irenaeus (*Haer.* 1.23:1–5) saw in Simon Magus the precursor of Menander, a Samaritan Gnostic active first in Antioch and whose doctrine seems to have traveled to Rome sometime before Justin (AD 139–65). Both Justin and Irenaeus (likely depending on Justin) set also Simon's activity in Rome itself during the reign of Claudius (AD 41–54), whom he would have convinced with his magical arts that he was a living god, the Senate dedicating him a statue in the Tiber Island. Beyond its fanciful character, the including of Peter in the plot with Simon in Rome, absent in Justin and Irenaeus, presupposes that the tradition of Peter in Rome

If the reader wanted to define further the death of Peter and strive to descend beyond the second half of the II AD, he could resort in two additional controversial sources, the apocalyptical passage of the Ascension of Isaiah, and the Vatican catacombs, outdoors cemetery in origin. The final editor of the apocryphal Ascension of Isaiah melded three, or at least two earlier sources. Its second susceptible source of being isolated, the Testament of Hezekiah (= Ascen. Isa. 3.13—4.18) prophecies Nero will kill one of the Twelve apostles, i.e., Peter (Ascen. Isa. 4.1–3).[97] In general, the Testament of Hezekiah parallels the NT, occasionally in primitive fashion: Ascen. Isa. 3.14//Matt 26:31; 28:4; 3.16//Luke 24:4; Jude 9; 3.17//Matt 28:19; 3.20// Matt 24:24; 3.21//1 Tim 4:12; 3.28//1 John 4:6. The first editor of the text dated it from late I AD to IV AD. It has also been proposed II AD though, in my opinion the text under consideration belongs preferably to the last part of II AD or even the start of III AD.[98]

As to the Vatican aedicule of Saint Peter, it may be dated to AD 150–160 and identified with Gaius' shrine reported ca. AD 200. The architectural

---

was already entrenched in the popular imagery, allowing to consider it a separate element which the author of the Acts of Peter exploited, thus preferably not before the beginning of the III AD.

97. The ms G^2, primitive copy of the original, goes back to the III–IV centuries. The missing letters between brackets in the following passage are restored thanks to the much more recent Ethiopic version (Charles, *Ascension of Isaiah*, xxxi–xxxiii): *καὶ νῦ[ν] ʽΕξ[ε]κία καὶ ʼΙασούβ υ[ἱ]έ μο[υ] αὐταί εἰσιν α[ἱ ἡμέ]ρα[ι] τῆς πληρ[ώσεω]ς τ[οῦ κ] όσμου. τος αὐτοῦ ἐ[ν εἴδει] ἀνθρώπου βασιλέως ἀνόμου μητρα λῴου ὅστις αὐτὸς ὁ βασιλεὺς οὗτος τὴν φυτ[ε]ίαν ἣν φυτεύσουσιν οἱ δώδεκα ἀπόστολοι τοῦ ἀγαπητοῦ διώξε[ι] καὶ [τ]ῶν δώδεκα [ἐκ] ταῖς χερσὶν αὐτοῦ [π]αραδοθήσεται* (And now Hezekiah and Josab my son, these are the days of the fulfillment of the world . . . in it(?) you see a man, a lawless king slayer (of his) mother (= Nero), who, the king himself, will persecute the plant (= the church) which planted the twelve apostles of the Beloved, and of the twelve (one) will be delivered into his hands; Ascen. Isa. 4.1–3). Albeit the sense is equal, Charles, *Ascension of Isaiah*, 95 restores *[τ]ῶν δώδεκα [εἷς]* (one of the twelve), though comments the Ethiopic demands *[τ]ῶν δώδεκα [ἐκ]*.

98. Hall, "Ascension of Isaiah," 296–306 opts for the beginning of II AD based in the common milieu to Ignatius, the epistles of John, and Revelation. I may agree with him in the earliest possible date of materials dispersed along the work, but adducing five reasons for delaying at least Ascen. Isa. 4.1–3 to the second half of II AD and even the beginning of III AD: (a) out of this passage, the reference to Peter's martyrdom in Rome appears in the second half of II AD; (b) it will be surprising that an apocryphal work would supply the earliest mention of a deed when the general rule is that apocryphal authors tend to draw themes from the popular mainstream; (c) the author knows the final edition of Matthew; (d) the context denotes the end of the charismatic church, whereas in Ignatius it is still strong (Ascen. Isa. 3.27: *and there will not be in those days many prophets . . . but one here and there*); (e) the Judeo-Christian ascendance of the author and the expulsion of Isaiah's disciples to Tyre and Sidon in Ascen. Isa. 5.13 fits the Second Jewish Revolt (AD 132–35) more than the First (AD 66–70) because then the Christians of Judaea fled eastwards, to the Decapolis.

features of the aedicule and at least two, perhaps three Petrine graffiti suggest it was given especial significance from its foundation to the IV century when Emperor Constantine (AD 306–37) built over it the Old Saint Peter's Basilica. The esteem that was bestowed to the aedicule during the several reformations of the area, where more decorated sepulchers were laid while the humble monument preserved during the III AD, and the setting of the apse's center of Old Saint Peter's just over it, indicate much more than the graffiti themselves and, with almost no shadow of doubt, that the emperor and his advisers identified the spot with Peter's shrine on the Vatican hill mentioned by Gaius when the works of the basilica started in around AD 333.

The aedicule was built against a brick wall 2.5 meters high, stuccoed and painted in red—called wall *r* or Red Wall, with three superimposed niches in the central part of its eastern face, N^1, N^2, and N^3, the lowermost (N^1) treasuring the famous bones mixed with earth and more than forty coins in a small cavity accessible from its bottom.[99] Over N2 a slab of travertine separating it from N^3, and two marble columns measuring not more than 1.5 meters high, would have formed the small shrine proper upon N1 against the Red Wall. Of one column, only the lower shaft was found displaced in secondary context, but the second was complete *in situ*. The space of N3 over the stone slab could have harbored a small statue or other funerary wares. Funerary rites associated with the aedicule seem close to reality in view of γ, one of the ten pit tombs in the sacred space P, where the shrine was erected, the area formed between the trajectory north to south of *r* in the west axis of P, and the surroundings mausolea S and O, which bounded P to the southeast. Pit γ is the deepest of area P and had a small pipe to pour libations into. It contained bones of a child in good condition and may be contemporaneous or earlier than N1 because it was underneath the foundations of *r*.[100]

The wall *r* was constructed upon a canal for rain water. Four equal brick slabs of the duct inscribed with the names of Aurelius Caesar (AD 140–81) and his wife Faustina Augusta (AD 147–75) provide the foundation date for *r* before Marcus Aurelius was granted the title of Imperator, thus AD 147–60.[101] This put *r* in the literary summit of Justin, who employed the same title of Aurelius in *1 Apol.*'s first lines.[102] Inasmuch as the wall foundations cannot be older than the water drain, the finding of the bones can be

99. Toynbee, "Shrine of St. Peter," 13–26. The bones counted some 250 pieces, large and small, with no skull (Walsh, *Saint Peter*, 58).

100. O'Callaghan, "Vatican Crypts," 72–87.

101. Walsh, *Saint Peter*, 66–67: five tiles.

102. The Roman titles of Marcus Aurelius have been discussed some notes above.

understood in two ways: (a) the bones were part of the original content of the lowermost cavity under niche N[1], deeper than *r*, and preserved there when the Red Wall and niches N2 and N3 over N1 were constructed taking the wall support;[103] (b) they were transferred in the second part of II AD from another spot, being favorite candidates in this supposition other pits of the close surrounding.

The aforementioned most relevant graffiti deciphered by the Vatican archaeological staff in the catacombs under Old Saint Peter's Basilica, studied between 1940s and 1950s—which we will call here n.1, n.2, and n.3—were very poorly carved or painted, undeniably popular in character.[104] Petty expertise in the field of epigraphy is required to note they are badly performed, not official engravings, with crooked lines, unequal letters, and poor proportioning, making it mysterious why Peter's aedicule didn't merit in the cemetery better Petrine references whereas these popular ones from visitors were authorized or permitted and the Roman bishops were provided of plainly identified tombs elsewhere, at Saint Callistus' catacomb throughout the III AD:[105]

(n.1) AD 160–200, right to the aedicule, over the plaster of the Red Wall itself: ΠΕΤ[Ρ] | ΕΝΙ. The most important graffito, interpreted as Πέτρος ἔνι (Peter is inside), appears in two levels, inclined from top left to bottom right. Interpreted from the next graffito, n.2, the reading of Πέτρος ἔνι seems certain. At any case, letters *omicron*/Ο, and *sigma*/Σ (or C, in rounded form), need reconstruction, the majuscule *rho*/Ρ could be a majuscule *iota*/Ι, a *gamma*/Γ, or not be a letter at all, whilst according to the distance between letters in the first level, the second level seems more the composition of two words than one: EN + I.[106] (n.2) Late III–early IV AD, to the north of the former, inwards the central niche of the Valerii mausoleum (H), a praying in five levels: PETRUS ROGA XS HS | PRO SANC[TI]S | HOM[INI]BUS | CHRESTIANIS AD | CORPUS TUUM SE[PULTIS] (Peter, pray Christ Jesus for the Saint Christian men at your buried body). Petrus was clearly readable, but the rest of the text decayed quickly during the excavations, though preserved entirely.[107] (n.3) Late III–early IV AD: XPE NICARIA.

103. Toynbee, "Shrine of St. Peter," 18: N[1]: asymmetric underground niche; N[2]: 1.4 meters high, 0.72 meters wide; N[3]: 0.92 meters high, 1.12 meters wide.

104. See Guarducci, *Tomba di San Pietro*, 44–75.

105. Saint Callistus, therefore, reduces the possibility that the ban of Christianity before the Edict of Milan (AD 313) gave reason for the absence of Petrine references in the Vatican necropolis. Apart, some identifiable paleo-Christian drawings, mosaics, and inscriptions, some secure, are seen in the Vatican cemetery proper.

106. See facsimile and picture n. XV in Guarducci, *Tomba di San Pietro*, 71.

107. Guarducci, *Tomba di San Pietro*, 50–51. The British J. M. C. Toynbee, one of

Sum of conjectures, this Christian graffito less useful for our purposes, will be studied at foot.[108]

Next to the Petrine hypothesis, which of course cannot be driven out since Constantine identified the spot with Peter's tropaion, it should also be considered that the aedicule could have belonged to a private family, one or more of whose members could have experienced violent death in the last third of I AD or first half of II AD. The tombs in area P and in area Q against the west face of wall *r* make this interpretation believable. Another pit in the open area Q where the water canal began, tomb *w*, held one stamped tile of Vespasian (AD 69–79) carrying the funerary character of the place well into I AD. More information is drawn from the iconography of T and U, mausolea south of O: a panther chasing a deer, a crowned Bacchid head, a dolphin, a peacock, the god Thanatos, Lucifer wielding a luminary and riding a horse, and the pipe for libations in the tomb of the child close to N^1; these express pagan benchmarks for the identification of the first owners of the Vatican cemetery.

Wall *r*, mausolea R and R1 to the southwest, one ramp and stairs in the close area to save the ground unevenness, are all of one fabric. This assortment of structures is called the *clivus*, and dated AD 150–170.[109] Deemed in its entirety, the construction of the Red Wall serves several structures, without being demonstrable in the degree that the intention of the builders was materialized by the architectural design that the shrine against *r*

---

the few external authorities permitted to follow some phases of the excavations, commented she was not allowed to read independently the inscription we call here n.2 in the spot where it was (see Toynbee, "Shrine of St. Peter," 5–6).

108. In wall *g* north to the aedicule too in its northern face, to the right of graffito n.2, the next invocation was read in a jumble of letters, some fifty Roman names, scratches, false tracings, and Christian symbols. Guarducci, *Tomba di San Pietro*, 64–66 reads: XPE NICARIA, a supposed Greek-Latin acronym for Ἰησοῦς Χριστός, Petrus, Maria, νίκη (Jesus Christ, Peter, Mary, victory!). The inscription portrays superimposed letters and symbol alleged to be read in four phases: (a) XP: the Chi-Rho meaning Ἰησοῦς Χριστός (Jesus Christ); (b) small Latin E to the right bottom of the Chi-Rho, that would compound the acronym PE for Petrus using the Greek *rho*/P of the Chi-Rho for the Latin *pee*/P; (c) reconstructed MARIA from the ARIA letters in the top level, where they form an inclined line to be read NICARIA, and a supposed M formed with what seems a majuscule *lambda*/Λ, the left to right tracing of the *chi*/X letter of the Chi-Rho, and a reconstructed vertical stroke to its left; (d) NICA, intended for the Greek NIKH—victory, but reading the majuscule *kappa*/K for the majuscule Latin *cee*/C. It seems that at least thirty times the Christian Chi-Rho was recognized in the plaster of this spot of wall g, and it may be that all the people who scratched their names there, Gaudentia, Ursianus, Bonifatia, Paulina, etc., were Christian (Walsh, *Saint Peter*, 47–48), but in my humble opinion the reading of Maria, so interspersed in the mess of scratches, is highly uncertain.

109. Toynbee, "Shrine of St. Peter," 4, 18.

was intended for one single person, i.e., Peter. Mausoleum F, the Caetenii, though later, for instance, was provided a funerary outstanding altar in its middle for members of the family and freedmen. The altar is not embedded against any wall, like Gaius' tropaion, but shows funerary pagan rites associated to one nearby family. It also has mosaic pavement with holes for pouring liquids, illustrating the rites that could have been performed in area P during its foundational phase, also supplied with a tomb with pipe for libations and small shrine. At any rate, the cult in the tropaion had to be executed not over the travertine slab itself, the expected place for standing objects but too high, 1.8 meters, for cultic rituals.[110] Assuredly, the floor mosaic of F is ornamented in a cross shape. The same form is seen in the vault of mausoleum G, supporting the paleo-Christian reading, despite that many other pagan figures in the same or similar contexts forestall the swift Christian identification.[111]

Early Christians of Roman family units could and did partake in pagan iconography and funerary customs. Peter's corpse after his martyrdom by Nero could therefore have rested among Gentile-Christian or even pagan inhumations and not in a Roman Jewish cemetery. But this hypothesis removes Peter from his Judeo-Christian background: no Judeo-Christian was there to honor the apostle in another way, for instance Mark, who according to 1 Pet 5:13 and later tradition was his companion in Rome and survived Peter, and on whom was the responsibility to take Peter's bones the year after his death to his kinsmen (m. Sanh. 6:6). On the other hand, funerary rites in honor to Peter seem alien to Jewish Christianity: Peter himself forbids Cornelius to bow before him according to Acts 10:25–26. Furthermore, none of the III AD Roman bishops and more startlingly neither of the IVseem attentive to the aedicule of the Vatican cemetery. On the contrary, the Roman episcopal burial tradition was to be found in the papal crypt of Saint Callistus' catacomb, some eight kilometers away.

Began by Zephyrinus (d. 217), who probably was inhumed in the plot but open field, the papal crypt comprised all the III AD Roman bishops excluding Callistus, who for circumstances related to his murder was interred in the Via Aurelia. Epigraphically attested in the III AD are: Pontianus (d. AD 235), Anteros (d. AD 235), Fabian (d. AD 250), Cornelius (d. AD 253), Lucius (d. AD 254), Eutychian (d. AD 285), and Caius (d. AD 296).[112] Following this line, the some fifty coins associated with the bones in the hole

110. Walsh, *Saint Peter*, 46.

111. It is impossible to study them here in full. For the chief symbolic funerary features of the area, see Basso, *Vatican Necropolis*, 73–114, 150–62.

112. Hertling and Kirschbaum, *Roman Catacombs*, 49–64. The Vatican tradition of papal burials only started with Gelasius (d. 496).

beneath N1 were for the most part from the years AD 285–325. Six of them were from AD 165–85, and only one was of Antoninus Pius (AD 138–61), suggesting that the place received attention only in the late III AD, the proposed date for inscription n.2.[113] Dated as early as AD 270–280, inscription n.2 was partly covered with the retaining wall of Old Saint Peter's by Constantine workers. It was drawn inside one of the niches in wall *g* of the Valerii mausoleum (H) in the alleyway to P, which, though pagan in design, appears to have sheltered one Christian grave.[114]

The late date for n.2 turns the reading of the incomplete inscription n.1., 5.7 centimeters high by 3.5 centimeters wide, contentious. Father A. Ferrua reported two versions of the finding: in one the plaster fragment etched with n.1 was inside the niche of wall *g* from the III AD, the same wall for inscriptions n.2. and n.3, a structure at a right angle constructed against the northern side of *r* to the east, but in the second version he recovered it among scattered detritus. Hence that the two versions induce us to believe n.1 was written in *r* before wall *g* was constructed.[115] I am inclined to assure the reading ΠΕΤ[Ρ] | ΕΝΙ in light of n.2, PETRUS ROGA XS HS. But the possibility that ΠΕΤ[Ρ] | ΕΝΙ were of the very age as *r*, contemporary to the aedicule's foundation, is untenable: the stucco workers would have marked the identity of the Petrine shrine better. This leaves n.1 to AD 160–200 at best accepting it belonged to the section of wall *r* that was later covered at a right angle by the projection of *g*.[116]

Graffiti n.1, n.2, and n.3, recall probe drawings, similar to the current sketches that lads or graffiti apprentices in possession of drawing material undertake on virgin walls. In the wall of the niche of n.2, and indeed forming part of the same composition, were found two heads, badly drawn. Beyond the clear reading of Petrus in n.2 next to the two heads denotes they can

113. For the coins I rely on O'Callaghan, "Vatican Crypts," 71; Walsh, *Saint Peter*, 62 reports two thousand coins in total in the surroundings of P, from the IV to the XV centuries for the bulk.

114. Toynbee, "Shrine of St. Peter," 4. The Christian term *deposito* (deposited) occurs in one sarcophagus of H, but the invocation to the Manes in the heading can be either paleo-Christian or pagan: D(IS) M(ANIBVS) | C(AII) APPAIENI CASTI QVI VIX(IT) ANN(IS) VIII M(ENSIBVS) X D(IEBVS) | XXVIII ALVMNO DVLC(ISSIMO) CVI LOCVM OPTVLIT C(AIVS) VAL(ERIVS) | HERMA IN FRONTE PED(ES) V SARCOFAGO TERRA DEPOSITO (To the gods Manes of the virtuous Caius Appaiens who lived eight years, ten months, twenty-eight days, the beloved student, for whom Caius Valerius Hermas offered a place five feet in front of the coffin deposited in earth; Basso, *Vatican Necropolis*, 122–23, 156).

115. Guarducci, *Tomba di San Pietro*, 69–70.

116. Wall *g* was settled in right angle to *r* after a vertical fault was formed in *r* eighty years after its foundation (Walsh, *Saint Peter*, 70).

be Christian in essence, the collation of these drawings with professional examples in the stucco of niches of mausoleum H points in the case of n.2 and n.3 to the prints of later occupants, visitors, or intruders.[117] It is adventurous to see the hand of the original owners of the cemetery in n.2 and n.3 insofar as the mess in which the graffiti were graved and their calligraphy contradict the economic investment in the sepulchers, the walls, the canal, stairs, and several reformations of the area. Only one scene in the cemetery, professionally made, accepts Petrine tints, in Mausoleum M. The Julii mausoleum is no doubt Christian: it shows off one mosaic of Helios-Christ riding a chariot along with the pictures of the Good Shepherd, Jonah in the ship, and the Fisherman, namely, a man armed with a fishing rod catching two fishes, and to their left, a rock. Peter was a fisherman and was foretold to be the rock upon which the church was to be established (Matt 16:18; Mark 1:16–17). Regrettably, the Petrine elements of the boat and the fishnet are lacking (Luke 5:3–11; John 21:3–11), whereas the small rock could display no special meaning. Several sure paleo-Christian tombs, many symbols, and inscriptions were set in the necropolis, but except the Fisherman none of those professionally made accepts Petrine readings. It seems, in conclusion, that not the sponsors of the area from late II AD to late III AD identified it with Peter the apostle. Accepting the Petrine identity of the Fisherman, we would only get confirmed inscriptions n.2 and n.3 because the Christian scenes in the tomb of the Julii are contemporaneous, late III AD to early IV AD.[118]

Setting ΠΕΤ[Ρ] | ΕΝΙ before III AD glues it to other readings, perhaps less convincing, although their evaluation turns statutory for the researcher. Without retiring the possibility of pilgrims to the Vatican hill honoring Peter in life of Gaius the Presbyter, Dionysius Alexandrinus (ca. AD 200) wrote that Christian parents named their children Peter or Paul. There is no firm reason to exclude that the custom could begin one or two decades before III AD, covering the proposed date for n.1. The text is scarcely quoted, but it has survived in Eusebius too (*Hist. Eccl.* 7.25:14).[119] Lastly, it is even possible

117. In Mausoleum H we find the goddess Earth, one satyr, a female dancer, and a male dancer, all well executed in stucco, professionally made (see Basso, *Vatican Necropolis*, 146–48 and figs. 54–58). The same plaster surface or very similar was used for inscriptions n.1, n.2, and n.3, wherein rest majorly the Petrine attribution of the small shrine in wall *r* to the period of its foundational stage, and even the late I AD.

118. One fish and several vertical lines were scratched into the brick wall of Mausoleum R, which could be representing the Eucharist. R is from the second half of II AD, but the fish must belong to the period of Christian visitors, not before III or late III AD. See Basso, *Vatican Necropolis*, 73–114, 161, and fig. 23.

119. Despite that he used the text in another discussion, I want to acknowledge again Black, *Mark*, 147–48.

though less probable for ΠΕΤ[Ρ] | ΕΝΙ cross the doorway into the pagan context of the primitive tombs because only for the period 99–31 BC assorted nomens beginning with PETI or PETR—Petillius, Petreius, Petronius, and Petrucidius—are attested in the imperial administration.[120] In sum: the archaeological context plants in the soil of certainty the aedicule's Petrine character in the first third of IV AD, and in view of Gaius' testimony and the Christian graffiti, returns it to around AD 200, strong still as to ensure Peter's Roman tradition in late I AD, but in origin, AD 160, it could also respond to a familiar shrine that the apostle's identity gradually superseded.[121]

Irenaeus of Lyon's Against Heresies (AD 180–190)

Scarce datable references for Irenaeus' utmost work have survived. The catalog of Roman bishops in *Adversus Haereses* 3.3:1 ends with Eleutherus, whose episcopate goes from about AD 177 to 192. Since Irenaeus tried to cool the spirits during the Paschal controversy between Rome and the Anatolian bishops and for that purpose held contact with Victor, the next Roman bishop to Eleutherus, the foregoing date must correspond to the composition of the work.[122] The Greek OT version Theodotion, not former to AD 184, is reported not far in *Haer.* 3.21:1, and ultimately Eusebius makes Irenaeus successor of Photinus in the chair of Gallia, martyr AD 177, *terminus post quem* for the work (*Hist. Eccl.* 5.5:8). The three dates drive to the second decade before the III century, AD 180–190, for the composition of the *Adversus*.

Adversus Haereses aims for the overthrow of heterodox streams. As depicted by the bishop of Lyon, heretics had usurped Christian categories which perverted assorting them with Gnostic tendencies

120. Broughton, *Magistrates of the Roman Republic*, 2:600.

121. Frend, *Archaeology of Early Christianity*, 267–75 proposed four reasons to leave for the field of faith the identification of the shrine with Peter's tomb: (a) the faint epigraphic proof reading ΠΕΤ[Ρ] ΕΝΙ for Πέτρος ἔνεστι (Peter is in) seems atypical in a place where other evident inscriptions or iconography should have denoted the Petrine ownership of the spot in the II AD; (b) in spite of its good preservation, between its foundation, ca. AD 160, and AD 290, the place didn't attract too much attention when the Petrine tradition was growing as shown by the unrepaired mosaic dated ca. AD 250 in fore of the aedicule, which would have not resisted the affluence of pilgrims; (c) in Rome the tombs of the martyrs were laid not beneath the floor of the church, but encased in marble and put in the focus within the nave as in the Holy Sepulcher of Jerusalem; (d) the successive popes didn't choose this place for burial (see distribution of early Roman Christian tombs in Lampe, *From Paul to Valentinus*, 25–38, 44–45).

122. Eusebius, *Hist. Eccl.* 5.5:8—6:4; Beaven, *Writings of S. Irenaeus*, 33; for Eleutherus, Grant, *Irenaeus of Lyon*, 5 prefers ca. AD 175–89.

(Simonians-Valentinians), Judaizing (Ebionites), or anti-Judaizing/Gnostic (Marcionites). Since for AD 180 heresies are well organized and their claims over Scripture are not new, the Christian discussions for canonical writings can be traced back some thirty to fifty years. Marcion on Paul ca. AD 140 and from another point of view Papias on Mark (and Matthew) around AD 130 should be considered the *terminus post quem* for issues soon related to the canon, but (Muratori apart) we must await until Irenaeus to be in possession of the earliest definition in the case of the four gospels.[123]

In the period of AD 130–180, the four-gospel canon has become a conquest for the church, already shaped with the traditional order that will stand unquestioned till the XVIII–XIX centuries:[124] "Now Matthew in the language of the Hebrews produced a scripture of the gospel, when Peter and Paul (were) evangelizing in Rome, and founding the church. But after their departure Mark, disciple and interpreter of Peter, himself had written and delivered to us the things preached by Peter. And Luke too, the follower of Paul, the gospel preached by this (Paul) put into a book. Afterwards, John the disciple of the Lord, the one who leaned on his breast, he himself has delivered the gospel (while) residing in Ephesus of Asia", says Irenaeus (*Haer.* 3.3:1).[125]

Apropos Mark's gospel, there is a slight enlargement from Papias to Irenaeus, who has used Papias as well as other sources: (a) the composition place is suggested: in Rome (ἐν ʽΡώμῃ), where Paul and Peter had been preaching (εὐαγγελιζομένων) and founding (θεμελιούντων) the church; (b) the occasion is plain for the first time: after their departure (*μετὰ δὲ τὴν*

123. According to Irenaeus, *Haer.* 1.27:1–2 and Eusebius, *Hist. Eccl.* 4.10:1—11:9, Marcion of Pontus flourished during the episcopates of Hyginus (AD 138–42) and Pius I (AD 142–57), and certainly was alive when Justin composed his *First Apology* (26.22–23; 58.1–5).

124. The first exegetes which questioned the chronological sequence for the composition of the gospels Matt, Mark, Luke, and John, bestowing priority to Mark, were Koppe (in 1782), Storr (in 1794), Herder (in 1796), Gratz (in 1812), Weisse (in 1837), and Wilke (in 1838); see the classical discussion in Schweitzer, *Quest of the Historical Jesus*, 35–36, 87, 120–35. The two main vindications in one of these fathers of the Marcan priority theory, C. H. Weisse, are kept with more or less variants in its current defenders: Matthew and Luke display a common plan solely in those parts which they have in common to Mark, whilst where they agree between them but not with Mark, what is disclosed is a common source of sayings (Q), lacking an order of events.

125. *Ὁ μὲν δὴ Ματθῖος ἐν τοῖς Ἑβραίοις τῇ ἰδίᾳ διαλέτῳ αὐτῶν καὶ γραφὴν ἐξήνεγκεν εὐαγγελίου, τοῦ Πέτροῦ καὶ τοῦ Παύλου ἐν ʽΡώμῃ εὐαγγελιζομένων, καὶ θεμελιούντων τὴν ἐκκλησίαν. μετὰ δὲ τὴν τούτων ἔξοδον Μάρκος, ὁ μαθητὴς καὶ ἑρμηνευτὴς Πέτρου, καὶ αὐτὸς τὰ ὑπὸ Πέτρου κηρυσσόμενα ἐγγράψως ἡμῖν παραδέδωκεν· καὶ Λουκᾶς δὲ, ὁ ἀκόλουθος Παύλου, τὸ ὑπ᾽ ἐκεῖνου κηρυσσόμενον εὐαγγέλιον ἐν βιβλίῳ κατέθετο. ἔπειτα Ἰωάννης ὁ μαθητὴς τοῦ Κυρίου, ὁ καὶ ἐπὶ τὸ στῆθος αὐτοῦ ἀναπεσών, καὶ αὐτὸς ἐξέδωκεν τὸ εὐαγγέλιον ἐν Ἐφέσῳ τῆς Ἀσίας διατρίβων* (*Haer.* 3.3:1; Eusebius, *Hist. Eccl.* 5.8:2–3).

τούτων ἔξοδον), presumably their death; (c) the position within the canon order is equally pointed by the interjection of μετά (after) and for what has been uttered formerly on Matthew: Matthew wrote while Peter and Paul evangelized Rome, therefrom it is conveyed Mark wrote after Matthew. At last, a controversial inference for scholarship, which today we will not develop, arises: since Matthew was first in writing the gospel in the dialect of the Hebrews, i.e., Aramaic (ἐν τοῖς Ἑβραίοις τῇ ἰδίᾳ διαλέτῳ αὐτῶν), Mark would be the first Greek gospel, unless it is agreed Irenaeus had in mind that Matthew's version was prior to Mark.[126]

Clement Alexandrinus (ca. AD 200)

According to Jerome, Clement managed the Alexandrian Ecclesiastical School and flourished under Severe (AD 193–211) and Caracalla (AD 211–17). His birth barely can be fixed in the mid II century AD, whereas more accuracy surrounds his demise ca. AD 215.[127] Securer is Clement's

126. Irenaeus on Matthew also depends on Papias (Eusebius, *Hist. Eccl.* 3.39:16): Ματθαῖος μὲν οὖν Ἑβραΐδι διαλέτῳ τὰ λόγια συετάξατο, ἡρμήνευσεν δ' αὐτὰ ὡς ἦν δυνατὸς ἕκαστος (Matthew then gathered the sayings (of the Lord) in the Hebrew dialect, but each interpreted them as was able). This is not the place for the massive plowing under the fathers' field searching this possible source of sayings (τὰ λόγια) in Aramaic. For now, it fulfills the objectives of the present Marcan study to simply underline the possible link between the first Aramaic gospel by Matthew (compilation of sayings/deeds uncertainly organized) and the sayings/reports of the Lord in Ignatius, Clement Alexandrinus, and the Gospel of Thomas. Entirely, this pre-Matthean source would have included apocryphal material later discarded, the fathers' quotations, as well as material inserted in the canonical gospels, eventually susceptible to be overlapped (Beatrice, "Gospel according to the Hebrews," 147–95). An analogue implication for the Aramaic Matthew is its identification, in part or totally, with the Aramaic Q, namely, material from the concurrence of Matthew and Luke against Mark retranslatable into Aramaic (for the plea of the Aramaic Q, see Casey, *Aramaic Approach to Q*, 2–50). Eusebius, *Hist. Eccl.* 3.25:5; 27:4 mentions that Jews who had accepted Jesus and Ebionites employed the so-called Gospel according to the Hebrews (καθ' Ἑβραίους εὐαγγέλιον), but the Aramaic Matthew should rather not be seen here, for the reading of Epiphanius, *Pan.* 30.13:2,6–8 conveys the Ebionites used a corrupted and maimed Hebrew version (νενοθευμένῳ καὶ ἠκρωτηριασμένῳ) of the canonical Matthew, hardly similar to the pre-Matthean Aramaic source. Nazoraeans and Ebionites were in origin sectarian Judeo-Christians opposed to Paul and possible renegades from James the Just's party (Acts 15:1–5; Gal 5:11–12). They fled to the Decapolis after the siege of Jerusalem in AD 70 (Epiphanius, *Pan.* 29–30).

127. Jerome, *Vir. Ill.* 38. Eusebius, *Hist. Eccl.* 6.11:6 and 14:8–9 holds two letters of Alexander, disciple of Clement and then bishop of Cappadocia and Jerusalem, which fix Clement's death. The former presupposes Alexander's ascension to episcopacy after the death of Severus (AD 211), and recommends Clement, the blessed elder (τοῦ μακαρίου πρεσβυτέρου), to the Antiochian church. The latter, addressed to Origen in

heyday, which can be estimated from the death of Commodus in AD 192, mentioned in the *Stromateis* or *Miscellanies* (1.21), work to be ended before the Severan persecution in AD 202 that triggered Clement's exit from Egypt. A stretch after, it is believed that Clement yielded the *Hypotyposeis.*[128] The work is almost completely lost.[129] But again it is owing to Eusebius that one valuable excerpt for the study of Mark has come down to us:

> That having Peter preached in Rome the word and in the Spirit expanded the gospel, those who were present, being many, implored Mark, as because for a long time he had followed him and remembered what had been said, to make a register of the things (that were) said: and (that) doing it, he gave the gospel to those who had asked him: and that (this) being precisely known to Peter he neither curbed it back nor he exhorted to be done. (Eusebius, *Hist. Eccl.* 6.14:6–7)[130]

Setting this first Marcan passage of Clement on a par with Irenaeus, additional developments over the common tradition come into light: (a) Clement makes explicit Rome, already strongly suggested or even taken for granted in Irenaeus, as the place where Mark composed the gospel; (b) but the scene is set before the departure of Peter; (c) Mark has been following Peter for a long time; (d) the gospel composition was requested apparently by the Roman Christians who begged Mark to write down what he remembered of his company with Peter; (e) Peter neither deterred it nor encouraged it.

AD 215, associates Clement with Pantaenus, certainly dead by this date, and speaks of them as those with whom Alexander will be soon (πρὸς οὓς μετ' ὀλίγον ἐσόμεθα).

128. Tollinton, *Clement of Alexandria*, 324–32 discussed the date for *Stromateis*, which is considered Clement's first title, casting the date of AD 192–95 for its first part and sometime before AD 202 for the accomplishment of the whole because when Clement deals with martyrdom it doesn't reflect yet the Severan persecution. In *Strom.* 1.11 Clement manifests that the work was intended for future preservation of the teachings he had accrued from his predecessors, something incongruent if he had written first the *Hypotyposeis*.

129. According to Osborn, *Clement of Alexandria*, 5, one complete copy of the *Hypotyposeis* was seen in the XVIII century at the library of the monastery of St. Macarius, north of Cairo, by the French diplomatist Comte d'Antraigues (d. 1812), who left the notice in a letter owned by the archive of Dijon, in mid-northeastern France. Osborn visited the monastery three times, finding no hint of the manuscript.

130. τοῦ Πέτρου δημοσίᾳ ἐν Ῥώμῃ κηρύξανος τὸν λόγον καὶ πνεύματι τὸ εὐαγγέλιον ἐξειπόντος, τοὺς παρόντας, πολλοὺς ὄντας, παρακαλέσαι τὸν Μάρκον, ὡς ἂν ἀκολουθήσαντα αὐτῷ πόρρωθεν καὶ μεμνημένον τῶν λεχθέντων, ἀναγράψαι τὰ εἰρημένα· ποιήσαντα δέ, τὸ εὐαγγέλιον μεταδοῦναι τοῖς δεομένοις αὐτοῦ· ὅπερ ἐπιγνόντα τὸν Πέτρον προτρεπτικῶς μήτε κωλῦσαι μήτε προτρέψασθαι.

Clement's testimony is quite restrained. But simultaneously and at first glance, it appears odd that the Roman Christians implored Mark to write the things he remembered of his company with Peter, being that Peter was still with them and being themselves capable to write what they heard of Peter himself or what they could ask Peter. This natural commentary of Clement and, properly, any of the canonical gospels, in the ornamented manner they have come down to us, fits better the aspirations of the third generation of believers, deprived of direct witnesses and in need of a narrative account of Jesus' soteriological event from its outset to its culmination.

The expression *τὸ εὐαγγέλιον μεταδοῦναι τοῖς δεομένοις αὐτοῦ* (he gave the gospel to those who had asked him) merits attention in this sense, since it recalls the reception of the second gospel by the Roman community. In a former occasion Eusebius takes the same sixth book of the *Hypotyposeis* and, though he doesn't quote it literally, offers the key for grasping the origin of Clement's tradition on Mark in the time when the public reading of the gospels was already established. There, Eusebius assigns Clement the statement that after Mark had already written the gospel down, "knowing the apostle (Peter) what had been done by revelation of the Spirit, was pleased for the eagerness of the men (and) sanctioned the scripture for the conference in the churches" (*Hist. Eccl.* 2.15:1).[131] Though *αἱ ἐκκλησίαι* (the churches) with geographical meaning is thoroughly consistent in Pauline literature, Clement seems to be understanding Peter from posterior contexts since the employment of written gospels in the churches belongs undoubtedly to the post-apostolic era, and in some probability was an innovation of Justin's generation during the first half of II AD.[132]

Further on, in the ongoing commentary about Peter's presence in Rome, Eusebius makes Clement say in the same work (*Hypotyposeis*) that Peter mentions Mark in his first epistle, and that Papias agrees with Clement

131. *γνόντα δὲ τὸ πραχθέν φασι τὸν ἀπόστολον ἀποκαλύψαντος αὐτῷ τοῦ πνεύματος, ἡσθῆναι τῇ τῶν ἀνδρῶν προθυμίᾳ κυρῶσαι τε τὴν γραφὴν εἰς ἔντευξιν ταῖς ἐκκλησίαις.*

132. Thayer, *Lexicon of the New Testament*, 195–96 picks more than fifty entries for church/churches. The references to geographical churches seal over the map the cradle of Christianity, a curved area where Anatolia occupies the center, Greece and Syria-Palestine the fringes: Acts 8:1 (Jerusalem); 15:41 (Syria and Cilicia); Rom 16:1 (Cenchreae); 1 Cor 1:2 (Corinth); 16:1 (Galatia); 16:19 (Asia); 2 Cor 1:1 (Corinth); 8:1 (Macedonia); Gal 1:2 (Galatia); 1:22 (Judaea); Col 4:16 (Laodicea); 1 Thess 1:1 (Thessalonica); 2 Thess 1:1 (Thessalonica); Rev 1:4 (Asia); 2:1 (Ephesus); 2:8 (Smyrna); 2:12 (Pergamum); 2:18 (Thyatira); 3:1 (Sardis); 3:7 (Philadelphia); 3:14 (Laodicea). Private churches: Rom 16:5 (of Prisca and Aquila, Rome); Col 4:15 (of Nympha, Laodicea); Phil 2 (of Philemon, Colossae?). Other uses of ἐκκλησία/ἐκκλησίαι: Matt 16:18; 18:17; Acts 5:11; 8:3; 20:28; Rom 16:4,16; 1 Cor 4:17; 7:17; 11:18,22; 12:28; 14:19,23,33–35; 15:9; 2 Cor 8:19; Gal 1:13; Eph 1:22; 3:10; 5:23–25,27,29,32; Phil 3:6; 4:15; Col 1:18,24; 1 Thess 2:14; 2 Thess 1:4; 1 Tim 3:15; Heb 12:23; 3 John 6; Rev 1:20; 2:7,11,17,29,3:6,13,22.

in rendering the expression ἀσπάζεται ὑμᾶς ἡ ἐν Βαβυλῶνι συνεκλεκτή (sends you greetings the co-chosen (church) in Babylon) of 1 Pet 5:13 as referred to Rome: "Clement in the sixth (book) of the *Hypotyposeis* presents the story, agreeing with him the bishop of Hierapolis named Papias, and (in that) Peter mentions Mark in the first epistle: which they say he composed in Rome itself, what he himself indicates, designing (it) more metaphorical(ly) Babylon by these (words), 'sends you greetings the co-chosen (church) in Babylon and Mark my son'" (Eusebius, *Hist. Eccl.* 2.15:2).[133]

Concerning Clement, Eusebius must be right. An anonymous Latin translation of the *Hypotyposeis*' commentary on 1 Peter shows a parallel to Eusebius, for its digression of 1 Pet 5:13 explains the motifs that on occasion of Peter's mission in Rome drove Mark to write the second gospel.[134] Despite the conversion into Greek is possible, the loss of the *Hypotyposeis* (and of Papias' works) foils the undisputed possession of the originals where Eusebius is reading, but the quotations in *Miscellanies* largely prove Clement employed 1 Peter.[135] Two hypotheses are lifted up.

First, to affirm Peter was preaching in Rome when Mark composed the gospel, for the bulk, Clement would depend on a reading over Irenaeus, where it is suggested though not explicitly stated. The possibility is not Martian since Clement did profit from the Irenaean arguments against the Gnostics, acknowledging the prompt reception of Irenaeus in Egypt.[136]

133. Κλήμης ἐν ἕκτῳ τῶν Ὑποτυπώσεων παρατέθειται τὴν ἱστορίαν, συνεπιμαρτυρεῖ δὲ αὐτῷ καὶ ὁ Ἱεραπολίτης ἐπίσκοπος ὀνόματι Παπίας, τοῦ δὲ Μάρκου μνημονεύειν τὸν Πέτρον ἐν τῇ προτέρᾳ ἐπιστολῇ· ἣν καὶ συντάξαι φασὶν ἐπ' αὐτῆς Ῥώμης, σημαίνειν τε τοῦτ' αὐτόν, τὴν πόλιν τροπικώτερον Βαβυλῶνα προσειπόντα διὰ τούτων "ἀσπάζεται ὑμᾶς ἡ ἐν Βαβυλῶνι συνεκλεκτὴ καὶ Μάρκος ὁ υἱός μου."

134. Zahn, *Supplementum*, 82–83 (= Stählin, *Fragmente*, 206; Zahn, *Supplementum*, 10–16 examines the fragment, perhaps traceable till the VI century): *Marcus, Petri spectator, praedicante Petro evangelium palam Romae coram quibusdam Caesareanis equitibus et multa Christi testimonia proferente, petitus ad eis, ut possent quae dicebantur memoriae commendare, scripsit ex his, quae Petro dicta sunt, evangelium quod secundum Marcum vocitatur* (Mark, Peter's witness, preaching Peter overtly the gospel in Rome before some Caesarean knights and bearing much witness of Christ, asking them, to learn by memory what was said, write for them what Peter said, the gospel that is proclaimed according to Mark). Black, *Mark*, 139 renders *Caesareanis* as *Caesar's*, but admits his translation has slightly modified the Latin meaning. The morpheme *-ea* denotes the root is feminine (Caesarea the town), and not masculine (the person of Caesar).

135. *Strom.* 3.11//1 Pet 2:11–12,15–16; 3.18//1 Pet 1:14–16; 4.7//1 Pet 3:14–17; 4.7//1 Pet 4:12–14; 4.20//1 Pet 1:6–9; 6.15//1 Pet 1:11. Besides, 1 Peter is alluded or mentioned without reference to the apostle in *Strom.* 1.27; 2.15; 4.18//1 Pet 4:8; 2.23//1 Tim 2:9–10//1 Pet 3:3; 3.6//Prov 3:34//Jas 4:6//1 Pet 5:5; 4.4//1 Pet 1:19; 4.26//1 Pet 1:24; 5.2//1 Cor 4:15//1 Pet 1:3,23; 5.10//1 Pet 2:3; 6.11//1 Pet 1:7; 7.7.10.12//1 Pet 2:9; 7.12//1 Pet 3:11.

136. Exhaustive approach to the subject may produce further parallels. Patterson,

Disgracefully, Eusebius also records Clement thought the gospels bearing genealogies were written first, bestowing priority to Luke over Mark against the list of Irenaeus.[137] Therefore, if Clement on Mark is depending on Irenaeus, he has questioned issues related to the tradition. Second, on Mark, Clement depends not directly on the bishop of Lyon, but on a common tradition to Irenaeus that he has received under different form, or that he has diversely interpreted or expanded in the case that Irenaeus and Clement were editors of the common source.

This source could well be Papias. Eusebius in fact has given this to understand, but the direct quotation of Papias in 3.39:15, contrarily, suggests that Eusebius in 2.15:2 is reading Papias in broad terms, i.e., that the tradition on Mark as the interpreter of Peter confirms the longer version of Clement, i.e., the writing of the second gospel in line with Peter's mission in Rome, in the sense that the particular statement is contained in the general, allowance that for ancient standards was enough to defend that the two were reporting the same. We are not told more details to elicit in which precise sense Papias of Hierapolis gives support to the testimony of Clement on Mark, but the more congruent option is that Clement's version of the second gospel in the *Hypotyposeis* was an expanded version of Papias on Mark as it is Irenaeus', but not the identical version. The other option, that Papias said something about Peter's mission in Rome beyond his supposed commentary on 1 Pet 5:13, is much less credible because Eusebius would have reflected it in the large commentary devoted to Papias (3.39:1–17).

We encounter, therefore, an enigma if Eusebius is reliable to restore his sources: did Papias relate 1 Pet 5:13 with the second gospel tradition? When commenting Babylon for Rome in 1 Pet 5:13, Eusebius apparently is equating Clement and Papias by means of a third plural present form of φημί (to say): ἣν καὶ συντάξαι φασὶν ἐπ' αὐτῆς Ῥώμης (which they say he (Peter) composed in Rome itself). Nor would it be surprising to find the

"Irenaean Themes in Clement," 498, 500–515; and Löhr, "Gnostic Determinism Reconsidered," 383–88 uncover the next Irenaean motifs copied by Clement, though shifting the weight to the divine pedagogy of the soul rather than to the Irenaean salvation of the bodily flesh. The dependence in Irenaeus seems out of doubt for II-century sources criticizing Gnosticism, Justin and Hippolytus present different argumentation: *Strom.* 2.10//*Haer.* 2.29:1; 4.37 (against Gnostic determinism); *Strom.* 3.1//*Haer.* 1.6:4 (on Gnostic teachings on marriage and sexuality); *Strom.* 3.3//*Haer.* 1.28 (on the Basilideans' libertinism); *Strom.* 7.18//*Haer.* 5.8:3 (comparison of the unclean animals in Lev 11:2–3//Deut 14:3 with the heretics). The fragment POxy 405 (= *Haer.* 3.9:3) bearing nomina sacra going back to the II AD, θs, χs, ιηs, is claimed to attest the reception of Irenaeus in Egypt by the early III century (Grenfell and Hunt, *Oxyrhynchus Papyri III*, 10; *IV*, 264–65; Stanton, "Fourfold Gospel," 329).

137. Eusebius, *Hist. Eccl.* 6.14:5.

rendering of Rome for Babylon seventy years before the Alexandrinus in Papias, witness of the Asian tradition, for Revelation accepted it soon in the II AD (14:8; 16:19; 17:5,18; 18:2,10,21). Eusebius doesn't disclose the fact when he stops largely at Papias and comments on the second gospel tradition (3.39:1–17), and this oddity makes the inclusion of Papias along Clement on 1 Pet 5:13 suspicious.

Heavier reason for the suspicion is the employment in a quite impersonal fashion of the narrative gadget φασί/φασίν (they say) when Eusebius includes oral traditions along his chronicle (2.2:2; 3.1:6; 4:7; 24:7,11; 4.5:2; 15:4; 29:6; 5.10:2; 6.29:2; 7.12:1; 17:1), leaving some taste of ambiguity in the scant instances when he refers the third plural of φημί to authoritative sources (2,15:2; 16:1).[138] Though the irrefutable answer will never be debugged, the next list of the fourfold gospel on the so-called NT canon of Origen, Clement's successor at the Catechetical School of Alexandria, sheds light over the way Eusebius, admittedly in a small proportion to his accurate comments, treated his sources.[139] Here the second gospel setting is associated with 1 Pet 5:13, where Eusebius' on Origen finds the relation of Mark with Peter and almost sure with Rome substantiated. The surviving Origenean parallels, particularly *Comm. Jo.* 1.4, do not mention 1 Pet 5:13, making Eusebius suspicious of implementing an adaptation of his sources under the purpose of defining with more support in the Scripture's authority the gospel canon inherited by the church.[140] If so, the nexus between Mark's gospel and 1 Pet 5:13 would be a device Eusebius took from Clement Alexandrinus (and/or Papias) to shield the four-gospel list of Origen:

> . . . as learning by tradition concerning the four gospels, which they alone are unquestioned in the church of God under the heaven, that first was written that according to whom once (was) a tax-collector, and then apostle of Jesus Christ, Matthew, delivered it to those from the Judaism (who) believed, (and)

138. The middle stage is the occurrence of φασί/φασίν among the quotations of the *Acta Martyrum* Eusebius collected: 5.1:62; 2:5,6. Sellew, "Eusebius and the Gospels," 117, 121 must be recognized for noticing the impersonal use of φασί/φασίν, though underrating Eusebius' general trend for accuracy.

139. Ferguson, "New Testament Canon," 318–19; Kalin, "Canon of Eusebius," 389. Clement knew the four-gospel list. *Strom.* 3.13: Πρῶτον μὲν οὖν ἐν τοῖς παραδεδομένοις ἡμῖν τέτταρσιν εὐαγγελίοις οὐκ ἔχομεν τὸ ῥητόν, ἀλλ' ἐν κατ' Αἰγυπτίους (First then, in the four gospels handed to us we don't have the thing, but in that according to the Egyptians).

140. Eusebius, *Hist. Eccl.* 6.25:6–7 is assigned by Eusebius to Origen's *Comm. Matt.* The work is lost and scholarship prefers to see there an adaptation of Origen's *Hom. Jes. Nav.* 7.1, only extant in Rufinus' Latin translation, or *Comm. Jo.* 1.4 (Kalin, "Canon of Eusebius," 390–92). See next note.

composed an Hebrew book. And second that according to Mark, as Peter instructed him, did it, and who (Peter) declared (his) son in the Catholic epistle saying "sends you greetings the co-chosen (church) in Babylon and Mark my son." And third that according to Luke, (who) has made the praised gospel by Paul for those from the Gentiles. And after all, that according to John. (Eusebius, *Hist. Eccl.* 6.25:4–6)[141]

Preliminary Assessment of the Papias-Clement Tradition on Mark

Papias on Mark is around AD 130 the earliest literary testimony for the second gospel authorship whilst for its place of composition is Irenaeus ca. AD 180 or with more explicitness Clement Alexandrinus ca. AD 200. 1 Pet 5:13 rolls back the association of Mark and Peter with Rome to the lifespan of Peter, but it depends on the doubly controversial presumption that 1 Peter is not pseudepigraphic and that the reading of Babylon for Rome in 1 Pet 5:13 must be accepted beyond what Eusebius says on Clement Alexandrinus and Papias. The connection of 1 Peter with Clement Romanus does exist, but the link of 1 Peter with Pauline theology is stronger, better fitting the position of the epistle's sender with a presbyter from the second to third generation of believers, a Hellenistic Judeo-Christian writing from the same region of his addressees or perhaps from Rome who has reached the faith through Scripture, rather than from direct witness of Jesus. Ignatius and Muratori ignore 1 Peter. Polycarp apparently knows it and not without likelihood does 2 Clem. in the east, but the first to acknowledge its Petrine authorship free of contest is Irenaeus, AD 180.

The correlation of 1 Peter and 1 Clem. rests on the header (1 Pet 1:2// 1 Clem. *Prae.*), the expressions *to be called out of/from darkness to light* (1

141. ὡς ἐν παραδόσει μαθὼν περὶ τῶν τεσσαρῶν εὐαγγελίων, ἃ καὶ μόνα ἀναντίρρητά ἐστιν ἐν τῇ ὑπὸ τὸν οὐρανὸν ἐκκλησίᾳ τοῦ θεοῦ, ὅτι πρῶτον μὲν γέγραπται τὸ κατὰ τόν ποτε τελώνην, ὕστερον δὲ ἀπόστολον Ἰησοῦ Χριστοῦ Ματθαῖον, ἐκδεδωκότα αὐτὸ τοῖς ἀπὸ Ἰουδαϊσμοῦ πιστεύσασιν, γράμμασιν Ἑβραϊκοῖς συντεταγμένον· δεύτερον δὲ τὸ κατὰ Μάρκον, ὡς Πέτρος ὑφηγήσατο αὐτῷ, ποιήσαντα, ὃν καὶ υἱὸν ἐν τῇ καθολικῇ ἐπιστολῇ διὰ τούτων ὡμολόγησεν φάσκων "ἀσπάζεται ὑμᾶς ἡ ἐν Βαβυλῶνι συνεκλεκτὴ καὶ Μάρκος ὁ υἱός μου"· καὶ τρίτον τὸ κατὰ Λουκᾶν, τὸ ὑπὸ Παύλου ἐπαινούμενον εὐαγγέλιον τοῖς ἀπὸ τῶν ἐθνῶν πεποιηκότα· ἐπὶ πᾶσιν τὸ κατὰ Ἰωάννην. The passage is reminiscent of Origen *Hom. Jes. Nav.* 7.1; *Comm. Jo.* 1.4, especially of this last, remarkably the beginning: Ἐγὼ δ' οἶμαι ὅτι καὶ δ΄ ὄντων τῶν εὐαγγελίων, οἱονεὶ στοιχείων τῆς πίστεως τῆς ἐκκλησίας, ἐξ ὧν στοιχείων ὁ πᾶς συνέστηκε κόσμος ἐν Χριστῷ καταλλαγεὶς τῷ θεῷ (For I believe that four are the gospels, as the principles of the faith of the church, from which principles the whole world is reconciled (and) set together with God in Christ).

Pet 2:9//1 Clem. 59.2*), love covers a multitude of sins* (1 Pet 4:8//1 Clem. 49.5; but see also 2 Clem. 16.4), *precious blood of Christ* (1 Pet 1:19//1 Clem. 7.4), and on the admonishment *be subjected to the presbyters* (1 Pet 5:5//1 Clem. 57.1). Despite the strong reasons to refute 1 Peter's early date and on the contrary to accept pseudonymity, the connection to Clement Romanus would strengthen its Roman origin and find support for Mark's association with Peter from 1 Pet 5:13 as part of the Roman tradition. The frame around AD 85–90 for 1 Peter suggested by the Anatolian persecutions reported in Pliny to Trajan (*Epistolae* 10.96) makes in fact viable the dependence of the common materials for 1 Clem. on 1 Peter. However, this makes in turn inconceivable the absence of 1 Peter in the group of Muratorian writings recognized by the Roman church or in the hand of Justin in the second half of II AD.

But something stays more striking: Mark seems from the position of 1 Peter known to the intended audience. Why should so many distant Asia Minor communities know altogether Mark in the 60s? Mark, discarded borrowing from Phlm 24 into Col 4:10 and 2 Tim 4:11, could have been known in Philippi, Ephesus, and Colossae, but the addressees in 1 Pet 1:1 represent a situation too ambitious, geographically, for one single epistle from the 60s. See the tardy verse Rev 1:11, whose scope is even lesser. On the other hand, pseudonymity from a later period when these Pauline epistles quoting Mark were familiar to the author of 1 Peter and expectedly in his mind by the intended recipients or even when the early reception of the tradition on the origin of the second gospel soon reported by Papias in AD 130 was a reality explains the resource to Mark in a work whose guise is, at all lights, pseudonymous.[142] The position thaT 1 Peter was a late document bridging Pauline and Petrine ecclesiastical patronages at the start of II AD saves, in fact, the problem of claimed Petrine authorship and Pauline themes.[143]

Secunda Clementis stands as another of the most primitive witnesses to 1 Peter and even as the first concurrence of materials ostensibly borrowed from 1 Peter, the gospel of Mark, and the epistle of Ephesians in one single document around AD 150, for 1 Clem. and Ignatius don't seem to attest the second gospel, and Irenaeus does but is more recent. Attached to 1 Clem.

142. P[46], recovered in the Fayum, Egypt, is the earliest preserved physical Pauline corpus. Already assembled in the early to middle II AD, it most likely attests that in the late I AD or beginning of the II the Pauline corpus was in circulation. It preserves in this order long extensions of Romans, Hebrews, 1 Corinthians, 2 Corinthians, Ephesians, Philippians, Colossians (including Col 4:10), and 1 Thessalonians (Comfort and Barrett, *Earliest NT Manuscripts*, 1:183–307).

143. Black, *Mark*, 66 may be hitting the target seeing 1 Pet 5:13 as a blend of Pauline and Petrine trends.

in the three mss where it has been preserved, A, H, and S, 2 Clem. was used majorly by eastern authors. Among them, Const. ap. 8.47:85 grouped it in the Syrian canon of sacred documents during the late IV AD, being also its eastern pedigree apparently proven by its appending to Codex Alexandrinus in the V AD, and by its absence in L, ms with Clementine writings, where if it were a western document it should have been natural to find it placed alongside the Latin version of 1 Clem. probably from the II to the III AD century (folios CV–CXVIII), as well as next to the Latin version of the *Clementine Recognitions* (folios I–CI), and to the apocryphal letter of Clement Romanus to James the Just (folios CI–CV).[144]

Secunda Clementis is, thus, one very early document from the Greek part of the Roman Empire which stresses the possible production in the same geographical area of 1 Peter and Mark. Further precision is even suggestible inasmuch as the Coptic mss which attest 1 Clem. in the IV and V AD, C and C[1], ignore 2 Clem., pointing powerfully for the latter Syrian, Greek, or Anatolian provenance against Egyptian.[145] Despite that, it must be remembered that raw materials from Mark or the second gospel itself are located in Rome contemporaneously by means of Justin, who has before him with all security Mark 3:16–17 (*Dial.* 106.16–19), ostensibly Mark 16:20 (*1 Apol.* 45.15–16), and less identifiable Marcan constituents, partly reversible into Matthean or Lucan readings.

The longer ending, Mark 16:9–20, belongs to the second half of II AD and was possibly affixed to the canonical gospel from an excerpt going back to the first half, but this source as a whole is doubtfully Justin for Mark 16:9–19 is not paralleled in his works, despite that Justinian inspiration could find some ground for Mark 16:20. Mark 16:9–20 is unknown by Clement Alexandrinus and his disciple Origen in the early III AD, and above all is absent in the two oldest mss for the whole second gospel, B and ℵ. Irenaeus acknowledges the source for Mark 16:19 in *Haer.* 3.10:5 (AD 180), suggesting the western origin of the longer ending because it is improbable that the early text of B and ℵ, traceable to the second half of II AD (in base of the concurrence to 85 percent of the text-type B and P[7]5 for Luke), dropped out verses 9–20 if they were original.[146]

144. Morin, *Clementis Romani*, iv–v.

145. Ehrman, *Apostolic Fathers*, 1:30, 161.

146. Metzger, *Greek New Testament*, 126 clinched the matter of the longer ending by means of the existence of the shorter one (Mark 16:8b–c): nobody would have refurnished the end of Mark if the longer ending were original. Seemingly, we are before western fabric again: Codex Bobbiensis (k), ca. AD 400, but with a text-type very akin to Cyprian of Carthage returns back Mark 16:8b–c to mid III AD (Metzger and Ehrman, *Text of the New Testament*, 102).

In some exegetical circles, Clement Romanus (AD 98) and Ignatius (before AD 120) are usually called in help of the Roman provenance of the gospel of Mark, inasmuch as they stand as possible early witnesses of Peter's death in Rome, where Mark would have accompanied Peter according to 1 Pet 5:13. Possibly Irenaeus (AD 180) and undoubtedly Clement Alexandrinus (AD 200) declare the Roman production of Mark. That notwithstanding, the silence of Eusebius when he is commenting at length on the early source for Irenaeus and the Alexandrine, Papias on Mark as the interpreter of Peter (*Hist. Eccl.* 3.39:1–17), force us to accept that this source said nothing on Rome, whilst the readings of Peter's death in Clement Romanus and Ignatius are not free of chiaroscuro, and neither are the secure datable mentions of Peter's martyrdom in Rome by Gaius and Dionysius when they are seen as witnesses of one-hundred-year-old facts.

Perhaps better headway is achieved from betting on the Roman reading of Col 4:10; 2 Tim 1:17; 4:11; and Phlm 24 over other alternatives, setting Mark in Rome along with Paul in the early 60s, which would bestow him the possibility to encounter Peter in the imperial see. The cross-reference is convoluted, but shows at any circumstance the consistency of Mark as NT character, to whom several documents resort, who was held a relevant companion of Paul in the first stage of his Christian career (Acts), in his last stage (Paul's epistles), and of Peter (1 Peter).

The association of Mark with Rome by means of Paul is firmer than the link by means of Peter, solely upheld in 1 Pet 5:13. It is fair to remind here that the motif for Peter's travel to Rome during Claudius (AD 41–54) continues to be the romance of Simon Magus in the IV century (Eusebius, *Hist. Eccl.* 2.13:1—15:1), and that the wizard's link with the Roman Gnosticism of Menander by Justin (*1 Apol.* 26.1–22) and Irenaeus (*Haer.* 1.23:1–5) may be based in the confused reading of a Latin stele in the Tiber Island between the two bridges (ἐν τῷ Τίβερι ποταμῷ μεταξὺ τῶν δύο γεφυρῶν; *1 Apol.* 26.8–11), which made Justin and Irenaeus following Justin suppose that Simon had traveled to Rome and convinced the Senate of his divinity. The stele was re-discovered in 1576 near the door of the Franciscan convent and remains in the Galleria Lapidaria of the Vatican Museum. It has a ten-lined inscription dedicated to the god of oaths, Semo Sancus: SEMONI | SANCO | DEO FIDIO. . . (To Semo Sanco God of Faith . . . ; CIL VI,567), which likely Justin erroneously registered ΣΙΜΩΝΙ ΔΕΩ ΣΑΓΚΤΩ (To Saint Simon God) in *1 Apol.* 26.11.[147]

147. The fact that in Eusebius the reason that drove Peter to Rome before his martyrdom was still his eagerness to win over the heresy of Simon Magus prompts one to believe that the tradition of Peter in Rome, certainly established from the second half of II AD onwards, was not built over solid historical accounts born in Rome itself one

The papyri facilitate external proof to tradition for the currency of the first Marcan fundamental, the authorship, doubtlessly in the III century AD, and with some probability in the second half of the II AD. Worthy of mention is P[45], the earliest four-gospel codex, dated ca. AD 250.[148] It comprised in origin 220 leaves of which 198 have been preserved. P45 holds, besides, the earliest uncontroversial Marcan physical remnants, comprising sections from Mark 4–13 in fifteen leaves (thirty pages).[149] P45 has the privilege to be the earliest full outward confirmation of the fourfold gospel tradition of Muratori, Irenaeus, and Clement Alexadrinus, though possibly the order reflected when the papyrus was taken to England was western typically—Matthew, John, Luke, Mark—differing from the former three.[150] This is curious and some justification for Muratori is required because there John ensues the gospel of Luke (line 10), and if Mark is accepted for the incomplete sentence before the third gospel (line 1), then the order is what later will be called eastern. But see Irenaeus in Lyon of Gaul, whose order is eastern

hundred years before, since otherwise it would have offered Eusebius a more rigorous report than Justin's, who probably was followed by Irenaeus and Eusebius because he was a written authority and there were not available better oral traditions concerning the same facts.

148. P[75] is contemporaneous to P[45], but its surviving material only includes the gospels of Luke and John.

149. Comfort, *Earliest NT Manuscripts*, 2:201, 333–34 claims P137 to be earlier to middle II AD. Found in Oxyrhynchus and very fragmentary, it contains single letters and very incomplete sentences of Mark 1:7–8,16–18. Comfort recognizes the text is too small to assess its type, but he doesn't hesitate to defend the resemblance to P[46], holding most part of the Pauline corpus and dated to AD 100–150. More problematic is 7Q5 (Comfort, *Earliest NT Manuscripts*, 2:298–99). This I AD Qumranite ms, claimed to be Mark 6:52–53, has sixteen to twenty scattered letters in five levels. Worth mentioning is the gap in line 3, which serves the hypothesis of a separation between two verses. Suggestive also is the inscription below the superior rim of one jar associated to the ms: רומא (Ῥούμας?; less probably, Ῥώμη?). Six letters or more in 7Q5 need reconstruction or a choice between two or three readings (O'Callaghan, "Papiros Neotestamentarios," 93–96; *Cueva 7 de Qumrân*, 22–23, 44–61), and the extant reconstructed text would only set forth two thorough words, ἤ and καί, too trivial to decode the ms.

150. P.Chester Beatty I (= P[45]) was purchased from local dealers in about 1930. It apparently came from the neighborhood of the Fayum or from Aphroditopolis, and originally measured 25.4 x 20.3 centimeters. It was composed of sewn single-sheet quires doubled in two, giving four pages for each quire (two leaves for both faces). Every leaf is mutilated and in some cases only few words are preserved on each page. Each page had thirty-nine lines. The preserved Marcan sections are: Mark 4:36—5:2,16–26; 5:38—6:3,15–25,36–50; 7:3–15; 7:25—8:1,10–26; 8:34—9:9,18–31; 11:27—12:1,5–8,13–19,24–28. According to the editor, the text of Mark is precursor of the Caesarean type with 107 agreements with uncial W and 65 with Θ, 54/A, 49/D, 44/B, 42/א, and 31/C (Kenyon, *Chester Beatty Biblical Papyri I*, 5–12; *II*, v–xviii); Comfort and Barrett, *Earliest NT Manuscripts*, 1:138–82. See list of II–III AD gospel mss in Elliott, "Greek New Testament Papyri," 15–20.

(*Haer.* 3.3:1) at the same early stage. Lastly, the entitled gospel codex $P^{6}6$ merits also some lines here: regardless that it is devoted to a single gospel, it introduces the four-gospel tradition some decades before into the II AD.

$P^{6}6$ is a codex papyrus antecessor of the format of the great IV–V-century vellum uncials (א, A, B, C, D, W). Professionally written, it preserves most of the fourth gospel, and bears pagination figures from 1 to 156. $P^{6}6$ is one of the two earliest issues of superscript gospel titles, being readable εὐαγγέλιον κατὰ Ἰωάννην (gospel according to John) in the upper part of the first leaf. It has been dated to the second half of the II AD. Among the calligraphic features adduced to the early date is the hook or apostrophe (') between double consonants, displayed in some mss of the second century (P.Mich 6871, P.Oxy 3013, BGU III 715.5).[151] The conservative date ca. AD 200 has also been established.[152] P^{4}, Egyptian codex dated ca. AD 200, holding Lucan fragments from chapters 1 to 6, preserves too the title κατὰ μαθ'θαῖον (according to Matthew) in a small single adhered fragment that possibly testifies the original dimensions of the codex comprising at least two complete gospels.[153]

$P^{6}6$ and P4 substantiate the following uttermost inference: the gospel mss were accompanied in the early III AD and possibly during the second half of the II AD by a tradition on their authorship and most probably of their provenance. If the gospel codices were indeed assigned to single

151. P.Bodmer II (= P^{66}) was discovered in Mount Abu Mana, east of the Nile River, in 1952. Comfort and Barrett, *Earliest NT Manuscripts*, 1:353–54 adduces that the form of the letters δ, θ, and ε, as well as the employment of apostrophe ('), find parallels in the II AD, and defends a date of ca. AD 150, brothering P^{66} with the earliest gospel fragment, P^{52} (P.Ryland 457), a remnant of John 18:31–33 dated in the first half of the II AD.

152. NA^{28} catalogues P^{66} ca. 200 AD. Gathercole, "Earliest Manuscript Title," 227–34 gathers some mss using the apostrophe in I–II AD, but sets preferably the apostrophe of P^{4} in II–III AD, maybe post–AD 200. In my opinion the date can be also subscribed for P^{66}.

153. Skeat, "Oldest Manuscript," 8–22, considering the calligraphic exactness, the same distance between columns, the virtually same height and number of words per column in accord with his calculation, was convinced that the Matthean fragments P^{64}/P^{67}, from AD 150–75 and assumed by scholarship to form separate parts of the same ms, should additionally belong to the same codex as the Lucan P^{4}. This polemical consortium, not yet resolved, would grant P^{64}/P^{67}/P^{4} the privilege to be the first example of a multi-gospel codex, earlier therefore than P^{45} and P^{75}. The discussion cannot be assumed here in full: see Comfort and Barrett, *Earliest NT Manuscripts*, 1:31–47 for a correlation of T. C. Skeat; Head, "Magdalen Papyrus of Matthew," 267–76 for an early III AD date for P^{64}; Head, "P^{4}, P^{64} and P^{67}," 451–57 for the objections to Skeat's theory foundations, especially the estimation of the codex format from the calculation of letters per column and leaf; and Charlesworth, "P^{64+67} and P^{4}," 587–602 on the problem of different fiber orientation of the recto and verso in P^{64}, P^{67}, and P^{4}.

authors at the beginning of III AD, then it becomes strongly conceivable that the oral tradition of their authorship can be retraced scarce decades, reaching Irenaeus in AD 180, Muratori in about AD 150–200, and finally Papias before the middle of II AD. Thus, it doesn't sound foreign to reality that the first recognizable attribution of authorship to the gospels (of Mark and Matthew) makes its appearance in Papias ca. AD 130, from whom all the later witnesses seem to depend.[154] If we bespeak of the second gospel as an independent physical document, and not of Mark as the NT character to whose paternity the document, once produced and in circulation, will be attributed, proceeding beyond this date, AD 130, requires caution, though it is plausible, offering the reader a final analysis on the internal coherence of Papias' testimony.

The name of the elder from whom Papias received the tradition, we said, is John the Presbyter. Eusebius presents Papias himself as instructed by direct disciples of the apostles, one of whom would be Ariston, and another this John.[155] John the Elder is a mysterious figure not reported before Papias. According to Eusebius and Jerome, John the Elder wrote Revelation and 2 and 3 John. Scrutiny of the sources on this John is not conclusive but it must be admitted that he is an undisputed character of the Anatolian tradition, especially related to Ephesus, the town were his tomb was located.[156] Forwarding his font of information to John the Presbyter, Papias buttresses the idea of an early II century Asia Minor, not Roman, origin of the tradition on the second gospel.[157]

154. This will match the early date for the Marcan P[137] (see note above).

155. Eusebius, *Hist. Eccl.* 3.39:1–14.

156. Eusebius, *Hist. Eccl.* 3.39:6; 7.24:17 mentions two tombs in Ephesus during the III and IV AD of two different Johns, likely one attributed to John the son of Zebedee, and the other to John the Presbyter, quoted by Papias. Discussed in the next note.

157. The letter of Polycrates, bishop of Ephesus, to Victor of Rome, during the Quartodeciman controversy (late II AD) restates the tradition of the beloved disciple leaning on Jesus' breast and states he died at Ephesus (John 13:23; Eusebius, *Hist. Eccl.* 5.24:2–7). Polycrates gives the name of the disciple, John, but also states he had been a Jewish priest wearing the sacerdotal plate (ἱερεὺς τὸ πέταλον πεφορεκώς). In the case the datum is glimpsed from the NT, Polycrates must be thinking of the disciple that took Peter into the palace of the high priest (John 18:15–16) and perhaps had him identified with John, a shadowy figure from the high-priestly family in Acts 4:6. Polycrates even appeals to Philip the Evangelist (Acts 5:6; 8:4–40; 21:8–9) in his intention to impose the Asiatic custom for the Passover, whom he erroneously calls *apostle* and one of whose daughters also died at Ephesus. Bauckham, "Papias and Polycrates," 25–65 focuses over the Asian tradition on Philip, also known to Papias (Eusebius, *Hist. Eccl.* 3.39:9–10), and drives the discussion on the several Johns to the assumption that John the beloved disciple is the author of the fourth gospel (John 21:24) and must be identified with John the Elder quoted by Papias, later substituted by the more authoritative son of the Zebedee (Irenaeus, *Haer.* 1.1:1). The tradition Polycrates retains is too suggestive to let it go

On the other hand, one of the strongest arguments in support of the tradition is that Mark was not Jesus' eyewitness, something that could not be invented if Papias' intention was to legitimize the gospel against heretic charges concerning its apostolic origin or, among the orthodox churches, against sheerer accounts of Jesus' life and sayings like Matthew's, which is much better attested in the early church fathers Justin, Ignatius, and Clement Romanus. This assessment is mirrored in the II–III AD mss evidence corroborating the scant popularity won by the Marcan mss with one single instance (P^{45}) against sixteen Johannine, twelve Matthean, and seven Lucan.[158] Contrariwise, the statement that in no respect Mark erred when he wrote some things as he recorded them (*οὐδὲν ἥμαρτεν Μάρκος, οὕτως ἔνια γράψας ὡς ἀπεμνημόνευσεν*) offset possible accusations, revealing in Papias the actual concern over legitimacy which every work pretending sacred inspiration should confront.[159] If the intention was to justify the gospel, it was preferable to say it came from a direct disciple of Jesus and not from Mark, whose authority rests in being Peter's interpreter. The conclusion from this insight is that Mark is not an invented name or, it is conceivable, that Papias wants to save the reputation of John the Presbyter.[160]

---

without lucubration and one is persuaded to agree with Bauckham. Polycrates defines John the beloved disciple as *μάρτυς καὶ διδάσκαλος* (witness and teacher). This would suffice for Bauckham, "Papias and Polycrates," 32 to declare him also the author of the fourth gospel and of the Johannine letters. The *μάρτυς/μαρτυρέω* word family is, doubtlessly, one of the favorites of the fourth gospel and the Johannine letters, deserving a separate study (John 1:7–8,15,19,32,34; 3:11,26,28,32,33; 4:39; 5:36; 8:13–14,17–18; 10:25; 15:26–27; 18:37; 19:35; 21:24; 1 John 1:2; 5:7–11; 3 John 3,6,12). Moreover, Revelation sets forth the concept related to one John who admonishes the seven churches in Asia (Rev 1:2,9; 19:10; 20:4; 22:16,18,20). But if we observe the usage of *martyr/witness* in Revelation, we perceive a less deep, presentist and communitarian tone, isolating its author from the remaining Johannine corpus. And since this John must be the source for Papias' millenarism (*1 Apol.* 20:1–7; Eusebius, *Hist. Eccl.* 3.39:11–12), he should be differentiated from the fourth gospel as Eusebius, Dionysius Alexandrine, and Jerome state (*Hist. Eccl.* 3.39:4–6; 7.24:6–27; *Vir. Ill.* 9; 18). The question is all in all puzzling. Revelation assumes the notion of the (Asiatic?) elders (Rev 5:8,11,14; 11:16; 19:4) to which John the beloved disciple, John son of Zebedee, and John the Elder are related. Furthermore, for the Canon Muratori John the disciple was pushed to write the fourth gospel by his fellow-disciples and bishops (*cohortantibus condescipulis et episcopis*; line 10; Tregelles, *Earliest Catalogue*, 32–35), one of whom could be this other John, i.e., John the Elder. See further sequels of this tradition in Eusebius, *Hist. Eccl.* 5.14:7 on Clement Alexandrinus and later on in Const. ap. 7.46:7.7.

158. Hurtado, *Earliest Christian Artifacts*, 20, 27–31; Elliott, "Greek New Testament Papyri," 15–20.

159. Eusebius, *Hist. Eccl.* 3.39:15; Taylor, *St. Mark*, 1–3.

160. Senior, *Swords and Clubs*, 11 brings an alternative, in my view less probable: the bishop of Hierapolis, preferring oral apostolic testimony to written tradition, is criticizing Mark for fixing a written account of Jesus, proving by the opposite way the independence of his source.

2

Internal Evidence

The Semitic Background

The Presence of Peter in the Gospel of Mark

The tradition on gospel authorship in the second half of I AD is fairly defensible, but it would be biased, neglecting further precisions, to identify it with the creation of the gospels instead of with their diffusion. Some sort of attribution should have accompanied each document from its very creation, but it seems improper to their nature to see then the signature of one apostle or companion. Out of Matthew and Mark, all NT documents bear grammatical remarks, original, pseudepigraphic, or indirect to their authors. It is reasonable to assign the difference to the public character of these texts, not in the sense that were targeted to faith communities, a shared aim with almost all the canon, but as a result of the evolution suffered during their editorial process. The opposite criterion is not, of course, applicable. Luke 1:3; John 19:35; 21:24–25; Acts 1:1; and 1 John 5:13 use a veiled first singular o plural, but it is observed that in general the NT documents are signed: Pauline epistles, all beginning with Παῦλος; Heb 13:23–24; Jas 1:1; 1 Pet 1:1; 2 Pet 1:1; 2 John 1; 3 John 1; Jude 1; Rev 1:4,9.

In the last part of I AD, the group of eyewitnesses and their followers was ending, and the next generation was in short of an authoritative representant of the Jesus tradition, assembled over the biographical framework, with the style of biblical scripture, that collected the available sources on Jesus in the oral circles, perhaps too, already available under the form of small written parables or lists of sayings, and that gave answer to the challenges the announcement of Jesus faced toward Judaism and Gentility. Even in the second gospel, the shortest of the four canonical, the stream of information gathered to build a new sacred biography, faithfully commited to historical deeds but simultaneously adjusted to biblical categories for their deep understanding, is ample. Of course this single reason doesn't necessarily account for plural authorship. The style of the second gospel is, for the bulk, fairly homogeneous, admitting one final editor who has smoothed the former narrative units belonging to tradition instead of leaving them united but grammatically untouched. It is his resource to sayings and biographical episodes of Jesus which raises the suspicion that he was not alone when the primary sources were assembled or that, if they belonged to an earlier document, his work relied on more than one font of information in origin.[1]

But, in spite of the view that the sole Peter's teaching Mark collected according to Papias should be something less elaborated than the actual shape of some second gospel episodes (Mark 5:1–20; 6:45–52; 9:2–8; 13:1–37; 16:1–8)—because while Peter was alive his personal testimony was not in need of literary dressing, even more, was inconvenient as it could be refuted by those who were still living witnesses of Jesus—the content of the current document demonstrates that the link with Peter is not invented and that neither is the general framework or chronological sequence. On the contrary, many of the Marcan sections have all the cards to come from Peter or from the postapostolic heir circle of Peter, eloquently represented in two expressions of the Marcan community that have been slipped into the first part of the document, Σίμων καὶ οἱ μετ᾽ αὐτοῦ (Simon and those with him; Mark 1:36) and τοὺς περὶ αὐτὸν κύκλῳ καθημένους (at those round him (= Jesus) sitting in circle; Mark 3:34). We have a less valuable τοῖς περὶ τὸν Πέτρον (to those around Peter) in the shorter ending as well (Mark 16:8b), perhaps not earlier than mid III AD according to its attestation in Old Latin *k*, although valuable to some extent as inspired in Mark 1:36; 3:34, or Ignatius, *Smyrn.* 3.2.

One full reading is sufficient indeed to see the dependence of the second gospel on Peter's figure, the most important character after Jesus in order of quotations, up to twenty-six instances.[2] Peter and his brother Andrew

1. On the proto-Mark theory, see discussion in footnotes in chapter 3.

2. The possible Aramaic birth name of Peter, Simon (Σίμων), equals the Hebrew שִׁמְעוֹן, Simeon (Συμεών), the son of Jacob (Gen 29:33) and one of the twelve tribes (Num 1:22; Josh 19:1). In Mark, Peter as Simon is mentioned six times, five by the evangelist (Mark 1:16,29,30,36; 3:16) and once by Jesus (Mark 14:37). After the institution of the Twelve and with the exception of Mark 14:37, Simon is called Peter twenty times including the shorter ending, nineteen by the narrator (Mark 3:16; 5:37; 8:29,32,33; 9:2,5; 10:28; 11:21; 13:3; 14:29,33,37,54,66,67,70,72; 16:8b) and one time by an angel (Mark 16:7).

are the first disciples to be called by Jesus (Mark 1:16–17), Capernaum near the Lake of Galilee was the place where Jesus began his ministry, the place where Peter dwelt (Mark 1:21–22,29), and the headquarters of the primitive mission in Galilee (Mark 2:1; 3:20; 7:17; 9:33). Simon is the first disciple to be named in the list of the Twelve (Mark 3:13–19), in the lists of the four (Peter, Andrew, James, and John: Mark 1:16–19,29; 13:13), and in the lists of the three (Peter, James, and John: Mark 5:37; 9:2; 14:33), concentric discipleships around Jesus lead by Peter where the apostolic nucleus of the second gospel stays in sight.

Only Peter, James the Great, and John are allowed to see a miracle demanding privacy (Mark 5:37). Peter, James, and John alone saw the transfiguration and it was only Peter who spoke in the mountain with Jesus (Mark 9:2–6). Peter speaks on behalf of the Twelve (Mark 10:28; 11:21). At intervals Peter asks Jesus, and Jesus answers for all (Mark 10:28–31; 11:21–25). Other times, looking to all, Jesus upbraids Peter (Mark 8:33; 14:37–38). Significant is the sequence of Mark 8:27–30: Jesus asks all, answers Peter, and Jesus gives a command to all. Mark 14:37, Jesus admonishing Peter, is the unique verse of the second gospel where Jesus pronounces a personal name. Peter is the first Christian, the first to declare Jesus is the Messiah (Mark 8:29). Peter, James, and John receive private instruction (Mark 9:9–13), and also the three with Andrew (Mark 13:3–37). Peter promised Jesus fidelity to the death (Mark 14:29–31). Peter, James, and John accompany Jesus on the Mount of Olives (Mark 14:32–34). Peter tried to fulfill his promise following Jesus to the very palace of the high priest (Mark 14:53–54), but like Jesus had foretold (Mark 14:30), he was not brave enough to confess Jesus thither (Mark 14:66–72). Finally, the message given by the angel to the women distinguishes Peter from the other disciples (Mark 16:7).

The House of Peter According to Mark 2:1–12

Beyond his theological importance, as regards Peter the gospel of Mark presents one of the NT episodes that archaeology has checked. The trustworthiness of the gospel has in fact one of its representants in the healing of the paralytic in Capernaum, which most likely occurred in the house of Peter (Mark 1:29–34) and could be rooted in direct witness (Mark 2:1–12).[3] According to Mark 2:3–4, a paralytic was let down in a mat to the drawing

3. The house of Peter in Capernaum (Mark 1:29–34) seems to be the several times mentioned where Jesus was lodged (Mark 2:1; 3:20; 7:17; 9:33). But it could be Levi's (Mark 2:15), or any when οἰκία/οἶκος lacks the article (3:20; 7:17; 2:1 seems an exception).

room where Jesus was, after his fellows had unroofed it (ἀπεστέγασαν τὴν στέγην) and dug out a hole (ἐξορύσαντες). Contrarily, Luke, seeing another building model in his mind, prefers the expression ἀναβάντες ἐπὶ τὸ δῶμα διὰ τῶν κεράμων καθῆκαν αὐτὸν (went up onto the housetop and through the tiles lowered him; Luke 5:19), depicting a wealthier settlement of better-constructed dwellings.

The archaeology in southern Capernaum the Franciscan Custody developed from 1969 to 1991 uncovered a large urban net of poor walls, not wide enough, made of rounded basaltic stones, unshaped, fixed by soil and pebbles, without true mortar and foundations that hardly could support a second storey or a heavy roof.[4] Believed to continue the first occupation stage from the Hellenistic epoch judging from ceramics and five coins of the II BC, two of Antiochus IV (175–64 BC), one of Demetrius II (146/145 BC), and two of Alexander Janneus (103–76 BC), all the I-century AD stratum in Capernaum actually is very humble.[5] The lack of arches, roof tiles, or other economic-level pointers like marble, mosaics, frescos, hydraulic systems, or columns confirms that the Marcan version of a simple roof of beams crossed by reed and topped with straw and mud that could be easily unroofed probably is, if likened with Luke's, the closest version to the original report.[6]

There are, however, a handful of hints as to curtail the image of a hamlet reduced to subsistence level and to consider inside the world of plausibility the fact that I AD Capernaum enjoyed some level of prosperity, but far yet from the urban wealthy districts of Palestine. Sherds of imported commodities, fine red wares of Eastern Terra Sigillata and stamped Rhodian jars from the Hellenistic Period (II–I BC), a full glassware set, and few fragments of large stone jars in the Early Roman Period (I AD) manifest that some or at least few families in Capernaum were assuredly not poor.[7] On the other hand, the second gospel subscribes this broader background: Zebedee was richer than his employers (Mark 1:20), reasonably equaled by Peter and Andrew, who apparently owned a boat besides fishing equipment (Mark 1:16; for Peter's boat see Luke 5:3); Jairus the archisynagogos

4. Corbo, *House of Saint Peter*, 37; Loffreda, *Recovering Capharnaum*, 20–21.

5. Loffreda, *Cafarnao*, 2:141.

6. For the discussion of this point see Reed, *Archaeology and the Galilean Jesus*, 148–60.

7. Reed, "Stone Vessels," 385–95 counted all the published and unpublished stone vessel fragments in hands of the Franciscan Custody in Capernaum, some 150, 2 percent of them residuals of large stone jars (so some three fragments), lathe turned and not locally made, for the big dimensions of the soft limestone block required for this type of stone vessel (up to 400 kilograms) obligated to place the workshop in or next to the quarry.

suggests a slightly superior level of prosperity (Mark 5:22), whereas Levi the tax collector (Mark 6:14–15) must be understood under a superior official, perhaps inhabiting the very Capernaum.[8]

Another interesting fact is that against all the other structures studied, one room in the archaeological area measuring 5.80 by 6.45 meters, normally attributed to the so-called house of Peter, was especially enclosed within an octagonal concentric plan during the IV–V centuries. Several trial trenches brought to light that its floor and possibly the walls were against all other structures in the close area several times coated between the second half of the I century AD and the beginning of the II, a date attested by the deepest layer of the room from Late Hellenistic Period underneath the painted levels, and typologically by some Herodian lamps mixed with the

8. I follow Mattila, "Revisiting Jesus' Capernaum," 90–129. She argues, notwithstanding, that Insula 2, one of the best preserved domestic agglomerates in the Franciscan side of Capernaum, including a large house shop (203 m^2) with a spacious triple courtyard, one doublet columned entrance, and stairs for a second storey belonging to the III–V AD, and another two-floored house measuring 121 m^2 from the III–VI AD, shows some level of richness traceable back to the I AD. Assuming these houses are supposed to have capitalized previous structures, the argument is defended onto three factors: (a) the houses in Insula 2 seem to have reached their smaller size in the Byzantine period, from where it is deducible that the original structures belonging to I AD were large units surpassing subsistence level; (b) the set of early Roman glassware was found in Insula 2; (c) the archaeology of Karanis in Egypt supports the notion of some level of prosperity within mud-brick houses adorned with decorated plastered inner walls; hence, the rough basaltic walls of I AD Capernaum could be but bare residuals of what they were one day. Though Mattila's discussion is really balanced, I deem that among the three reasons only (b) is consistent and (c) tenuously probable. (a) is not, because the trend to reduce size might to have occurred not before the Levantine economic decay of the III AD (strong coinage debasement, eclipse of luxury trade with India, South Arabia, and the Horn of Africa, and wane/final abandonment of the fortifications in the southeastern Roman limes in the V–VI AD), and the large I AD tracings under the Byzantine houses, to be the case, could have belonged to more than one family unit. In addition, we have mortar walls in the Byzantine period of Insula 2, as we see in other Byzantine enclosures, but the device is unknown in I AD foundations, which had to seal the basaltic stones with the same mud used in the thatch. As for (c), fragments of Herodian lamps (late I BC–early II AD) and a coin of Antiochus IV (175–64 BC) acknowledge the habitation under Insula 2 in the foundational stage of Capernaum (Loffreda, *Cafarnao*, 2:125–28, 186). Despite the fact, drawings in the walls with mud-revetment of Karanis are not secure indicative of prosperity, and otherwise, like the mud-bricks, are less probable in Peter's Capernaum due to humidity during the rainy season, and above all, as a consequence of the general I AD stream in the urban landscape out of the Palestinian Hellenized cities, which was to avoid representations and foreign fashions, proven by the disappearance of imported wares in the turn to the I AD and its substitution by stone vessels, among other indicatives of concern over religious purity (Berlin, "Jewish Life before the Revolt," 429–53). In conclusion: Insula 2, placed between Peter's house and the synagogue, was occupied during the I AD, but its level of prosperity remains uncertain.

plaster. The plaster, some Christian graffiti, and the plan of the most recent walls in accordance to ancient authorities reveal the conversion of a II BC house into a *domus ecclesia* by the beginning of the II AD at the latest and finally embellished in the IV–V centuries.[9]

More walls from the I AD preserved in the perimeter of the octagonal basilica, part of them aligned with the sacred room, ease the recovering of the original design of Peter's house, or of the one recorded as Peter's by the Judeo-Christians of the II AD. The comparison with the nearby preserved houses manifests a nearly square structure, with several roofed rooms around an 84-m2 central courtyard, probably shared by more than one family occupying each compartment. Strikingly, only Mark among the synoptics (Matt 8:14; Luke 4:38) says that Peter's house also belonged to his brother Andrew (τὴν οἰκίαν Σίμωνος καὶ Ἀνδρέου; Mark 1:29). Nothing can undeniably prove it, but the archaeological data confirm the Marcan narrative of Peter with his wife, his mother-in-law, and Andrew (Mark 1:29,31) dwelling in a II BC house, already built when the brothers moved from Bethsaida as the Johannine tradition states (John 1:44).[10]

The narration of Mark shows the crowd blocking the doorway, forcing the four friends of the paralytic to dig a hole in the roof (Mark 2:1–4). The archaeological park reveals a system of narrow accesses in an east-west axis aligned with the lakeshore, not more than three meters wide, perpendicular to the main street of I-century AD Capernaum.[11] The house attributed to Peter was flanked on the side looking to the east by the main (north-south) street, but it had an additional open space between the main street and the door leading to the courtyard, next to the plastered room, in the northeastern side, in the junction of the house farthest from the lake.[12] One entrance

9. Corbo, *House of Saint Peter*, 8–34, 55–70; Loffreda, *Recovering Capharnaum*, 50–67. Peter the Deacon, in his *Liber de Locis Santis* of the XII century, a work describing the holy places of Palestine based in more ancient sources, registers an important report when he gets the turn to Capernaum: *In Capharnaum autem ex domo apostolorum principis ecclesia facta est cuius parietes usque hodie ita stant, sicut fuerunt* (In Capernaum the house of the prince of the apostles is now a church whose walls are still standing as they were; PL 173:1128/2B).

10. For the fact that Peter was married and his wife living when he met Jesus, compare Mark 1:30 and 1 Cor 9:5. Indirectly: Mark 10:28.

11. Loffreda, *Recovering Capharnaum*, 8–9, 24; Mattila, "Capernaum," 220.

12. In other words: when Peter and Andrew exited from their house, they stepped first into an open space in fore of which the main street and the sunrise in the horizon were visible, and crossing the street and some to the right were the low buildings of Insula 3, dated also to the Early Roman Period to judge from ceramics (Loffreda, *Cafarnao II*, 100, 121–25, 141–43). Then, if they wanted to go toward the lake, they turned right, to the south, leaving the wall of their house to the west and Insula 3 to the east; and if they wanted to go to Insula 2 or farther to the synagogue, they turned left, that

there dovetails well the narrative of Mark 2, being more accurate to set the multitude endeavoring to enter the house in that open space and not in the main street, to which the private room belonging to Peter had no direct access because it was some meters away.[13] If the reconstruction according to the excavations is correct, the healing of the man affected by palsy would have occurred in the same room later converted into a *domus ecclesia*.

Related Early Christian Traditions

The Marcan healing of the paralytic breathes the atmosphere of the small Jewish village. Estimation of the urban area of Capernaum in the I century AD reaches a size no more than ten hectares in which the type of buildings doesn't support a population superior to 100–150 persons per hectare. The village of Peter and his companions would therefore hold a maximum of 1,500–1,700 inhabitants.[14] Mark's narrative in Capernaum and its surroundings, extended to Bethsaida five kilometers to the east and to Gennesaret three to the west, outlines the narrow medium where Jesus did not pass unsuspected. The reluctance of Jesus to be made known (Mark 1:25,34,43–44; 3:11–12; 5:43; 7:36; 8:26,30; 9:9–10), usually interpreted in the light of the suffering Son of Man (Mark 8:29–33; 9:30–32), can reciprocally be accounted from the physical conditions the reduced space imposed to Jesus' ministry.

The area formed by the three villages Gennesaret, Capernaum, and Bethsaida, abutting the natural track along the fringe of the lake and sharing few paths for wares, flocks, and transients, was inclined to the impulsive propagation of Jesus' miracles (Mark 1:28,45; 3:8; 7:36–37) and to the misappropriation of their meaning. The pressure at Simon's house (Mark 2:2,4) and additional references of crowds going in seek of Jesus in the Galilean part of the gospel (Mark 1:32,33,37,45; 2:13; 3:7–10,20,32; 4:1,36; 5:21; 6:31–34.53–56; 8:1; 9:14) must rather in fact be judged from the reduced geographical space and not from an overpopulated area. The quickness of motion the narrative conveys to the reader and what outwardly appears an exaggeration acquire historical flavor when the relative conditions

is, to the north. The longest axis of the lake is the north-south (twenty-one kilometers), the same orientation as I AD Capernaum's cardo, but the shore there is perpendicular to this axis because the lake, after a curvature, runs from east to west.

13. Loffreda, *Recovering Capharnaum*, 50–57.

14. I am indebted again to Reed, *Archaeology and the Galilean Jesus*, 148–52.

of reduced space for a ministry of teaching and healing in I-century AD Capernaum are taken into consideration.[15]

Surely, deeply behind this motif of the second gospel survives the substratum of personal testimony rich in detail and motion of characters, easily perceived in the continuous reading. The episode of the paralytic (Mark 2:1–12), the girl restored to life and the healing of the bleeding woman (Mark 5:22–43), the epileptic boy in Caesarea Philippi (Mark 9:14–27), the discussions with Pharisees at Levi's house (Mark 2:15–22), in the field (Mark 2:23–28), or in the synagogue (Mark 3:1–6), and the disagreements in Nazareth and with the kinsmen of Jesus in Capernaum (Mark 3:21–35; 6:1–6) can be encompassed in the category of narratives in small spaces of proportionately plenty of people based on personal testimony.[16] The expression *οἱ παρ' αὐτοῦ ἐξῆλθον κρατῆσαι αὐτόν· ἔλεγον γὰρ ὅτι ἐξέστη* (his relations went forth to hold him: for they said he was out of minds) referred to Jesus in Mark 3:21, for instance, Peter's denial anathematizing and abjuring he didn't know this man Jesus (*ἀναθεματίζειν καὶ ὀμνύναι ὅτι οὐκ οἶδα τὸν ἄνθρωπον τοῦτον*), and Jesus' despairing cry hanged in the cross (*ὁ θεός μου, ὁ θεός μου, εἰς ἐγκατέλιπές με*; my God, my God, why hast thou forsaken me?)—the last two beyond the Galilean part of the gospel (Mark 14:71; 15:34)—hardly could be invented if the intention of the second evangelist were to disseminate in his targeted audience faith in Jesus' divinity.[17] It is

15. It is a pity Boring, *Mark*, 67–69, 75–78, 81, 97–99, 106, assuming the whole ministry of Jesus in Galilee is modeled from the Easter and missionary experience of the church, doesn't ponder the historical reliability of the paralytic healing episode and of the crowds going in seek of Jesus.

16. Taylor, *St. Mark*, 102 considers the passion, including the report of the empty tomb, Mark 14:1—16:8, of the same type of vividly told narratives, but his list of sections based on Petrine testimony differs in some points: Mark 1:21–39; 4:35—5:43; 6:30–56; 7:24–37; 8:27—9:29.

17. It is not our intention to comment on the entire literary groove of the second gospel. At this point however, it is convenient to lay out the backdrop of the tripartite scene of Mark 3:20–35, brimful of contrast, disparate characters, motion, and historical plausibility, as an example of what we have called vivid Galilean traditions of the second gospel. Outside a house (3:20)—preferably it could be Peter's (1:29,33; 2:1) or Levi's (2:15)—it has crowded a tumult again (3:20; see 3:7–9) trying to access Jesus, impeding the disciples even to eat bread (3:20). In the tumult are Jesus' kinsmen, saying he is out of his mind (3:21). Scribes from Jerusalem capitalize (if not provoke) the rampage: Jesus is demon-possessed (3:22). But Jesus counteracts their impact and instructs the multitude crowded at the doorway with one parable (3:23–29). His mother and brothers are there, and send someone calling him out (3:31). Inside are Jesus and his first companions, *τοὺς περὶ αὐτὸν κύκλῳ καθημένους*, those sitting round him in circle (3:34; observe Matt 12:48 read *τοὺς μαθητάς αὐτοῦ*, his disciples). The Marcan adverb *κύκλῳ* (in circle) is in fact no more than a reinforcement of *περί* (round/around), grammatically avoidable after the preposition, but possibly Mark wants to stress what was the

natural to see in Peter the pivot of this tradition, though broadly understood, because we can afford to the count some other witnesses of Jesus, the rest of the Twelve excluding the Iscariot, Jesus' relatives, and the anonymous characters who encountered Jesus, then Christianized.

For tradition, Mark or John Mark was a Judeo-Christian of the second generation, who would have done the job of Peter's interpreter for the community of Rome, composed by Judeo-Christians and believers of Gentile origin. These last, unfamiliar with the Aramaic Peter spoke, entailed Mark's job as compiler of the Galilean traditions of Jesus' ministry into Greek. It has been long held by scholars that the second gospel bears many and noticeable Semitic grammar features and that in some parts it seems to be addressed to believers from the Gentile milieu. Highly startling is the presence among the abundant Semitisms of the gospel of a number of Latinisms that ostensibly confirm the testimony of Papias completed by Clement Alexandrinus stating that Mark wrote down the memories of Peter under an Italian context.

However, and in spite of the Petrine alignment of the gospel, the Papias-Clement tradition can be challenged from the grammatical standpoint and on the ground of Scripture when it pretends to climb high degrees of certainty. Semitisms and Latinisms are obvious features in the second gospel, but their total scope is notwithstanding disputed.[18] A first revision of Semitisms and geographical references will assure whether the author of the second gospel shared the Semitic background of Peter and Jesus, and will be useful to check in a second step if the Latin imprint in the gospel does justice to the Papias-Clement tradition or points out another direction.

Semitic Words and Commentaries on Jewish Customs

The Semitic milieu of the author and at times his position regarding the intended recipients of the second gospel can be glimpsed from text markers. The most popular are the Aramaic words, some rendered by Mark, and

---

vivid remembrance of disciples hearing Jesus. The image of people sitting inside the house clashes with the crowd outdoors seeking for Jesus in standing position, unless we ought to see two different moments, and not less nipping are the Jerosolimite scribes in remote Capernaum. Mark has not made great effort here to smooth and even the narrative thread. But, out these combination of factors, literarily, Mark has put into context with great achievement what are likely several data from the primitive tradition: the first disciples, gathered at Peter's house—often surrounded by villagers, strangers, and even foes since Jesus came to Capernaum—were at the occasion sat in a circle whose center was Jesus, magnetized by his teaching. For Mark 15:34 see commentary in next subheading.

18. On the problem of alleged Marcan Semitisms see Maloney, *Semitic Interference*, 7–50.

the commentaries on Jewish customs. In the face of the second gospel Aramaic words' popularity, it is not unbecoming an individual mention of all of them. The verses rendering Aramaic words are eight: (1) Βοανηργές (בְּנֵי רֶעֶשׁ, sons of the thunder; Mark 3:17);[19] (2) ταλιθα κουμ (טְלִיתָא קוּם, girl, stand up!; Mark 5:41); (3) κορβᾶν (קָרְבָּן, Jewish voluntary offering to God; Mark 7:11);[20] (4) εφφαθα (אֶתְפַּתַּח, you, open!; Mark 7:34); (5) Βαρτιμαῖος (בַּר-Τιμαῖος, son of Timaeus; Mark 10:46);[21] (6) αββα (אַבָּא, father; Mark 14:36); (7) Γολγοθᾶ (גֻּלְגֻּלְתָּא, Skull; Mark 15:22); (8) ελωι ελωι λεμα σαβαχθανι (אֱלָהִי אֱלָהִי לְמָה שְׁבַקְתַּנִי, my God, my God, why hast thou abandoned me?; Mark 15:34).[22]

19. The retranslation of Βοανηργές into Aramaic leads to a dilemma since no Semitic word is exactly equivalent to the second part of the word. The key for the answer is found in Moulton and Howard, *Grammar of New Testament Greek*, 2:108–9: gamma/γ in the LXX and NT period was generally aspirant. Thus, it could occasionally translate an ayin/ע as in Γόμορρα for עֲמֹרָה (Gen 10:19) or in Φόγωρ for פְּעוֹר (Gen 36:39). According to the anterior rule, the normal retranslation of Βοανηργές can be בְּנֵי רֶעֶשׁ, *sons of (the) quaking (heavens)* (Rook, "Boanerges," 94–95). Other convincing possibility is בְּנֵי רְגֶשׁ, *sons of the agitation* (Taylor, *St. Mark*, 231–32).

20. In Mark 7:9–13 Jesus is denouncing the hypocritical vow of a son who consecrates—declares qorban (קָרְבָּן)—the possible help his father could call for him over the fourth commandment: *Honor thy father and mother*. The qorban formula of Mark 7:11, κορβᾶν, ὅ ἐστιν δῶρον, ὃ ἐὰν ἐξ ἐμοῦ ὠφεληθῇς (qorban, that is, an offering (to God), whatever might benefit (you) from me), invalidated the possible benefit the father could extract from the thing declared qorban under the threat of trespass against the temple's treasury taboo. The son, therefore, was not pretending a real dedication to the temple but to make invalid the demand of assistance from his parents and in consequence he was violating the fourth commandment (Mark 7:13; see discussion in Benovitz, *Kol Nidre*, 16–27). The word קָרְבָּן is attested in several burial inscriptions from the NT period (CIIP 8,17,287,466,528). The best example is a Kidron Valley ossuary inscription in two lines from the I century BC to the I century AD bearing the same formula of Mark 7:11. CIIP 287: כל די אנש מתהנה בחלתה דה | קרבן אלה מן דבגוה (whatever benefit a man may derive from this ossuary is a qorban to God from him who is in it; Benovitz, *Kol Nidre*, 27–29).

21. Taylor, *St. Mark*, 448 proposed בַּר טִמְאַי, Bar Timay, but there is no strong reason to refuse a Greek-Aramaic hybrid name. Βαρθολομαῖος (Mark 3:18) possibly is בַּר תַּלְמַי, Bar Talmay (see 2 Sam 3:3), but also Bar Πτολεμαῖος (son of Ptolemy).

22. Jesus is crying (MT Ps 22:1): אֵלִי אֵלִי לָמָה עֲזַבְתָּנִי, *my God, my God, why did thou forsake me?* Again Taylor, *St. Mark*, 593 skillfully thinks in an original Hebrew by Jesus because the confusion of אֵלִי (God) with (the Greek variant) Ἠλείας (אֵלִיָּה, Elijah) is more understandable than if it comes from אֱלָהִי (ελωι), namely, the Aramaic אֱלָהּ (God) plus the first possessive suffix ִי., but a confusion of any kind with so similar words is perfectly possible attending to the oral context. The bystanders understood Aramaic but were in fact not well instructed in the Hebrew Psalms since they didn't guess the general sense of the cry. The abandonment of Jesus by God was likely a big ado for the first apologetic Christians. Luke 23:46 and John 19:30 alter thoroughly the import of the cry, ancillarily attesting that in Mark 15:34–35 we are over firm historical ground, like Cranfield, *Saint Mark*, 458 recalled. The reading is even earlier than D,

A ninth Aramaic word, not explained, is ῥαββί, appearing four times in Mark (רַבִּי, teacher; Mark 9:5; 10:51; 11:21; 14:45). A tenth is γέεννα, three times (גֵּי הִנֹּ, hell; Mark 9:43,45,47).[23] An eleventh is Βεελζεβούλ, one time (בְּעַל זְבוּב, Aramaic name of the devil; Mark 3:22), and a twelfth is ὡσαννά, twice in an exclamation of praise taken from the OT (הוֹשִׁיעָה נָּא, hosanna; Mark 11:9–10; Ps 118:25).[24] We have σατανάς, the Hebrew equivalent to Beelzebul, six times (שָׂטָן, Satan, the Adversary; Mark 1:13; 3:23,23,26; 4:15; 8:33), and the frequent Hebrew terms Sabbath and amen, that are so naturalized that the reader usually doesn't perceive the Semitism. Σάββατον/σάββατα is quoted twelve times (שַׁבָּת; Mark 1:21; 2:23,24,27,27,28; 3:2,4; 6:2; 15:42; 16:2,9) and ἀμήν eleven times, always in the compound form ἀμὴν λέγω ὑμῖν and ἀμὴν λέγω σοι, introducing some of the most famous predictions of Jesus (אָמֵן; Mark 3:28; 9:1,41; 10:29; 11:23; 12:43; 13:30; 14:9,18,25,30).[25] Lastly, the sixteenth Aramaic word is πάσχα (פִּסְחָא; Passover), five times in the section which antecedes the Last Supper, referring

---

who corrected into a full Hebrew sentence instead of part Hebrew and part Aramaic as it stands (Metzer, *Greek New Testament*, 70, 119–20).

23. גֵּי הִנֹּ, would be the Aramaic retranslation of γέεννα. The Aramaic form equates to the Hebrew גֵּי הִנֹּם, the valley Hinnom (Ἐννόμ) west of Jerusalem where Moloch was worshiped (2 Kgs 23:10). Hinnom was converted into a metaphor for hell because the Ammonites offered their children to Moloch and threw them into the fire (Jer 7:31; 39:35; see 2 Kgs 3:26–27 on Mesah, the Moabite king).

24. בְּעַל זְבוּב, Baal Zevuv means *Lord of the flies* or *bees* and is the denigrated name given by the Israelites to the god of Ekron in Philistia (2 Kgs 1:2). Taylor, *St. Mark*, 238–39 signals בְּעַל זְבֻל, Baal Zevul, *Lord of the dwelling*, in concordance with Matt 10:25. הוֹשִׁיעָה נָּא, *hosanna*, means *(God) save, I pray!*

25. The romance languages have an extra handycap to note the Semitism Sabbath in their Bible versions since they inherit the Hebrew שַׁבָּת through the Latin Graecism *sabbatum*—Spanish: *sábado*; French: *samedi*; Portuguese: *sábado*; Romanian: *sambata*. The twelve Marcan quotations of Sabbath are seven singulars including one in the longer ending (σάββατον; Mark 2:27,27,28; 6:2; Mark 15:42; 16:2,9) and five plurals (σάββατα; Mark 1:21; 2:23,24; 3:2,4). Casey, *Aramaic Sources of Mark*, 139–40 considers the neuter plural σάββατα an assimilation from the Aramaic singular definite state שַׁבְּתָא (the Sabbath) and alludes to LXX Exod 16:29: ἴδετε, ὁ γὰρ κύριος ἔδωκεν ὑμῖν τὴν ἡμέραν ταύτην τὰ σάββατα (look, for the Lord gave us this day, the Sabbath). We have similar usages of the plural σάββατα for the MT singular שַׁבָּת in Lev 23:3; Deut 5:12–13; Isa 56:2; 58:13, etc. But the sound of the Hebrew שַׁבָּת is very akin to the singular neuter σάββατον, which only adds the -*ον* ending of the neuter. According to Doudna, *Greek of the Gospel of Mark*, 10–12 the plural for singular names of feasts are also known in Greek authors (γάμοι, weeding; νυμφεῖα, engagement). Even Mark has an example (τοῖς γενεσίοις, the birthday; 6:21). The plural σάββατα could have been, thus, normally obtained from its Greek singular, being this last a faithful rendering of the Hebrew שַׁבָּת. What appears clear is that σάββατα doesn't come from the Hebrew plural שַׁבָּתוֹת (Sabbatoth).

either to the Passover day (Mark 14:1.16) or to the Passover lamb that was eaten at sunset (Mark 14:12,12,14).[26]

Mark explains four Jewish customs (underlined). (1) In Mark 7:2–4: *καὶ ἰδόντες τινὰς τῶν μαθητῶν αὐτοῦ ὅτι κοιναῖς χερσίν, τοῦτ᾽ ἔστιν ἀνίπτοις, ἐσθίουσιν τοὺς ἄρτους, οἱ γὰρ Φαρισαῖοι καὶ πάντες οἱ Ἰουδαῖοι ἐὰν μὴ πυγμῇ νίψωνται τὰς χεῖρας οὐκ ἐσθίουσιν, κρατοῦντες τὴν παράδοσιν τῶν πρεσβυτέρων, καὶ ἄλλα πολλά ἐστιν ἃ παρέλαβον κρατεῖν, βαπτισμοὺς ποτηρίων καὶ ξεστῶν καὶ χαλκίων καὶ κλινῶν* (and seeing some of his disciples that with profane hands, this is unwashed, eat the breads—for the Pharisees and all the Jews if they don't wash the hands to the fist don't eat, holding the tradition of the elders, and many other things are that they received to hold, washings of cups and of basins and of vessels and of beds; a long commentary on the Jewish purifying of pots and hands before eating).[27] (2) In Mark 12:18: *καὶ ἔρχονται Σαδδουκαῖοι πρὸς αὗτὸν, οἵτινες λέγουσιν ἀνάστασιν μὴ εἶναι* (and (some) Sadducees come to him, who say there is no resurrection; a remark on a particular Jewish belief). (3) In Mark 14:12: *καὶ τῇ πρώτῃ ἡμέρᾳ τῶν ἀζύμων, ὅτε τὸ πάσχα ἔθυον* (and on the first day of the Unleavened, when they sacrificed the Passover (lamb); a precision about the first day of the Unleavened Bread feast). (4) In Mark 15:42: *καὶ ἤδη ὀψίας γενομένης, ἐπεὶ ἦν παρασκευὲ ὅ ἐστιν προσάββατον* (and already being evening, since it was the Parasceve, that is the day before Sabbath; a comment on the Jewish Friday).

Both markers, Semitic words and explained Jewish customs, suggest that the *Sitz im Leben* of the second-gospel author differs from the recipients' milieu because he takes the trouble to define words and customs to those that appear unacquainted with them. This observation plus a survey of the grammar steadfastly underscores that the author is a Judeo-Christian, whereas the recipients or part of them are believers coming from a Gentile environment. Among the eight Aramaic renderings above, Mark 5:41, 15:22, and 15:34 are accompanied by the verb *μεθερμηνεύω* (translate), of the same

26. In the LXX, *τὸ πάσχα* renders the Hebrew פֶּסַח from the phonetic of the Aramaic פִּסְחָא (Taylor, *St. Mark*, 527). Note the Aramaic is in the emphatic state, i.e., the noun + א (Johns, *Grammar of Biblical Aramaic*, 9–10). The postpositive Aramaic article א (the) covers the pre-positive Hebrew article ה (the), thus פִּסְחָא for הַפָּסַח or הַפֶּסַח (MT Num 9:2,4,6,13,14). In the MT it is usually the binomial פֶּסַח לַיהוָה (Passover to Yahweh = Passover of Yahweh). Exod 12:11: פֶּסַח הוּא לַיהוָה (is Passover to Yahweh = is the Passover of Yahweh); LXX Exod 12:11: *πάσχα ἐστὶν κυρίῳ* (is the Passover to the Lord= of the Lord); Lev 23:5; Num 9:10,14; 28:16; 2 Kgs 23:21. LXX 2 Chr 30:1 and 35:1 have the variant *τὸ φάσεκ κυρίῳ*.

27. The variance between mss makes Metzger, *Greek New Testament*, 93–94 consider *καὶ κλινῶν* improbably original, perhaps added by copyists, understanding the verse from Lev 15:4–5 was intentionally omitted in view of the context or unintentionally due to *homoioteleuton*.

root as ἑρμηνεύς, the term Papias uses to call Mark the interpreter of Peter. Against scholars who don't grant much value to the Papias-Clement tradition, it must be conceded that the Aramaic renderings and the clarifying of Jewish customs are absolutely consistent with a Judeo-Christian gospel destined to an audience embodying Gentile converts.

Further confirmation of Mark's interest in expounding is found in the parentheses, a characteristic feature of Mark, who really is fond of them. The translations of Aramaic and the remarks on Jewish customs are indeed specific types of parentheses. In cases, parentheses can be a literary resource and in this way might not be rare to them to sound repetitive. Elsewhere are sign of deference and precision towards the tradition Mark comments (Mark 5:22,42; 7:26; 12:42; 14:10,43; 15:16,21,43), being in this category that the translations and incisions on customs must be included.[28] Undoubtedly, the explained words or customs are obvious Marcan Semitisms but many others have been acknowledged in the order of syntax and semantics.

Grammatical Semitisms in the Second Gospel

The list below within the central body of the text brings three examples of each type of Semitism in Mark, and in one case four. In some grammatical specimens Semitisms can be Greek constructions from either Hebrew or Aramaic. In others, a single instance can be vernacular Greek or possible classical Greek, but the overuse or its proximity to clear Semitisms expresses Semitic usage. The list has been simplified to a general summary of the question, comprising thirty-one instances, but continues to be appropriately functional for NT scholarship. Who is speaking every time a Semitism is quoted—the evangelist or a character of the second gospel—and the more detailed account in footnotes of the selected categories of Semitism are likewise supplied to be of aid in complementary studies.[29]

28. The instances above add new information not deducible from the previous sentences. More apodosis: Mark 2:10; 2:15; 5:15,33; 6:14,48; 7:25; 10:32; 11:13,32; 12:12; 13:14; 14:40; 16:4. In the sayings: Mark 2:26; 7:19.

29. Except for category (I), the types of Semitisms and circa half of the Marcan quotations are taken from Turner, "Style of Mark," 224–31; Taylor, *St. Mark*, 46–65; Moulton and Howard, *Grammar of New Testament Greek*, 2:411–77; Doudna, *Greek of the Gospel of Mark*, 63–127; and Black, *Aramaic Approach to the Gospels*, 50–142. They have been checked against Maloney, *Semitic Interference*, 51–196 when possible, from whom I take some of the MT and LXX examples. To be more schematic, I only include parallels from Matthew whenever the Semitism is avoided or corrected. Parallels from Luke, examples from D, and less clear categories of Semitisms or instances are excluded. Lastly, OT fundamentals and instances go beyond what is merely representative of each Semitism whereas Marcan examples are exhaustive.

(A) Parataxis. True parataxis is the linking of clauses without employing subordinating conjunctions. Very frequent in biblical prose, however, is the secondary parataxis, namely, the overuse of the copulative Hebrew *waw*/ו to coordinate chains of clauses and sentences, stressing copulative style. In Mark, the overuse of *καί* (also called paratactic *καί*) is the most characteristic stylistic feature and it is usually ascribed to this second paratactic category.[30] Despite the plethora of *καί* most probably responds in Mark to Semitic interference, the possibility that it could also respond to Greek, Latin, or oral influence asks for independent discussion and will be examined in chapter 3.

Now, we only deem the use of *καί* requiring a subordinate function in an apparent coordinate clause, resembling the flexible Hebrew *waw*/ו in the OT anywhere it doesn't adopt the normal conjunctive meaning (and).[31] Mark 4:27 (speaks Jesus): *καὶ καθεύδῃ καὶ ἐγείρεται νύκτα καὶ ἡμέραν, <u>καὶ</u> ὁ σπόρος βλαστᾷ καὶ μηκύνηται ὡς οὐκ οἶδεν αὐτός* (and he might sleep and gets up night and day, <u>then</u> the seed sprouts and grows as he doesn't know; compare with Matt 13:26). Mark 8:34 (Jesus): *ἀπαρνησάσθω ἑαυτὸν <u>καὶ</u> ἀράτω τὸν σταυρὸν αὐτοῦ καὶ ἀκολουθείτω μοι* (let him deny himself, <u>then</u> take his cross and follow me). Mark 15:25 (narrator): *ἦν δὲ ὥρα τρίτη <u>καὶ</u> ἐσταύρωσαν αὐτόν* (it was the third hour, <u>when</u> they crucified him).[32]

(B) Asyndeta. Many Marcan verses omit Greek connectors. In spite of the contrast with the high paratactic style of Mark, cases of asyndeton are universal in oral speech and can be found in written Greek, Latin, and biblical Hebrew.[33] Juxtaposition quickens discourse when the addresser and

30. Coordination and subordination are mirror concepts with hypotaxis and parataxis. The first two define the link existing between two or more clauses: if they stand at the same syntactic level, usually by a coordinating conjunction, they are called coordinate; but if dependence exists, usually expressed by a subordinating particle, they are called subordinate. The term *hypotaxis* (ὑπὸ-τάξις, under-level) equates to subordination, and *parataxis* (παρὰ-τάξις, same-level) to coordination, being legitimate to employ them as synonyms, but they technically refer to the existence of subordinate particles (hypotaxis) or to the lack of them (parataxis).

31. MT 1 Sam 3:2: וַיְהִי בַּיּוֹם הַהוּא וְעֵלִי שֹׁכֵב בִּמְקוֹמוֹ (and came to pass in this day <u>that</u> Heli slept in his place). The LXX renders it conservatively: *καὶ ἐγένετο ἐν τῇ ἡμέρᾳ ἐκείνῃ <u>καὶ</u> Ἠλὶ ἐκάθευδεν ἐν τῷ τόπῳ αὐτοῦ* (and occurred in that day <u>that</u> Heli slept in his place); MT Hos 3:3 (because). Maloney, *Semitic Interference*, 70–72 brings Exod 14:10 (so); 2 Kgs 8:1 (which); Jer 31:31 (when); Dan 7:14 (so that); 7:20 (which, whose).

32. To the use of subordinating *καί* Turner, "Style of Mark," 224 adds in degree of possibility the next instances, all in narrative verses, but the unforced Greek makes the Semitism difficult to ascertain: Mark 1:6,11; 4:38; 5:21; 7:30. Taylor, *St. Mark*, 59 sums Mark 1:19 (narrator; cf. Matt 4:21 who prefers a circumstantial clause).

33. *Asyndeton* (ἀ-σύνδετος, *un-tied*) means absence of conjunctions between words or clauses. Juxtaposition *(iuxta-positio, side by side* or *near-position*) can be employed

emitter share the immediate communicative context, making superfluous the resource to syntactic linkers. Thus, Mark's asyndeta are not unequivocally Semitisms, but the density of adjoining Semitisms and overall secondary parataxis advocate for their inclusion in the list. Asyndeta in Mark are divided in juxtaposition between clauses and direct speech lacking introductory particles. The second, common in biblical Hebrew as well as in the LXX, is considered here.[34] Mark 2:17 (Jesus): *οὐκ ἦλθον καλέσαι δικαίους ἀλλ' ἁμαρτωλούς* (I didn't come to call righteous but sinners; compare with Matt 9:13, who has *γάρ*). Mark 12:37 (Jesus): *αὐτὸς Δαυὶδ λέγει αὐτὸν κύριον* (David himself calls him Lord; compare with Matt 22:45, who adds *εἰ οὖν*). Mark 13:7 (Jesus): *μὴ θροεῖσθε· δεῖ γενέσθαι* (don't be disturbed: it must happen; compare with Matt 24:6, who adds *γάρ*).[35]

(C) Parallelism, redundant speech, and tautology. Semantic proximity, in words and clauses, gives the impression of saying the same thing again, but an effect of reinforcement is produced, intensity, or opposition. It is a classic Hebrew scheme of thinking, plentiful in poetry and sapientia, plain

---

to denote contrast or emphasis between two syntactical elements, but in broad terms is a synonym of asyndeton.

34. MT Exod 7:26: וַיֹּאמֶר יְהוָה אֶל מֹשֶׁה בֹּא אֶל פַּרְעֹה וְאָמַרְתָּ אֵלָיו כֹּה אָמַר יְהוָה (And said Yahweh to Moses ( ) go to Pharaoh and you will say to him ( ) thus says Yahweh). MT usually has asyndeton after verbs of saying: Num 2:2; 3:6,15,39; 6:23. Deut 5:6–21 combines asyndetic verses with others beginning with *waw*/ו consecutive; etc. LXX 1 Sam 3:6 is an interesting instance, including asyndeta after verbs of saying and one asyndeton formed by two consecutive imperatives: *καὶ προσέθετο κύριος καὶ ἐκάλεσεν* ( ) *Σαμουηλ Σαμουηλ· καὶ ἐπορεύθη πρὸς Ἡλὶ τὸ δεύτερον καὶ εἶπεν* ( ) *Ἰδοὺ ἐγώ, ὅτι κέκληκάς με· καὶ εἶπεν* ( ) *Οὐ κέκληκά σε, ἀνάστρεφε* ( ) *κάθευδε* (and the Lord presented himself and called him ( ) Samuel, Samuel; and he went to Heli a second time and said ( ) Here I am, because you have called me; and said ( ) I haven't called you, return ( ) sleep). Biblical asyndeta between clauses are usually found in poetry: Deut 33:11; Judg 5:9,20,21,26,27; but not only: Isa 7:1; 60:1.

35. In the sayings: Mark 2:8 (Matt 9:4, *ἱνατί*); 2:9 (Matt 9:5, *γάρ*); 2:25; 3:34; 4:24,28; 5:39 (Matt 9:24, *γάρ*); 6:38; 8:2,15 (Matt 16:6, *καί*); 10:14 (Matt 19:14, *καί*); 10:24,27,28; 11:28; 12:27,36; 13:6 (Matt 24:5, *γάρ*); 13:8b (Matt 24:7, *καί*); 13:8c (Matt 24:8, *δέ*); 13:9b (Matt 10:17, *γάρ*; 24:9, *τότε*); 13:17,34 (Matt 25:14, *γάρ*); 14:6,8 (Matt 26:12, *γάρ*). NA[28] considers the asyndeton probable in Mark 3:35 (Matt 12:50, *γάρ*); 12:9 (Matt 21:40, *οὖν*); 13:15, but has between brackets the less probable conjunctions, *γάρ*, *οὖν*, *δέ*, respectively. In direct speech out of Jesus: Mark 8:29 (Peter); 9:24 (father of the boy with a spirit); 9:38 (John); 10:28 (Peter); 11:28 (chief priests/scribes); 14:19 (disciples); 14:61 (chief priest); 14:63 (chief priest); 16:6 (angel; Matt 28:5, *γάρ*; 28:6, *γάρ*). Examples from D, up to four, are not counted (see Black, *Aramaic Approach to the Gospels*, 58). Asyndeta in narrative parts falls into good Greek and may not be a Semitism, but the synoptic comparison continue to show the Matthean preference for connectives: Mark 8:29 (Matt 16:6, *δέ*); 9:24; 10:25,27 (Matt 19:26, *δέ*); 10:28 (Matt 19:27, *τότε*); 10:29 (Matt 19:28, *δέ*); 12:20 (Matt 22:25, *δέ*); 12:23 (Matt 22:28, *οὖν*); Mark 12:24 (Matt 22:29, *δέ*); 12:29 (Matt 22:37, *δέ*); 12:31 (Matt 22:39, *δέ*); 12:32; 14:3 (Matt 26:7, *καί*); 14:6 (Matt 26:10, *γάρ*); 14:19.

in the sayings of Jesus and in the narrative parts of Mark.[36] Mark 4:39 (narrator): *καὶ διεγερθεὶς ἐπετίμησεν τῷ ἀνέμῳ καὶ εἶπεν τῇ θαλάσσῃ* (and being woken up he rebuked the wind and told to the sea; Matt 8:26 lacks *εἶπεν*). Mark 6:4 (Jesus): *οὐκ ἔστιν προφήτης ἄτιμος εἰ μὴ ἐν τῇ πατρίδι αὐτοῦ καὶ ἐν τοῖς συγγενεῦσιν αὐτοῦ καὶ ἐν τῇ οἰκίᾳ αὐτοῦ* (a prophet is not dishonored except in his homeland and among his kindred and in his home; Matt 13:57 lacks *ἐν τοῖς συγγενεῦσιν αὐτοῦ*). Mark 12:44 (Jesus): *αὕτη δὲ τῆς ὑστερήσεως αὐτῆς πάντα ὅσα εἶχεν ἔβαλεν ὅλον τὸν βίον αὐτῆς* (but this one of her want, all that she had, threw, all her living).[37]

(D) Pleonastic *ἤρξατο/ἤρξαντο* (he/they began to) accompanying an infinitive, to which it adds very little meaning, although a slight verbal motion can be felt.[38] Always in narrative parts, Mark has up to twenty-six

36. Parallelism can be broadly divided into synonymous, synthetic, and antithetic. Frequently tautology (*τὸ-αὐτὸς-λογία*, *the-same-saying*) and parallelism (*παρὰ-ἀλλήλων*, *same-one-another*) are interchangeable terms. Synonymous parellelism: MT Isa 6:7: וְסָר עֲוֺנֶךָ וְחַטָּאתְךָ תְּכֻפָּר (and loosed your iniquity and your sin expiated). Progressive tautology: LXX Gen 8:16: Ἔξελθε ἐκ τῆς κιβωτοῦ, σὺ καὶ ἡ γυνή σου καὶ οἱ υἱοί σου καὶ αἱ γυναῖκες τῶν υἱῶν σου μετὰ σοῦ (Go out of the ark, you and your wife and your sons and the wifes of your sons with you). More: Gen 12:1; 26:5; 28:3; 40:5; Ruth 1:1; 1 Sam 1:27; Isa 9:1–2; 43:6; 66:12; Zeph 2:3. Inasmuch BH poetry and sapientia seek the emphatic style, parallelism converts there into one of the most common devices. MT Ps 18:2b–3a: יְהוָה חִזְקִי יְהוָה סַלְעִי וּמְצוּדָתִי וּמְפַלְטִי אֵלִי צוּרִי (Yahweh my strengh, Yahweh my rock and my fortress and my safety, my God, my refuge). LXX Prov 6:7 *ἐκείνῳ γὰρ γεωργίου μὴ ὑπάρχοντος, μηδὲ τὸν ἀναγκάζοντα ἔχων, μηδὲ ὑπὸ δεσπότην ὢν* (for it has no owner of the field, neither has one ruler, nor is under lord). More in BH poetry and sapientia: Ps 6:2; 9:19; 11(10):4; 15(14):1; 16(15):11; 19(18):11; 24(23); Prov 1:8,20; 4:12; 7:1; 22:24; Sir 4:4–5; 6:5; 15:16–17, etc.

37. Mark 1:28 (evangelist; compare Matt 4:24); 1:32 (evangelist; cf. Matt 8:14); 1:35 (evangelist); 2:20 (Jesus; cf. Matt 9:15); 2:25 (Jesus; cf. Matt 12:3); 4:2 (evangelist; cf. Matt 13:3); 4:30 (Jesus; cf. Matt 13:31); 5:19 (Jesus); 5:39 (Jesus; cf. Matt 9:24); 6:25 (evangelist); 7:13 (Jesus; cf. Matt 15:6); 7:21 (Jesus); 7:33 (evangelist); 8:17 (Jesus); 9:2 (evangelist; cf. Matt 17:1); 11:28 (chief priests/scribes/elders); 12:14 (Pharisees/Herodians); 12:23 (Sadducees; cf. Matt 22:28); 13:19 (Jesus; cf. Matt 24:21); 13:20 (Jesus; cf. Matt 24:22); 13:35 (Jesus; cf. Matt 24:43); 14:18 (Jesus; cf. Matt 26:21); 14:30 (Jesus; cf. Matt 26:34); 14:61 (evangelist; cf. Matt 26:63); 15:26 (evangelist; cf. Matt 27:37). With less confidence Aramaic reflection based on repetitions can also be seen in the redundant participle *ἀποκριθείς* + verbal form of *λέγω* to introduce a saying: Mark 9:5; 11:14 (cf. Matt 21:19); 12:35; similar instances: Mark 3:33; 6:37; 7:28; 8:29; 9:19; 10:3; 11:22,33.

38. MT Judg 17:11: וַיּוֹאֶל הַלֵּוִי לָשֶׁבֶת אֶת הָאִישׁ (and was willing the Levite to rest (= to live) with the man). In BH the verb וְאַל + infinitive expresses willing for a result (the inf.), but the LXX does not always render with *ἤρξατο/ἤρξαντο* + inf. Two LXX exceptions are Deut 1:5 (*ἤρξατο διασαφῆσαι*, began to explain); Judg 17:11 (*ἤρξατο παροικεῖν*, began to live). Forms of הֵחֵל (begin) + inf. also can be found: Judg 16:2 (*ἤρξατο ἀνατεῖλαι*, began to grow); 1 Sam 3:2 (*ἤρξαντο βαρύνεσθαι*, began to be impeded); Others: LXX Hos 7:5 (*ἤρξαντο θυμοῦσθαι*, began to be anger).

examples. Mark 4:1: καὶ πάλιν ἤρξατο διδάσκειν παρὰ τὴν θάλασσαν (and again he began to teach by the sea). Mark 10:41: καὶ ἀκούσαντες οἱ δέκα ἤρξαντο ἀγανακτεῖν περὶ Ἰακώβου καὶ Ἰωάννου (and having heard it the ten began to be angry with John and James; see Matt 20:24, who has the aorist ἠγανάκτησαν). Mark 15:8: καὶ ἀναβὰς ὁ ὄχλος ἤρξατο αἰτεῖσθαι καθὼς ἐποίει αὐτοῖς (and coming up the crowd began to ask as he (usually) did for them).[39]

(E) The expression καὶ ἐγένετο followed by circumstantial complement is usually temporal, in impersonal fashion (and it happened/came to pass that), to introduce a past event. The source Hebraic idiom is וַיְהִי (and it come to pass), which when rendered in the Septuagint is usually followed by circumstantial ἐν. καὶ ἐγένετο is not registered in Greek authors, who employ by rule forms of συμβαίνω (occur).[40] Mark has four true Semitisms of this sort, and some reminiscent expressions, but unrelated syntactically, almost always in narrative parts. Mark 1:9 (narrator): καὶ ἐγένετο ἐν ἐκείναις ταῖς ἡμέραις (and it happened in those days; compare with Matt 3:13 who has τότε). Mark 2:23 (narrator): καὶ ἐγένετο αὐτὸν ἐν τοῖς σάββασιν (and it came to pass him in the Sabbath; compare with Matt 12:1, who uses ἐν ἐκείνῳ τῷ καιρῷ). Mark 4:4 (Jesus): καὶ ἐγένετο ἐν τῷ σπείρειν (and it happened in the sowing; Matt 13:4 drops καὶ ἐγένετο).[41]

(F) Redundant pronouns: after relative, emphatic, or resumptive following a *casus pendens* due to the Aramaic *de*/דִי and to the Hebrew *'asher*/אֲשֶׁר

39. Mark 1:45; 2:23; 5:17 (cf. Matt 8:34); 5:20; 6:2 (cf. Matt 13:54); 6:7 (cf. Matt 10:1); 6:34 (cf. Matt 9:35); 6:55 (cf. Matt 14:35); 8:11 (cf. Matt 16:1); 8:31,32; 10:28 (cf. Matt 19:27); 10:32 (cf. Matt 20:17); 10:47 (cf. Matt 20:30); 11:15 (cf. Matt 21:12); 12:1 (cf. Matt 21:33); 13:5 (cf. Matt 24:4); 14:19,33,65 (cf. Matt 26:67); Mark 14:69 (cf. Matt 26:69); Mark 14:71; 15:18 (cf. Matt 28:29).

40. MT Exod 2:11: וַיְהִי בַּיָּמִים הָהֵם (and it happened in those days); LXX: Ἐγένετο δὲ ἐν ταῖς ἡμέραις . . . ἐκείναις; Exod 12:41; 18:13; 1 Kgs 14:25, etc. The LXX sometimes renders וַיְהִי by the passive καὶ ἐγενήθη (and it was happened): Gen 11:1; 1 Sam 4:1; 28:1; 2 Sam 2:1; 1 Kgs 6:1, etc. The MT knows other uses of the idiom too: in the tale of creation it is employed two by two: Gen 1:5: וַיְהִי עֶרֶב וַיְהִי בֹקֶר יוֹם אֶחָד (and it came to pass an afternoon, and it came to pass a morning, the day one); the LXX has: καὶ ἐγένετο ἑσπέρα καὶ ἐγένετο πρωί, ἡμέρα μία; Gen 1:8.13.19.23.31. As a matter of fact, the idiom וַיְהִי is a crutch so commonly employed that the list can be easily augmented: Gen 7:10,17; 1 Sam 8:1; 18:9; 30:1; 1 Kgs 15:21; 18:1, etc.

41. In the fourth instance the narrator employs the middle present καὶ γίνεται (and it happened; Mark 2:15). Beyond the four secure circumstantial uses of καὶ ἐγένετο/καὶ γίνεται registered by Maloney, *Semitic Interference*, 81–86, the second gospel has some more instances where the imitation of LXX style is suggested: one more καὶ γίνεται in Mark 4:37 (narrator; cf. Matt 8:24); three paratactic καὶ ἐγένετο: Mark 9:7a (narrator; Matt 17:5a, ἰδού); 9:7b (narrator; Matt 17:5b, ἰδού); 9:26 (narrator); and four instances of ἐγένετο where the verb has been displaced from καί and, like the last four anterior examples, it is not impersonally employed: Mark 1:11 (narrator; cf. Matt 3:17); 4:10 (narrator; cf. Matt 13:10); 9:3 (narrator); 11:19 (narrator).

constructions.[42] Mark 7:25 (narrator; after relative): ἀλλ᾽ εὐθὺς ἀκούσασα γυνὴ περὶ αὐτοῦ, ἧς εἶχεν τὸ θυγάτριον αὐτῆς πνεῦμα ἀκάθαρτον (but immediately having a woman heard about him, whose daughter of her had an unclean spirit; Matt 15:22 prefers the direct speech ἡ θυγάτηρ μου). Mark 6:17 (narrator; emphatic): Αὐτὸς γὰρ ὁ Ἡρῴδης (For himself, Herod; Matt 14:3 lacks αὐτός). Mark 11:23 (Jesus; casus pendens): ὃς ἂν εἴπῃ τῷ ὄρει τούτῳ· ἄρθητι καὶ βλήθητι εἰς τὴν θάλασσαν . . . ἔσται αὐτῷ (whoever says to this mount: be removed and be thrown into the sea . . . it will be (given) to him).[43]

42. In BH and in the LXX, the *casus pendens* or dislocation is a discursive skill that reinforces the apprehension of a first nominative (the *pendens*), usually drawing on a pronoun (the resumptive) that takes again the meaning of the first constituent at the cost of leaving it grammatically out (without predicative). It has been stated that the Hebrew idiom was marked through intonation (Naudé, "Dislocation in Biblical Hebrew," 118; Westbury, *Left Dislocation*, 66–67, 87–88). Hellenistic Greek knows the idiom, but hardly always resumes the *pendens* with a demonstrative resumptive (forms of οὗτος and ἐκεῖνος). On the contrary, according to Maloney, *Semitic Interference*, 88–89, the LXX *pendens* followed by a personal pronoun probably responds to Hebrew interference, where the resumptive (here underlined), usually rendered with a form of αὐτός, is always followed by personal pronoun and never by demonstrative. MT Gen 3:12: וַיֹּאמֶר הָאָדָם הָאִשָּׁה אֲשֶׁר נָתַתָּה עִמָּדִי הִוא נָתְנָה לִּי מִן הָעֵץ (and said the man: the woman whom you gave to stay with me, she gave me from the tree). LXX Gen 3:12 renders the third singular resumptive (הִוא, she) by a demonstrative (αὕτη, this): καὶ εἶπεν ὁ Αδαμ· Ἡ γυνή, ἣν ἔδωκας μετ᾽ ἐμοῦ, αὕτη μοι ἔδωκεν ἀπὸ τοῦ ξύλου (and Adam said: The woman, whom you gave (to be) with me, this one gave me from the tree); Judg 17:5: καὶ ὁ ἀνὴρ Μιχα, αὐτῷ οἶκος θεοῦ (and the man Micah, to him (is) a house of God = he has a shrine); Ec 3:16: καὶ τόπον τοῦ δικαίου, ἐκεῖ ὁ ἀσεβής (and the place of the righteous, there the impious; adverbial resumptive). Andrews, "Aramaic *dî* in the Greek Bibles," 15–51 exhaustively studied the Greek rendering of the polyvalent Aramaic particle *de*/די in LXX and Theodotion Dan 2:4—7:28 (and in several parts of Ezra). He finds two translated resumptive pronouns after dislocation in fourteen renderings of Aramaic casus pendens involving the relative די: (1) Θ´ Dan 5:23: καὶ οὐ γινώσκουσιν, ἤνεσας καὶ τὸν θεόν, οὗ ἡ πνοή σου ἐν χειρὶ αὐτοῦ (and they don't know, (nor) having praised God, whose your spirit (is) in his hand; LXX renders καί for די); (2) Θ´ Dan 6:3: καὶ ἐπάνω αὐτῶν τακτικοὺς τρεῖς, ὧν ἦν Δανιηλ εἷς ἐξ αὐτῶν (in front of them three strategists, of whom was Daniel one of them; LXX καί).

43. Redundant pronoun after relative: Mark 1:7 (John the Baptist; cf. Matt 3:11); emphatic: Mark 1:19 (narrator; cf. Matt 4:21); 5:37 (narrator); 12:36 (Jesus; cf. Matt 22:43); 12:37 (Jesus; cf. Matt 22:45). A special kind of Hebrew dislocation, is the general relative statement (beginning with אֲשֶׁר, which, that; מָה, what; and מִי, who) followed by resumptive personal pronoun, as we see in MT Exod 32:33: מִי אֲשֶׁר חָטָא לִי אֶמְחֶנּוּ מִסִּפְרִי (who that has sinned against Me, I will blot him out of my book) rendered by LXX εἴ τις ἡμάρτηκεν ἐνώπιον μου, ἐξαλείψω αὐτὸν ἐκ τῆς βίβλου μου (whoever have sinned before Me, I will erase him of my book). Maloney, *Semitic Interference*, 101 brings also Josh 15:16; Judg 7:5; Isa 44:10–11. The above Marcan example and the next ones, all in the sayings, enter the category: Mark 4:25a; 4:25b; 8:38; 9:42.

(G) Repetition of the preposition in a series, slowing down but burdening the mental digestion of the text.[44] Mark 3:7–8 (narrator): *καὶ πολὺ πλῆθος ἀπὸ τῆς Γαλιλαίας, καὶ ἀπὸ τῆς Ἰουδαίας καὶ ἀπὸ Ἱεροσολύμων καὶ ἀπὸ τῆς Ἰδουμαίας* (and many people from Galilee, and from Judaea and from Jerusalem and from Idumaea; Matt 5:25 keeps the series with only one *ἀπό*). Mark 6:56 (narrator): *καὶ ὅπου ἂν εἰσεπορεύετο εἰς κώμας ἢ εἰς πόλεις ἢ εἰς ἀγρούς* (wherever he went to, to the villages or to the towns or to the fields). Mark 11:1 (narrator): *ὅτε ἐγγίζουσιν εἰς Ἱεροσόλυμα εἰς Βηθφαγὴ* (when they approach to Jerusalem to Bethphage).[45]

(H) Use of adjectives, numerals, distributives, and adverbials. The positive adjective for the comparative due to lack of grade in the Semitic adjective, except in the Arabic.[46] In numbering, the cardinal for the ordinal

44. MT Isa 2:12–16: עַל (upon; LXX *ἐπί*) up to ten times; MT Num 1:1: בְּ (in; LXX *ἐν*). LXX Num 1:20,22,24, etc. (*κατά*); Hos 1:7 (*ἐν*); 2:20 (*μετά*); 4:3 (*σύν*).

45. Same preposition in a series: Mark 5:1 (narrator); 11:1 (narrator); 13:9 (Jesus). The style is similar to the heavy or perhaps emphatic repetition of the article: Mark 9:2 (narrator): *παραλαμβάνει ὁ Ἰησοῦς τὸν Πέτρον καὶ τὸν Ἰάκωβον καὶ τὸν Ἰωάννην* (Jesus takes along Peter and Jacob and John); 8:31 (narrator; cf. Matt 16:21); 10:33 (Jesus; cf. Matt 20:18); 14:33 (narrator; cf. Matt 26:37); 14:43 (narrator; cf. Matt 26:47). The next instance is also not especially Semitic but resembles the reiteration of the preposition (see also note in section on Latin parataxis): Mark 3:16–19 (narrator; syndetic *καί* and to a lesser extent repetiton of the article). Other less perceptible Semitisms for the reader with prepositions are: (a) instrumental *ἐν*, rendering the preposition *be*/בְּ: Mark 4:30 (Jesus; meaning *with*); 14:1 (narrator; meaning *with*; Matt 26:4, *ἵνα*). An instrumental sense of *ἐν* may be understood in Mark 1:23 (narrator); 5:2 (narrator; cf. Matt 8:28); (b) imperatival *ἵνα*, accompanying subjunctive: Mark 5:23 (narrator; the verse has two *ἵνα* and clauses in subjunctive, both eluded by Matt 9:18 who prefers imperative and future tenses); 10:51 (Bartimaeus); 14:49 (Jesus); (c) explicative *ἵνα*. The turn occurs in Greek but not to such an extent as in biblical literature. Sometimes it is changeable for *ὅτι* but the sentence normally can go without the preposition. Matthew is confortable and keeps the epexegetical *ἵνα* around one of every two parallels. The frequency in Mark, redundant depending on cases, responds to explicative tendency. Twenty of twenty-eight times speaks the narrator: Mark 3:9,12; 5:10 (cf. Matt 8:31); 5:18,43; 6:8 (cf. Matt 10:5); 6:12 (cf. Matt 11:1); 6:25 (Herodias' daughter; cf. Matt 14:8); 7:26 (cf. 15:22); 7:32,36; 8:22,30; 9:9 (cf. Matt 17:9); 9:18 (cf. Matt 17:16); 9:30 (cf. Matt 17:22); 10:35 (John and James; cf. Matt 20:20); 10:37 (John and James); 10:48; 11:16,28 (chief priests/scribes/elders; cf. Matt 21:24); 12:19 (Sadducees; cf. Matt 22:24); 13:18 (Jesus); 13:34 (Jesus); 14:35 (cf. Matt 26:39); 14:38 (Jesus); 15:21.

46. Hebrew uses the preposition *min*/מן usually *of* or *from*, to express the idea of *than* in constructed form. MT Gen 3:1: וְהַנָּחָשׁ הָיָה עָרוּם מִכֹּל חַיַּת (and the snake was cunning than nothing living = and the snake was the most cunning of the animals). MT Song 1:2: טוֹבִים . . . מִיָּיִן (are good than wine = are better than wine). The Semitism randomly is kept by LXX. MT Ps 78:31 is an interesting conservative case where we find an attempt to be literal in the LXX rendering of prepositions: וַיַּהֲרֹג בְּמִשְׁמַנֵּיהֶם (and he killed than robust among of them = and he killed the most robust among them); LXX (77:31): *καὶ ἀπέκτεινεν ἐν τοῖς πίοσιν αὐτῶν* (and he killed among the robust of them). More instances: MT Gen 29:19; LXX Ps 117:8; LXX Jon 4:3.

for the first day of the week is a Hebraism.[47] The repetition of the noun to express distribution instead of the preposition κατά or ἀνά chaining the accusative doesn't appear in Greek.[48] The frequency of the plural neuter πολλά (many things) with adverbial meaning (much) may be due to Aramaic too. Mark 9:43 (Jesus): καλὸν ἐστίν σε κυλλὸν εἰσελθεῖν εἰς τὴν ζωὴν ἢ . . . (better is for you to enter disabled into the life than . . .). Mark 16:2 (narrator): καὶ λίαν πρωῒ τῇ μιᾷ τῶν σαββάτων (and very early on the one after the Sabbath). Mark 6:39 (narrator): συμπόσια συμπόσια ἐπὶ τῷ χλωρῷ χόρτῳ (groups groups (= in groups) on the green grass). Mark 3:12 (narrator): καὶ πολλὰ ἐπετίμα αὐτοῖς ἵνα μὴ αὐτὸν φανερὸν ποιήσωσιν (and he severely ordered them that they should not make him known; compare with Matt 12:16).[49]

47. In BH, with the exception of the number two, from one to ten the ordinal is obtained adding the suffix י to the cardinal form (see Hostetter, *Grammar of Biblical Hebrew*, 55–57). MT Gen 1:1—2:4a has the cardinal for the first day of the week and the ordinal for the remainder: יוֹם אֶחָד (day one; LXX ἡμέρα μία); יוֹם שֵׁנִי (day second; LXX ἡμέρα δευτέρα); יוֹם שְׁלִישִׁי (day third; LXX ἡμέρα τρίτη); etc. LXX Num 1:1,18 (ἐν μιᾷ τοῦ μηνὸς δευτέρου, in the (day) one of the second month). Doudna, *Greek of the Gospel of Mark*, 92–96 takes up to twenty examples of εἷς for the first day of the month but the precedent in LXX Gen 1:5 (ἡμέρα μία) and Ps 23:1 (τῆς μίας σαββάτων; MT Ps 24:1 lacking) contradict his statement that this Semitism in BH is reduced to the first day of the month.

48. The idiom is Hebrew or Aramaic. Sometimes the Septuagint renders the Semitism conservatively. MT Gen 7:8–9: מִן הַבְּהֵמָה . . . שְׁנַיִם שְׁנַיִם בָּאוּ אֶל נֹהַ אֶל חֵתֵּבָה; LXX: καὶ ἀπὸ κτήνιων . . . δύο δύο εἰσήλθον πρὸς Νωε εἰς τὴν κιβωτόν (and of the animals . . . two (by) two went to Noah into the ark). See also MT Exod 8:10: חֳמָרִם חֳמָרִם; θιμωνιὰς θιμωνιάς (heap (by) heap); MT Num 9:10: אִישׁ אִישׁ; LXX ἄνθρωπος ἄνθρωπος (man (by) man); MT 2 Kgs 17:29: גּוֹי גּוֹי ; LXX: ἔθνη ἔθνη (nation (by) nation).

49. Positive adjective for comparative: 9:45 (Jesus); 9:47 (Jesus); 14:21 (Jesus). Maloney, *Semitic Interference*, 192–96 finds 14:21 correct Greek because a conditional clause accompanies the positive adjective, an attested usage in Greek: καλὸν αὐτῷ εἰ (good for him if). The other three would be an attempt to render the Semitic adjective followed by the preposition *min*/מִן. See that the comparative grade is known by Mark: 2:9 εὐκοπώτερον (Jesus); 4:31 μικρότερον (Jesus); 4:32 μείξον (Jesus); 9:34 μείξον (narrator); 10:25 εὐκοπώτερον (Jesus); 12:33 περισσότερον (a scribe); 12:31 μείξον (Jesus); 12:40 περισσότερον (Jesus); in adverbial compound Mark 7:36 μᾶλλον περισσότερον (Jesus). The cardinal for the adverbial in Mark 4:8 (Jesus); 4:20 (Jesus) likely comes from translation of the first Aramaic number *heth*/ח (cf. Matt 13:8,23, who corrects over the first ordinal of each duo but not adding adverbials). It is also remarkable that Mark 14:12 (narrator) employs the ordinal for dating events: καὶ τῇ πρώτῃ ἡμέρᾳ τῶν ἀζύμων (and on the first day of the Unleavened); also in the longer ending, Mark 16:9: πρώτῃ σαββάτου (first (day) after the Sabbath). Distributive idea made up with noun repetition: Mark 6:7 (narrator); 6:40 (narrator) presents the Semitic usage along the Greek: καὶ ἀνέπεσαν πρασιαὶ πρασιαὶ κατὰ ἑκατὸν καὶ κατὰ πεντήκοντα (and they sat groups groups (= in groups) of hundred and of fifty); similarly Mark 14:19 (narrator; cf. Matt 26:22). Except one case, the used of πολλά belongs to the evangelist. Adverbial πολλά: Mark 1:45; 5:10 (cf. Matt 8:31); 5:23 (cf. Matt 9:18); 5:26,38 (cf. Matt 9:23); 5:43; 6:20; 9:26. Halfway between adverbial and adjectival: Mark 6:34 (dependent on Mark

(I) The expression ὁ υἱὸς τοῦ ἀνθρώπου (the Son of the Man) is never found in Greek authors.[50] Its distant or general prototypes are the homonym Hebrew בֶּן אָדָם (son of man) and the Aramaic בַּר נָשָׁא (son of man), set phrases meaning a man, mankind, or a simple man, whilst its closest parallel to the Marcan usage is the expression כְּבַר אֱנָשׁ (like a son of man) in Dan 7:13, where the common Semitic expression is dressed with eschatological functions.[51] Always by Jesus or in indirect speech asigned by the narrator to Jesus, the expression is coined fourteen times in Mark, employed by rule as a christological title (the Son of the Man).[52] Mark 2:10 (Jesus): ἵνα δὲ εἰδῆτε

1:45); 15:3 (cf. Matt 27:12). Adjectival (not Semitism): Mark 6:13; 7:4,13 (Jesus); 8:31 (Jesus); 10:22.

50. ὁ υἱὸς τοῦ ἀνθρώπου is rendered *the Son of Man* by most English Bibles. Here, in *the Son of the Man*, the second article (τοῦ), redundant in English, is kept to show its Greek grammatical force. ὁ υἱὸς ἀνθρώπου will suffice for *the Son of Man*, covering the preposition *of* the genitive case of ἀνθρώπου (see next to following note).

51. The anarthrous בֶּן אָדָם (son of man) indicates man in the sense of one simple man or man in general. Ezekiel peruses this elemental sense, i.e., a particular man: MT Ezek 2:1: וַיֹּאמֶר אֵלָי בֶּן אָדָם עֲמֹד עַל רַגְלֶיךָ וַאֲדַבֵּר אֹתָךְ (and He said to me: "son of man, stand on your feet and I will speak you"); 2:6,8; 3:1,3,4,10; 4:1,16; 5:1; 6:1; 7:2, etc. Except for (the Aramaic) Dan 7:13, in the rest of biblical instances, the singular בֶּן אָדָם (son of man) or the plural בְּנֵי אָדָם (children of man) denotes similarly a man or men as simple descendant of mankind, sometimes forming a Hebrew parallelism with the term אִישׁ (man): MT Num 23:19; Ps 80:18; or with אֱנוֹשׁ (man), this last denoting the mortal essence of mankind: MT 2 Sam 7:14; Job 25:6; Ps 8:4; 90:3. As a rule, the Greek OT renders the singular בֶּן אָדָם with the anarthrous phrase υἱὸς ἀνθρώπου: LXX: Ps 143:3: τί ἐστιν ἄνθρωπος, ὅτι ἐγνώσθης αὐτῷ, ἢ υἱὸς ἀνθρώπου, ὅτι λογίζῃ αὐτόν; (what is the man, that he was known (by Thee), or a son of man, that you took him into account?). The Greek plural equivalent to בְּנֵי אָדָם (children of man) shows more variance: υἱοὶ τῶν ἀνθρώπων (LXX Ps 10:4; 11:2); υἱοὶ ἀνθρώπων (LXX 2 Sam 7:14; Ps 89:3).

52. Casey, *Aramaic Sources of Mark*, 112–18 discusses twelve usages of the Aramaic בַּר נָשָׁא (son of man) or בַּר אֱנָשָׁא (son of the man), Qumranic and Syriac, proving it was a general expression for man in the I AD, equivalent to the Hebrew בֶּן אָדָם discussed above. On this budget, Casey, *Aramaic Sources of Mark*, 126–29 understands the use of ὁ υἱὸς τοῦ ἀνθρώπου in Mark 9:12 in general terms, i.e., *son of man* referred to the man in his state of weakness upon this earth (reading supported by Isa 40:6–8 and Job 14). The same conclusions are offered in Casey, *Aramaic Sources of Mark*, 138–39, 158–64 for the idiom in Mark 2:10 and 2:28, whereas Casey in 193–252 defends that Jesus used the expression in Mark 10:45 and 14:21 referring to himself but still playing the ambiguity of the general Aramaic and Hebrew meanings. Certainly, ambiguity on the side of Jesus should have accompanied the employment of ὁ υἱὸς τοῦ ἀνθρώπου. Indeed, Matthew has been aware of the ambiguity accompanying the expression: the commentary of Matt 9:8 understood the general meaning in Mark 2:10 (Matt 9:6), and his corrective adverb οὕτως in Matt 17:12 seems destined to evade the ambiguity of Mark 9:12–13, where the Son of Man can be confused with Elijah. However, in my view this doesn't exclude that all the occurrences that have come to Mark are intended to mean christological titles likewise. They should be read accordingly from the apocalyptic use of Dan 7:13, supported by 1 En. 69–71, which justify the existence of messianic attributions to the

ὅτι ἐξουσίαν ἔχει ὁ υἱὸς τοῦ ἀνθρώπου (but to show you that the Son of the Man has authority). Mark 10:45 (Jesus): καὶ γὰρ ὁ υἱὸς τοῦ ἀνθρώπου οὐκ ἦλθεν διακονηθῆναι (and for the Son of the Man didn't come to be served). Mark 14:41 (Jesus): ἰδοὺ παραδίδοται ὁ υἱὸς τοῦ ἀνθρώπου (look!, the Son of the Man is delivered).[53]

---

expression in the I AD and before, even though the term continued to be employed in the popular substratum bare of theological significance. Dan 7:13 is expressly used in Mark 13:26 and 14:62, and in the latter expressly identified with Jesus, meaning which very likely is kept in the mind of Mark in all the gospel instances of the idiom, even in the more ambiguous Mark 2:10,28 and 9:12 (see further discussion below). The authority attributed to the title in Mark 2:10 (forgiveness of sins) and 2:28 (be over the Sabbath commandment), the christological use in Mark 9:9 (the beloved Son of God of Mark 9:7 is identified in 9:9 with the Son of Man, who will rise from the dead), and the personal way the title is used in Mark 14:41 read from 14:42 exclude a great degree of ambiguity in the level of redaction. In this sense, Cortés and Gatti, "Son of Man," 468–70 divide the expression ὁ υἱὸς τοῦ ἀνθρώπου in two components, the Semitism υἱὸς ἀνθρώπου rendering the Hebrew בֶּן אָדָם or Aramaic בַּר נָשָׁא, and the emphasis given by the two articles, ὁ and τοῦ, under which the messianic implications are hidden. Cortés and Gatti, "Son of Man," 481–83 suggest that if Jesus wanted to remove the popular ambiguity adhered to the Hebrew expression *son of man* (בַּר נָשָׁא), he would have chosen the determined state, בֶּן הָאָדָם (Son of the Man) in similar fashion to the second tale of creation, Gen 2:4b—4:1, denoting Jesus saw himself like the son of Adam, of the first man, the representative of humankind, lecture sustained by 1 Cor 15:45–49 and other loci (Schweizer, "Son of Man," 471–72).

53. The remaining eleven second gospel occurrences of ὁ υἱὸς τοῦ ἀνθρώπου are: Mark 2:28 (Jesus); 8:31 (narrator; cf. Matt 16,21, αὐτόν); 8:38 (Jesus); 9:9 (narrator); 9:12 (Jesus); 9:31 (narrator); 10:33 (Jesus); 13:26 (Jesus); 14:21a (Jesus); 14:21b (Jesus); 14:62 (Jesus). The phrase being a christological title, Matthew doesn't avoid the Semitism; on the contrary, he keeps thirteen of the fourteen Marcan occurrences and adds some more (Matt 8:20; 10:23; 11:19; 12:32,40; 13:37,41; 16:13,28; 19:28; 24:27,30,39,44; 25:31; 26:2). Vermes, "Jewish Aramaic," 321–25 brings two most interesting usages of the Aramaic בַּר נָשׁ (son of man) from the Palestinian Talmud (IV AD) in which the third person (son of man, i.e., *a man*) is a circumlocution for the first singular, *me* or *I*, enlighting the possible usage of Jesus. It's enough to provide here the first of the two, an edifying story in y. Berakhot 2:8, where Rabbi Zeïra complains before the sages about the wicked custom of a butcher who didn't want to sell him meat unless the rabbi accepted to be slapped: אֲמַר לְזוֹן רַבָּנָן מַה בִּישׁ מִנְהֲגָא דְהָכָא דְּלָא אָכַל בַּר נַשׁ לִיסְרָא דְקוּפָּד עַד דְּמָחֵי לֵיהּ חַד קוּרְסָם (said to the rabbis: what evil custom is here that a son of man cannot eat a pound of meat until they hit him!). This sort of circumlocution still now is very frequent in popular language: *I know of one who is going home*, intended to mean *I know of one—me—who is going home*. Some of the usages of Jesus should have played, as Casey points, with the general Aramaic meaning of *son of man*, but the context surrounding the expression converted it into a christological title within the group of the Twelve, where it was impossible to be indefinitely ambiguous. The shift from ambiguity to the unequivocal use of *the Son of the Man* in first person by Jesus is indeed registered in the second gospel. After Peter's declaration of Jesus' messiahship (Mark 8:27–30) it was superfluous to keep the secret anymore, and Jesus teaches that the Son of the Man, he, was to suffer, die, and after three days rise again: καὶ παρρησίᾳ τὸν λόγον ἐλάλει (and he spoke the thing openly; Mark 8:32).

(J) Other Semitic expressions. Some Greek idiomatic verses betray the Jewish thought but the reader seldom acknowledges them due to Christian assimilation. We can add to this miscellaneous last category the use of *θάλασσα* (sea), the term for salty waters, instead of λυμνή (lake) for the Lake of Galilee; the metaphorical υἱοί (sons) for friends; the consideration of the demons like impure spirits (that defile the man); and other usages.[54] Mark 1:16 (narrator): *καὶ παράγων παρὰ τὴν θάλασσαν τῆς Γαλιλαίας* (and going by the sea of Galilee). Mark 2:19 (Jesus): *μὴ δύνανται οἱ υἱοὶ τοῦ νυμφῶνος . . . νηστεύειν* (the friends of the bridegroom cannot . . . fast). Mark 5:2 (narrator): *εὐθὺς ὑπήντησεν αὐτῷ ἐκ τῶν μνημείων ἄνθρωπος ἐν πνεύματι ἀκαθάρτῳ* (immediately met him from the tombs a man with an impure spirit; compare with Matt 5:28).[55]

54. MT Josh 13:27: יָם כִּנֶּרֶת (Sea of Chineret; LXX τῆς θαλάσσης Χενερέθ); MT Num 34:3: יָם הַמֶּלַח (the Salt Sea = Dead Sea; LXX τῆς θαλάσσης τῆς ἁλυκῆς); Josh 15:5; 18:19; Ezek 47:8,18. Doudna, *Greek of the Gospel of Mark*, 73–74 called attention to the Marcan variants of the plural οἱ οὐρανοί (the heavens): Mark 1:11; 12:25; 13:25. In BH *heaven* is always the plural word שָׁמַיִם (heavens): Gen 14:19: בָּרוּךְ אַבְרָם לְאֵל עֶלְיוֹן קֹנֵה שָׁמַיִם וָאָרֶץ (blessed Abram by God the Most High who made the heaven and earth); Gen 1:1,8; Judg 5:4; Isa 1:2, Ezek 1:1; etc. Doudna, *Greek of the Gospel of Mark*, 74 admits posible influence from the Greek book of Psalms in Mark because of about 450 instances the LXX renders more of 410 with the singular ὁ οὐρανός (Deut 10:14; 1 Kgs 8:30) and of the remaining thirty-six where the plural is chosen, twenty-seven are in the Psalms (2:4; 8:2,4; 32:6; 68:35). The plural in Mark 14:62, ἐκ δεξιῶν (at the rights), on the contrary, is used as a substitution of God and suggests a kind of plural of majesty. The notion is clear in some OT instances of שָׁמַיִם (Deut 10:14; 1 Kgs 8:27; Ps 148:4) and may be extended to its general use, denoting boundless extent and majesty (Ember, "Pluralis Intensivus in Hebrew," 199–201). Notwithstanding, contrast Mark 1:11; 12:25; and 14:62 with Mark 15:27 ἐκ δεξιῶν and 16:5 ἐν τοῖς δεξιοῖς (in/at the rights) (this last is noted by Doudna, *Greek of the Gospel of Mark*, 12 and is not especially intensive), and Mark 13:25, possible middle case. The Hebrew majestic is evident in the rendering of אֱלֹהִים (Elohim, plural of אֱלוֹהַּ; Gen 1:1; 5:1, Ex 1:20; Job 1:1,5, etc.) by θεός, but it is possible in inanimate objects like תְּהֹמוֹת (abysses), a term employed to designate the Red Sea in Isa 63:13; Ps 78:15; 106:9, where it is rendered by the singular ἄβυσσος; and others (Ember, "Pluralis Intensivus in Hebrew," 195–98).

55. Θάλασσα instead of λυμνή, in most cases by the evangelist: Mark 2:13; 3:7; 4:1,39; 4:41 (the disciples); 5:1,13,21; 6:47,48,49. Perhaps Jesus has in mind the icon of the lake in the sayings Mark 9:42; 11:23. Metaphorical υἱοί/τέκνα: Mark 10:24 (Jesus); perhaps Mark 3:17 (narrator); The accusing expression πνεῦμα ἀκαθάρτος undoubtedly belongs to the religious sphere of Mark: 1:23 (narrator); 1:26 (narrator); 1:27 (the public); 3:11 (narrator); 5:8 (Jesus); 5:13 (narrator; cf. Matt 8:32); 6:7 (narrator); 7:25 (narrator); 9:25 (narrator).

Palestinian Geographical References

Aramaic was the official scripture of the Persian Empire and despite the conquests of Alexander spreading the Greek scripture in its western half, forms of Aramaic remained the mother tongue of many Levantine folks at the rise of the first millenium. Ordinary citizens from Syria, Nabataea, Transjordan, Israel, and Phoenicia spoke Aramaic dialects, and also Greek for the more cultured if they were engaged in international business, travels, the army, or local politics. If the Marcan Semitisms would have solely been Aramaic in character, we could not be in a condition to specify much more the provenance of the author of the second gospel. Fortunately, the presence of Hebraisms and the association of lexical turns with the LXX and the Jewish religion point to a Judeo-Christian and not to an author coming into the Christian faith from Semitic paganism. The Papias-Clement tradition, once again, appears to be confirmed, but the geographical references in Mark, notoriously wrong in a pair of occasions and ambiguous in other three, gain ground for the hypothesis of a Syrian, Phoenician, or less probably Transjordan provenance.

Geographical references in chapters 5–6 of the gospel show little acquaintance with the region surrounding the Lake of Galilee. Mark places Gerasa opposite to Capernaum (Mark 5:1–21) and confuses Gennesaret with Bethsaida (Mark 6:45–53), suggesting that the precise and vivid portrait of many Galilean traditions around Capernaum have been sewn to the narrative net by one who is alien to Galilee. The first instance, 5:1, presents one serious geographical mistake, confirmed by ancient mss and the synoptic comparison. The passage which opens, 5:1–20, narrates the healing of a demoniac. The territory of the Gerasenes, today Jordan Jerash, the site where it took place according to the narrative, is sixty kilometers southeast of the Lake of Galilee. Surprisingly, the narrator tells that Jesus encounters the possessed once he crosses the lake to the opposite shore to Capernaum. Mark 5:1–2 reads: *καὶ ἦλθον εἰς τὸ πέραν τῆς θαλάσσης εἰς τὴν χώραν τῶν Γερασηνῶν. καὶ ἐξελθόντος αὐτοῦ ἐκ τοῦ πλοίου εὐθὺς ὑπήντησεν αὐτῷ τῶν μνημείων ἄνθρωπος ἐν πνεύματι ἀκαθάρτῳ* (and they came to the other side of the sea to the country of the Gerasenes. And as he was going out of the boat immediately met him from the tombs a man with an unclean spirit).

Hence, the action of the healing happens in the very eastern shore of the Lake of Galilee. Mark 5:11–13 repeats the same location and 5:10,20 focus the action unmistakably (but in general terms) in the Decapolis. In 5:11–13 the spirits expelled from the man entered a swine herd that rushed into the sea from a cliff that modern explorers have attempted to identify. The movements of Jesus and his disciples across the Lake of Galilee are usually along the west-east axis, not north-south, impelling one to deduce that the episode of the demoniac in Mark 5:1–20 took place in the mid-northern part of the eastern shore.[56] Just opposite to Magdala, today Mejdel, is Khersa, a good place for pasturage and unique in that there is a cliff on the eastern shore, two kilometers south of Wady Semakh, entering the border of the lake. Excluding this cliff, the hills are recessed a minimum of eight hundred meters from the water's edge, making it impossible to locate 5:1–20 anywhere else on the eastern shore.[57]

There are no tombs in Khersa, but it is not quite far from Gadara, a town in the Decapolis, and it can be supposed that the owners of the herd were from this territory, not from Jerash. Anyhow, it is not guessable whether Mark confuses Khersa-Gadara with the name of Jerash or whether he thinks Jerash of the Decapolis was bordering the lake. More precisely, Gadara rests over the Yarmuk River, some miles away from the lake, southwards from Khersa. The Yarmuk, which leads to Gadara and dies into the Jordan River after it leaves back the lake, forms steep walls, and can fit as a better setting for Mark 5:14. The mistake made by Mark is further attested by the parallel Matt 8:28, more correctly reading *εἰς τὴν χώραν τῶν Γαδαρηνῶν* (to the country of the Gadarenes). Comparison of mss also gives priority to a Mark 5:1 original *Γερασηνῶν* against corrections with *Γαδαρηνῶν* influenced by Matt 8:28.[58] We can infer therefore that Mark either ignores the exact location

56. The western shore was more familiar to Jesus and his disciples than the eastern shore. The western territory between Bethsaida in the entrance of the Jordan River to the lake—the town of Philip, Capernaum—the village of Peter, Andrew, John, James the Great, and Levi, the plain of Ginnesar, and Magdala, is the setting for Jesus' motions in the Jewish quarter of the lake (Mark 1:21; 2:1,13; 3:1; 6:53; 8:10). Except for Bethsaida, which can be considered neutral for the division (although Mark thinks about it in eastern terms probably due to its heathen population; see Mark 8:13,22), the other settlements are in the mid-north of the western shore. Jesus moved to the eastern side seemingly because the crowds didn't let him rest in the western shore (Mark 4:35; 6:32–34; 7:31; 8:13).

57. Dalman, *Sacred Sites and Ways*, 176–79; Wilson and Warren, *Recovery of Jerusalem*, 283–89.

58. The original reading *Γερασηνῶν* of Mark 5:1 is established thanks to Codex Sinaiticus (א), a IV-century AD parchment ms; and supported by Codex Vaticanus (B), from the mid IV century; Codex Bezae (D), V century; the entire Latin Tradition, containing ancient versions from the III to IV centuries; and the Sahidic Tradition, reaching back to the IV century. Readings of Mark 5:1 *Γαδαρηνῶν*, inferred by Matt 8:28, appear later. The most representative are Codex Alejandrinus (A), an uncial from the V century, and Codex Ephraemi (C), a V-century palimpsest. Another reading of Mark 5:1 *Γεργυστηνῶν*, bad supported, is found in Codex Washingtonianus (W), from the IV to early V centuries. Finally, the reading *Γεργεσηνῶν* occurs in the version Syrus Sinaiticus between the III and IV centuries and much later witnesses, like a correction on א from the VII century. *Γεργεσηνῶν* does not belong to the original Mark but

of Gerasa or that he confuses it with Gadara. The arguments above explain why Matthew, who seems to have better grasp of the eastern shore, corrects Mark, and why Luke (8:26), who neither is hither advised by Galilean traditionalists, doesn't save the mistake made by Mark.[59]

Mark 6:45 confirms the inexactness of Jesus' travels across the lake. The expression προάγειν εἰς τὸ περὰν πρὸς Βηθσαϊδάν (they go ahead to the other side, toward Bethsaida) indicates a shift from one shore to another. According to the foregoing miracle of the breads (Mark 6:30–44), Jesus is in a desert spot of the oriental shore. But when the action in 6:45 finishes in 6:53, Jesus moors in Gennesaret, not in Bethsaida, which doesn't correspond to any of the two opposite shores but to the northern mouth of the lake. To dodge the problem, some authors consider this Bethsaida other than Bethsaida-Julias, but it seems not the case attending to the unequivocal Bethsaida-Julias of Mark 8:22–27 on the way to Caesarea Philippi. On the other hand, the use of Mark 6:45 by Matt 14:22 repeats the same words but lacks πρὸς Βηθσαϊδάν. Obviously, the handier explanation is another correction of Matthew over Mark or a mistake by Mark if both depend on a common source better retained in Matthew.[60]

The geographical imprecisions of Mark don't conclude with the surroundings of the lake. The less commented cross-references of Mark 9:33 and 10:1,10—which we save for later discussion in the course of chapter 3—reveal incongruence in the spatial design of the narrative and with all likelihood the fallible creative hand of Mark, who is not always entirely successful fusing independent units. Besides, the second gospel appears not to be acquainted with the whereabouts of the temple's treasury (Mark 12:41), and with the route from Jericho to East Jerusalem (Mark 10:46; 11:1). In the latter, Mark 11:1, the order of toponyms and the prepositions εἰς and πρός seem to say that Jesus was going up to Jerusalem, by way of Bethphage and Bethany: Καὶ ὅτε ἐγγίζουσιν εἰς Ἱεροσόλυμα εἰς Βηθφαγὴ καὶ Βηθανίαν

---

it conceivably derives from the comments of Origen (died c. AD 254) on Matt 8:28 (NA²8 119; Metzger, *Greek New Testament*, 84; Metzger and Ehrman, *Text of the New Testament*, 62–73, 80–81, 96–98, 101–5, 110–13).

59. Strikingly, the original parallel Luke 8:26 Γερασηνῶν to Mark 5:1, attested by early Latin versions, the Greek papyri P⁷5 from the early III century, and B are absent from ℵ. Codex Sinaiticus supplies the original reading to Mark 5:1 Γερασηνῶν, but not to Luke 8:26, reading there Γεργεσηνῶν (NA²8 214; Metzger and Ehrman, *Text of the New Testament*, 58–60).

60. The second miracle of the breads, Mark 8:1–10, similarly ends with a motion from the oriental shore εἰς τὰ μέρη Δαλμανουθά (to the districts of Dalmanutha), a reading well attested by ℵ, A, and B (NA²8 134). The Matthean parallel to Mark 8:10, Matt 15:39, has εἰς τὰ ὅρια Μαγαδάν (to the territories of Magadan), assimilated to Magdalan by W, and simply to Magdala by later mss, Regius (L), Sangallensis (Δ), or Koridethi (Θ) from the VIII to IX centuries (NA²8 50).

πρὸς τὸ ὄρος τῶν ἐλαιῶν (when they were approaching to Jerusalem, to Bethphage and Bethany at the Mount of Olives). In the construction πρὸς τὸ ὄρος τῶν ἐλαιῶν the preposition πρός can be rendered *to*, *toward*, *near*, or *at the Mount of Olives*.[61]

The first reading, πρός meaning *to*, can be discarded considering Mark adds a new preposition to εἰς, whereas πρός meaning *at*, is backed up by Mark 1:33; 2:2, the proximate verses Mark 11:4; 14:54, and with less confidence Mark 4:1. πρός with εἰς occurs in Mark 6:45,51, but there it can be either rendered by *to*, *toward*, or *with* if we distinguish πρός and εἰς in the same verse. Then, πρὸς τὸ ὄρος in Mark 11:1 is more consistent rendered *at the mount* or *near the mount*, though the meaning *toward the mount* in πρός followed by the accusative is possible. In conclusion: it is consistent in view of the use of πρός that in Mark 11:1 the author is thinking that Bethany and Bethphage are on the Mount of Olives or near it on the way from Jericho to Jerusalem. Ancient Bethphage, today et-Tur, was indeed on the Mount of Olives, and Bethany, today El-Azariyeh, near it, but not on the main road from Jericho to Jerusalem.

As one gets to Jerusalem from Jericho, the eastern part of Mount of Olives appears in the foreground. In the I century AD, the track from Jericho took, nevertheless and against Mark 11:1, the northern side of the eastern slope of the Mount of Olives, whereas Bethany was near the southern side. A detour could be chosen by Bethany, where Jesus had some friends, itinerary taken by John 12:1–12, more respectful towards the distance permitted to be walked on Saturday, but then it would be better to say Jesus was approaching Jerusalem by way of Bethany and Bethphage because Bethphage was a suburb nearer to the town than Bethany and this last was not on the shortest access to the temple coming from Jericho. In other words: the route to the esplanade by means of the direct way wherein Jesus was acclaimed Messiah (Mark 11:8–9) avoided Bethany. The next approach will see it in more detail.[62]

The ancient road from Jericho entered Jerusalem from the east. The area near Jerusalem is urbanized and the outright itinerary cannot be discerned,

61. πρός, meaning *to/toward*, accompanying verbs of motion, is the most frequent use, highly consistent in the second gospel, up to thirty-six instances: Mark 1:32,40; 2:3,13; 3:7,8,13,31; 4:1; 5:15,19,22; 6:25,30,48,51; 7:1,25; 9:14,17,19,20; 10:1,14,50; 11:7,27; 12:2,4,6,13,18; 14:10,53; 15:43. πρός, meaning *near:* Mark 4:1 (near/at); 6:3 (with/near).

62. Initial light on this theme has been taken from Roskam, *Purpose of the Gospel of Mark*, 97–99, to whom I am greatly obliged for the paragraph above and the last idea of the former. The grammatical and the next developments are mine. Roskam defends the Galilean origin of the second gospel. One of his cornerstones is the Galilean setting for Mark 13:9–13, which I will discuss in chapter 3.

though open field surveys done the last century, ancient literary sources, and some old remains—Roman milestones, steeps hewn in the rock, foundation stones, cisterns, and ruins—permit the adequate reconstruction of almost all the road. In the last stage coming from Jericho, past Qasr Ali—a village six kilometers to the east of Jerusalem—the route continued by Wadi es-Shid to modern Sheik Inbar. At this point, with the eastern slope of Mount of Olives to its left and the eastern slope of Mount Scopus in front, the road bifurcated. Both hills form a tiny range that runs north-south opposite to the eastern wall of Jerusalem, which was the same eastern wall of the temple's esplanade, serving at this point as a defense. The eastern wall was separated from Olives and Scopus by the Kidron Valley, a small depression. From Sheik Inbar, the most direct way to Jerusalem can be traced up to the lowest joint between Olives and Scopus, where the construction in 1950s of the road to Augusta Victoria's hospital unearthed foundations of an ancient (Roman) road whose clipped profile in five strata showed that it could have been built over what can be considered the Jewish access to the temple.[63]

The alternative and longer way to Jerusalem turned left from Sheik Inbar, bordering Mount of Olives in the eastern side, and then turned right again, leaving Bethany to its left and Bethphage, which belonged to the most peripheral quarter of Jerusalem and was situated in the same Mount of Olives, what today is et-Tur, to its right. The normal option from Bethany was to continue straight to the temple from the south, crossing the Kidron Valley and going up to the Huldah Gates. On the contrary, the shortest alternative for the pilgrim, along which Jesus was acclaimed Messiah, possibly went straight from Sheik Inbar through the separation between Olives and Scopus to the esplanade through the Shushan Gate, the direct access to the temple in the middle part of the eastern wall, a little southwards from the actual Golden Gate. Thus, the shortest way went down from the pass between the two hills, turning left in the Kidron Valley and then directly to the Shushan Gate by a bridge.[64] The not-entirely-clear expression of Mark

63. Beauvery, "Route Romaine de Jérusalem a Jéricho," 73–75. The 1950s road went from the Kidron to the Hospital Augusta Victoria. The chopped profile, 1.10 meters high, was made on the west slope of Olives. The absence of more recent structures, loose cobblestones over the surface of stratum V, several more here and there, and Roman sherds in the northern small depression of Olives allow the identification of the Roman road, just south of the hospital. My statement that this road possibly leveraged the Jewish road is based on the possible shortest way to the temple. By Bethany was anyway longer, and by the northwestern corner of Scopus towards the Antonia, much the same long and where some sort of path is supposable (see next note), faced the problem of lengthening the way by the Kidron Valley, much more rugged in the I AD than today.

64. Even so, the way to the temple from Sheik Inbar should have allowed one new bifurcation turning right, to the northern part of the temple's esplanade. In the

11:1 may be the cause of why, when Matthew resorts in the common tradition, he says nothing about Bethany (Matt 21:1). The literal understanding is awkward and the translators tend to amend the involved prepositions in one way or another.[65] Albeit not everyone knows the homeland well, these notions are expected if the author of the second gospel is John Mark, Judeo-Christian disciple of Peter and Paul, son of Mary, the believer who dwelt in the suburbs of Jerusalem.

---

northwestern side of the esplanade stood the Antonia Tower, and further west the Sheep Gate. It is possible that for security reasons from the southern part of Augusta Victoria's hospital, the last spot where the ancient pilgrims' road can be reconstructed with certainty, a lesser way conducted to Antonia keeping the straight line from this spot just south of the hospital to the campanile of Saint George's Cathedral (Beauvery, "Route Romaine de Jérusalem a Jéricho," 73–78; Dalman, *Sacred Sites and Ways*, 245–55; Wilkinson, *From Jerusalem to Jericho*, 10, 21–23; Safrai and Avi Yonah, "Temple," 613).

65. NRSV: *When they were approaching Jerusalem, at Bethphage and Bethany, near the Mount of Olives . . . .* REB: *They were now approaching Jerusalem, and when they reached Bethphage and Bethany, close by the Mount of Olives . . . .* NJB (Spanish version): *Cuando se aproximaban a Jerusalén, cerca ya de Betfagé y Betania, al pie del Monte de los Olivos . . . .* NV: *Et cum appropinquarent Hierosolymae, Bethphage et Bethaniae ad montem Olivarum.* The Greek εἰς Ἱεροςόλυμα εἰς Βηθφαγὴ καὶ Βηθανίαν must be literally translated *to Jerusalem and to Bethphage and (to) Bethany* if we consider similar constructions meaning *to* in very proximate verses, Mark 11:11: Καὶ ἐισῆλθεν εἰς Ἱεροςόλυμα εἰς τὸ ἱερὸν . . . ἐξῆλθεν εἰς Βηθανίαν; and 11:15: Καὶ ἔρχονται εἰς Ἱεροςόλυμα. Καὶ εἰσελθὼν εἰς τὸ ἱερὸν; and the use of ἐν with the dative Βηθανίᾳ when Mark wants to say *at Bethany* in Mark 14:3. Furthermore, Mark 11:1 ἐγγίζουσιν (approaching) is a dynamic verb that requires a preposition like εἰς. Grammatically, Mark 11:1 is correct, and what the translators try to straighten is the locative sense of the construction.

3

Internal Evidence

The Latin Background

Latin Loans Κοδράντης (Mark 12:42) and Πραιτώριον (Mark 15:16)

Two more Marcan passages concerning Jerusalem involving geographical depictions, the vague image of the temple's court in the episode of the widow's mite (Mark 12:41–44) and the purportedly imprecise literary framework during the stay of Jesus in Pilate's headquarters (Mark 15:1–20), have been alleged to disprove that the second gospel was addressed to a Judaean community.[1] In the judgement of the author of these pages, we have general descriptions, but not errors as we have seen formerly. On the contrary, the spatial scrutiny throws light on the elemental geographical coherence of Mark in these two portions of the narrative.[2] Rather, the striking

1. This is the position of Roskam, *Purpose of the Gospel of Mark*, 97, to whom again I am beholden for the first approach to the subjects.

2. The scene of Mark 12:41–44 occurs in the court of women, the only authorized hall for the widow. The Talmud of Jerusalem reports that thirteen chests were displayed in the temple, six of them for voluntary gifts (y. Shek. 6:1,7). Besides, there were two lodges for voluntary offerings, the room of votive vessels (of precious materials), and the room *of the silence*, where poor sin-fearers could do anonymous offerings if desired (y. Shek. 5:7). The exact location of the treasuries is unknown, but some had to be accessible from the court of women, especially those for voluntary offerings. The gospel says that Jesus, *καθίσας κατέναντι* (having sat in front; Mark 12:41), saw the woman and other people doing voluntary offerings. The reader has the impression of a unique treasury. The reality of the temple was more complex and some additional details could have been given by the author of the second gospel, but in big lines Mark 12:41–44 is

side of Mark 12:41–44 and 15:1–20 is the presence of Latinisms fastened to the same idiom used for the explaining of Aramaic words (ὅ ἐστιν), namely, the fact that Mark explains Greek terms by means of Latin equivalents.

Mark 12:42 bothers with the worth of the offering the widow threw into the temple's treasury: *καὶ ἐλθοῦσα μία χήρα πτωχὴ ἔβαλεν λεπτὰ δύο, ὅ ἐστιν κοδράντης* (and one poor widow came and threw two copper coins, which is a quadrans). Mark 15:16 presents the same turn when Jesus is taken prisoner to Pilate: *οἱ δὲ στρατιῶται ἀπήγαγον αὐτὸν ἔσω τῆς αὐλῆς, ὅ ἐστιν πραιτώριον* (and the soldiers led him inside the palace, which is (the) praetorium). Furthermore, in the latter instance, the Latinism can respond to the attempt to be geographically precise.[3] The praetorium was the residence of the Roman governor and the reference to the praetorium in Mark 15:16 would thus be an attempt to define which kind of building is the palace where Jesus is taken, since the palace of Caiaphas the high priest has been previously reported (τὴν αὐλὴν τοῦ ἀρχιερέως; Mark 14:54,66,68), not the rendering of an unknown concept.[4] But in the former case, the Latinism

coherent with the context. According to y. Shek 6:7, every chest had its own function depending on the material sacrifice for whose suffrage the money was destined. As a result, it was possible for Jesus to know if a person was doing voluntary offering. In the case Jesus did not directly see the mite of the widow, he could have guessed the quantity from the manner in which she took it out from her garments (less probably from the sound of the small coins dropping in the chest) or from previous experiences with poor donors. The major incoherence might be here the mention of the treasury in singular with no further specification, γαζοφυλάκιον.

3. On the question of the vague references of Jesus' movements in the praetorium during his arrest (Mark 15:1–20), Mark is sparse in words, but doesn't make any explicit mistake. In comparison with the other evangelists, Mark is not incoherent, and neither is he if we enlarge the passage to the previous and next geographical spots (Mark 14:53–72; 15:21–22). The other gospels add some information to this long section, but don't positively correct it. From the arrest in Gethsemane to the place where Jesus was hanged on the cross, Mark has six local references: the high priest's palace (Mark 14:53–54); presumably the Sanhedrin (Mark 15:1a); a place where Pilate is, presumably the palace or its surroundings (Mark 15:1b); inside the praetorium (Mark 15:16); outside the praetorium, apparently the street (Mark 15:20); and the Golgotha (Mark 15:22). Matthew, who tends to rectify Mark, keeps the scheme, with six moves (Matt 26:57; 27:1; 27:2; 27:27; 27:31; 27:33). Luke adds one motion to the itinerary, an unidentified spot where Herod Antipas was (Luke 23:7); and takes out another, the scene with the soldiers inside the praetorium. John adds four: the house of Annas, father-in-law of Caiaphas (John 18:13), a spot in the praetorium from where Jesus crowned with thorns was shown to the populace (John 18:5), inside the praetorium a second time (John 18:9), and the pavement of judgment where Jesus was sat (John 19:13). Luke and John add different information to the movement of Jesus during his arrest, but yet conserve the general scheme of Mark and Matthew (Luke 22:54; 22:66; 23:1; 23:11; 23:26; 23:33; John 18:24; 18:28; 19:1; 19:16; 19:17).

4. Depending on Josephus, the main site the Roman prefect of Judaea occupied when he lodged in Jerusalem was two-winged and protected all around by a wall and

κοδράντης is not a concept that belongs to the story-telling time. Mark is clarifying the worth of two small copper coins by means of a denomination that belongs to the mental universe of his audience.

The word λεπτόν names the small copper coin. Deeming the context and the given comparative value, two leptons for one quadrans, λεπτόν must amount in Mark 12:44 to the Jewish prutah, whose average weight was 1.90 g during the Roman governors of Judaea before Agrippa I (AD 41–44), ranging mostly from 1.5 to 2.5 g in that period.[5] The quadrans was the smallest Roman denomination, worthing the fourth of the as, with a standard around 3 g crossing the I century AD. It was western currency, mainly struck in Lugdunum (Lyon) and Rome, instituted by Augustus (27 BC–AD 14), and issued until Antoninus Pius (AD 138–61).[6] Its lower value,

---

three defensive towers, Phasael, Hippicus, and Mariamne (Josephus, *B.J.* 1.21; 5.4). This fortified complex, southwest to the temple's enclosure and first built by Herod the Great, has been excavated by archaeologists since 1970s in what today is the southern area to the Tower of David and the Jaffa Gate, where the old Ottoman police Kisleh stays (Peleg-Barkat, "Herod's Western Palace," 57–60). A fill of compacted earth and stones in three distant points, one amid two retaining walls and seven meters high in a north-south axis, recently exposed along forty meters and dated by associated sherds to the second half of the I century BC, gives an idea of the massive structure raised by Herod to set the plateau for the palace (Re'em, "Second Temple Period Fortifications," 140–42). Over the plateau, apparently 140 meters extent from north to south, the complex had to be divided in a several-building residential area and a small camp for soldiers. On its western side, a small fortified gate in two phases with turrets has been identified as the proper spot for the conversation of Pilate with the chief priests and as one of the accesses to the praetorium (Gibson, "Jerusalem Praetorium," 104, 110). Mark 15:2–15 doesn't identify where Jesus was delivered to Pilate, but it had to be a neutral area to avoid the ritual defilement that would have prevented the chief priests from eating the Passover lamb (John 18:28). A gate in the wall next to the street where the two parties could meet and the higher level within the praetorium concur with the gospel, enabling the dialogue between Pilate, the priests, and the populace, and the sway of the situation by the soldiers (Gibson, "Jerusalem Praetorium," 111–18). With this sense at the back, Mark 15:16 can be considered an attempt to be precise. When Jesus was taken into Pilate's headquarters, ἔσω τῆς αὐλῆς (inside of the palace), Mark says ὅ ἐστιν πραιτώριον (which is the praetorium) to distinguish this building from Caiaphas' palace, where Jesus had been before (Mark 14:54,66,68), or from the peripheral fortified gate, where the high priests delivered Jesus to Pilate (Mark 15:1b).

5. Hendin, "Judaean Small Bronze Coins," 115–17; Jensen, "Message and Minting," 75. Since the coins circulated for decades, it is impossible to determine the kind of prutot in which the offering of the widow consisted. The candidates are the small bronze prutot with double cornucopia of the last Hasmoneans and Herod the Great, the bunch of grapes-helmet coin of Archaelaus, the barley-palm tree type of the Roman governors before AD 26, and the simpulum-lituus prutot of Pilate (Jacobson, "Roman Governors of Judaea," 73–82; Wacks, *Biblical Numismatics*, 21–47).

6. King, "Quadrantes from the River Tiber," 60–82; Sutherland, *Roman Imperial Coinage I*, 3–6, 21–187.

in comparison with the larger imperial copper coins, the as, dupondius, and sestertius, discarded its hoarding and (depending on the finds of stray issues) made it very scarce beyond its area of minting where provincial denominations substituted it. The mints of Ephesus, Pergamus, and Antioch struck aes in the second half of the I century BC and during the first half of the I AD that widely circulated, but not quadrantes.

The larger Roman copper denomination, the as, would have been known in large Roman centers in the east and surrounding areas, but attending to the precedent the quadrans itself would have been rare to see for Greek citizens not in touch with the Roman community. It has been hinted that, to understand what is the second evangelist doing in Mark 12:44 we must return to Plutarch, who beginning the II AD explains the smallest Roman denomination to the Greek readers of his Life of Cicero in a way just the opposite to Mark: *τὸ δὲ λεπτότατον τοῦ χαλκοῦ νομίσματος κουαδράντην ἐκάλουν* (and the smallest copper coin was called quadrans).[7] Mark 12:44 suggests an audience well acquainted with the smallest Roman denomination, and no doubt, which seem to be more in contact with Roman currency than Plutarch's Greek readers. There are other possibilities but Mark 12:42 furnishes enough evidence to suppose, confidently, a western origin of Mark's Gentile audience, including Roman provenance properly.

The Marcan Latinisms have been for long defended proofs of a Roman composition. They can be mainly clustered in loans, transliterations of Latin expressions, and possible Latin syntactic style.[8] The morphological loans, including the two discussed, are the following eleven in nineteen occurrences: (1) *κράβαττος* (*grabatus*; bed; Mark 2:4,9,11,12; 6:55); (2) *μόδιος* (*modius*; a container for measurement holding a sixth of the Attic *medimnus* or some 8.75 liters; Mark 4:21); (3) *λεγιών* (*legion*; Mark 5:9,15); (4) *σπεκουλάτωρ* (*speculator*; a scout of the body-guard, executioner; Mark 6:27); (5) *δηνάριον* (*denarius*; Mark 6:37; 12:15; 14:5); (6) *κῆνσος* (*census*; tax; Mark 12:14); (7) *ξέσται* (*sextarii*; the sextarius is a measure for solids or liquids of some 0.5 liters; Mark 7:4); (8) *κοδράντης* (*quadrans*; commented above; Mark 12:42); (9) *φραγελλόω* (*fragellare*; lash; Mark 15:15); (10) *πραιτώριον* (*praetorium*; commented above; Mark 15:16); (11) *κεντυρίων* (*centurio*; Mark 15:39,44). Mark holds too one semantic Latinism wherein the stem is Greek but not the meaning, *αἰτία* (*causa*; reason of an accusation; Mark 15:26);[9] and one

7. Plutarch, *Cicero et Demosthenes* 19.4. This exegetical insight, certainly a jewel, is first attributed to Hengel, *Studies in the Gospel of Mark*, 29.

8. Turner, "Style of Mark," 235–36, from whom I draw the morphological loans, and further on the listed transliterations.

9. In the NT *αἰτία* is a quite common word expressing the reason or cause of something (Luke 8:47; Acts 10:21; 2 Tim 1:6,12; Titus 1:13; Heb 2:11), or the charge of an

possible Latin-fashioned neologism, Ἡρῳδιανοί (*Herodiani*; the likely Latin gens adopted by the Herodian family and their supporters; Mark 3:6; 12:13).[10]

Latin Loans Κῆνσος (Mark 12:14) and Δηνάριον (Mark 6:37; 12:15; 14:5)

The Roman taxation in the provinces generally consisted in tribute over lands (*tributum soli*) and tribute over persons (*tributum capitis*). For the latter a census over population was necessary because it was levied from every male at a fixed cash amount, whereas the taxation of lands was based on a property registration quite independent and common to be exacted upon a fixed percentage or amount of crop over the established productivity of the soil. The tributum soli was the rule from ancient times in the Near East (see 2 Kgs 23:35), but the tributum capitis in addition to traditional taxation

accusation (Matt 19:3,10; 27:37; Mc 15:26; John 18:38; 19:4,6; Acts 13:28; 22:24; 23:28; 25:18,27; 28:18,20; Thayer, *Lexicon of the New Testament*, 18 keeps αἰτία for cause in Acts 22:24; 28:20). Mark 15:26 is readable with αἰτία/causa as well as with αἰτία/charge, making insecure the Latinism. Van Tine, "Avoiding the αἰτία of Adultery," 401–8 discusses a comparable case, Matt 19:3 and Matt 19:10, wherein the sway of the later Latin tradition over the Greek αἰτία is recognizable. Matt 19:3 has εἰ ἔξεστιν ἀνθρώπῳ ἀπολῦσαι τὴν γυναῖκα αὐτοῦ κατὰ πᾶσαν αἰτίαν, usually rendered as *is it lawful for a man to divorce his wife for any cause?* (NRSV), or by similar expressions where αἰτίαν can be rendered by the Latin *causam*. But literally the verse can be equally translated: *is it lawful for a man to divorce his wife for any charge* (of adultery)*?* Matt 19:10 has εἰ οὕτως ἐστὶν ἡ αἰτία τοῦ ἀνθρώπου μετὰ τῆς γυναικός. The NRSV's *if such is the case of a man with his wife* can correspond to an understanding of αἰτία from the Vulgate *causa*, but interpreted secondarily from 1 Cor 7 and transformed into *status*, that is, *case* or *situation*. In my opinion, if the Greek term exists, there is no reason to suppose a Latin reading for the fact that it improves the meaning. A more idiomatic expression does not always represent the original. This kind of error thoroughly crossed the classical article Couchoud, "Marc a été Écrit en Latin?," 161–92, wherein he points out more than 150 Latinisms in Mark. The author, assuming Bobbiensis (k) and Palatinus (e), from the IV to V centuries, are later witnesses of the first ms, tried to demonstrate Mark was originally Latin. Couchoud compared Greek witnesses against the Latin—as a rule the contemporary B, D, and W, projecting over the Greek text the judgment that a better Latin reading necessary represented the original and that any difference between Greek mss must be explained from a Latin original degraded in the act of copying or translation.

10. Here, the exegetical gemstone comes from Casey, *Aramaic Sources of Mark*, 186–87, who reconstructs the possible Aramaic equivalent הֶרֹדִיאַנֵי (vowels mine). As he pointed out, the expected Greek term would be Ἡρωδείων, which Josephus, *B.J.* 1.16 employs. The *-i* end is typical of the second declension nominative plural: *Herodianus-Herodiani*, plural genitive *Herodianorum*. If this Latinism acutely noted by Casey is accepted, Ἡρῳδιανοί would come from the popular Aramaic imitation of the Latin nominative, since the Latin genitive would require a longer word. There are three only known instances of the idiom: Mark 3:6; 12:13; and its parallel Matt 22:16.

on the basis of the census was a novelty introduced by Augustus in the Roman East upon the Italian model. Well documented in the papyri of Roman Egypt since 24 BC, its proper terms there were λαογραφία (registration of villagers), and the more general ἐπικεφάλαιον (head tax), and it consisted in a cash poll-tax imposed on the λαοί (adult males of the countryside). The imposing rate went from 16 denarii to 20 for men from the age of fourteen, giving a renovation of the census over a fourteen-year cycle in operation from Tiberius to the III century AD. Roman citizens were exempted and inhabitants of the nomens' capitals paid at a reduced rate rounding 8 denarii.[11]

The use of κῆνσος and δηνάριον by Mark 12:14–15 seems, accordingly, to represent the tribute over heads, excise though well attested in neighbor Egypt is under dispute for Palestine in times of Jesus. The complete disappearance of I AD Jewish tax registration papyri, the inconclusive ancient sources on the question, and the theological Jewish problem of paying taxes to the foreign power—that must be admitted as soon as the taxation under Quirinius in AD 6 raised the zealot party, makes thorny the dilemma that whether the taxation under Mark 12 consisted in the head-tax similar to the Egyptian λαογραφία or only in a land-tax for the sake of Rome.[12] It must be said that outside Mark 12:14 and Matt 17:25; 22:17,19, the word κῆνσος to express a taxation in the I century AD is absent anywhere else in ancient literature and archaeology. We must wait to the II–III centuries, invariably under eastern epigraphical military contexts.[13]

11. Rathbone, "Roman Taxation," 86–99.

12. Josephus utters that after Archelaos' banishment in AD 6, Quirinius was sent to Syria and to Judaea as assessor of the properties (τιμητὴς τῶν οὐσιῶν), after which Judas of Gamala (*the Galilean*) rose in rebellion (*A.J.* 18.1–10.23–26; *B.J.* 2.118). Josephus mentions another Roman tribute over the sales of fruits (τὰ τέλη τῶν ὠνουμένων καρπῶν) in Jerusalem just after Pilate, with Vitellius, AD 36 (*A.J.* 18.90), and a third one (τὴν εἰσφοράν) during Agrippa II in AD 66 (*B.J.* 2.403–4).

13. To my knowledge, epigraphical instances of κῆνσος before the IV AD are reduced to three. The nearest to Palestine is an inscription dated ca. 200 AD in seven lines with round sigma (C instead of Σ) of Mendes (today Tell el-Rub'a), north of Cairo. It covers the whole professional career of the Alexandrian idiologus, who has been in charge of several censuses (Milne, "Greek Inscriptions," 291 = I,1107) T.ΑΥΡΗΛΙΟC ΚΑΛΠΟΥΡΝΙΑΝΟC ΑΠΟΛΛΩΝΙΔΗC | ΧΙΛΙΑΡΧΟC ΛΕΓΙΩΝΟC ΙΑ ΓΕΜΙΝΗC ΧΙΛ ΛΕΓ | ΙΓ ΓΕΜΙΝΗC ΕΠΙΤΡΟΠΟC ΓΑΛΛΙΑC ΑΚΟΥΙΤΑΝΙΚΗC | ΕΠΙ ΚΗΝCΩΝ ΕΠΙΤΡΟΠΟC ΜΥCΙΑC ΤΗC ΚΑΤΩ ΕΠΙ | ΘΡΑΚΗC ΕΠΙ ΔΕΛΜΑΤΙΑC ΕΠΙ ΑΙΓΥΠΤΟΥ ΙΔΙΟΥ | ΛΟΓΟΥ | ΖΗCΑC ΕΤΗ ΝΕ (*T. Aurelius Calpurnianus Apollonides chiliarch of the Legion XIV Gemina, chi(liarch) (of the) Leg(ion) XIII Gemina, procurator of Gallia Aquitania pro(curator) of the censuses, procurator of Mysia the Inferior, pro(curator) of Thracia, pro(curator) of Dalmatia, pro(curator) of Egypt (and) idiologus lived 55 years*). The second occurrence is an inscribed base for a statue in Ephesus, AD 120–150, honoring one Gavius Balbus of the knighthood order, imperial procurator over the censuses of Galatia and Paphlagonia in central Anatolia (ἐπίτροπον

Before AD 70 Roman denarii are very scant in Palestinian finds in comparison to the Phoenician currency, whereas it is known that in AD 70, Vespasian transformed the previous Jewish contribution to the temple of half Tyrian shekel into a Roman tax paid in denarii[14]—making possible to re-think the Marcan account of a tax paid in the Roman coin during Jesus' time as the projection into the earlier Palestinian taxes of this later context. The identification Matthew has done of the *δηνάριον* with the coin for the *κῆνσος* in 22:19, his parallel verse to Mark 12:14, as well as the technic vocabulary for taxes we glean from Josephus (ἀποτιμάω/evaluate; ἀποτιμήσις/assessment; ἀπογράφω/register; ἀπογραφή/registration; τελέω/pay; τιμητής/assessor; φόρος/tribute; εἰσφοράς/contribution), the NT (Luke 2:1–2: ἀπογράφω/register; 20:22: φόρος/tribute; Acts 5:37: ἀπογράφω/register; Rom 13:7: φόρος/tribute; τέλος/tax), and the Babatha Archive before the Second Revolt (AD 132–35; ἀπογράφω/register; ἀπογραφή/registration; ἀποτιμήσις/assessment) reinforce this interpretation.[15]

Seen from this perspective, the use of *κῆνσος* in pre-AD 70 Palestine is dubious and the term seems a Latinism from Mark's own time and legal context in substitution of *ἀπογραφή*, *ἀποτιμήσις*, *ἐπικεφάλαιον*, *τέλος*, or *φόρος*, the expected Greek terms to express the administrative situation in times of Jesus. Hereby, the passage Mark 12:13–17 would be an adaptation of the discussion concerning the payment of taxes over productive holdings or commercial activities to Rome in Judaea to the post-AD 70 context when a *tributum capitis* in cash was added to the tribute over lands or sales, done in kind or/and for preference in other coins in circulation like the Tyrian drachma. Needless to say, some scholars attribute both *κῆνσος* and *δηνάριον* in Mark 12:14–15 to the post-AD 70 period claiming that the Roman census in operation, i.e., a *tributum capitis* in cash, and the denarius for the payment in Jesus' time are doubtful references.[16] Assuredly, very few denarii have been recovered in I AD Palestine in comparison with the abundance of Tyrian silver coins. The Qumran hoards found during the Roland

Σεβαστοῦ ἐπὶ τῶν κηνσῶν Γαλατίας καὶ Παφλαγονίας; Reisch, *Forschungen in Ephesus*, 3:48). The third inscription testifies to the career of Alphenus Arignotus, who was appointed over the imperial census (*ἐπὶ κῆνσον τοῦ Σεβαστοῦ*) and governor (*ἔπαρχος*) of several wings and legions of the army. Very similar in context to the foregoing, it comes from an inscribed marble in Anatolian Thyatira under the emperor Caracalla, II to III century AD (*CIG* 3497= IV,1213). Out of the NT, *κῆνσος* in literature jumps to the VI century with the retrospective note of Ioannes Lydus on the administration of Constantine the Great (*Mag. Rom.* II,30; see Mason, *Greek Terms for Roman Institutions*, 61).

14. Exod 30:13; Josephus, *A.J.* 18.312; *B.J.* 7.218.

15. Josephus, *A.J.* 17.317–19; 18.2.90; 20.102; 20.181.206 (*ἱερέων δέκαται*: priests' tithes); *B.J.* 2.118.383.386.403–4,16; P. Yadin 16 (AD 127).

16. Udoh, *To Caesar What Is Caesar's*, 223–36.

de Vaux's campaigns in 1950s, for instance, only have eight denarii in 561 silver coins.[17] Judging the date from one Tyrian shekel minted in 12/11 BC and countermarked in AD 52/53 and from another coin minted as late as AD 65/66, at least one of the three lots bearing 223 units that formed the treasure seems to have been hidden before AD 70, showing that for that period the denarius was aversed by the Khirbet Qumranites for the storing of cash.[18]

The Isfiya hoard found in Mount Carmel in 1960, containing one of the largest silver coin amounts in the Levant is perhaps, the unique strong proof of a measurable quantity of Roman denarii in circulation in Palestine formerly to AD 70. It contained 160 units, of them 130 Augustan and 30 Tiberian, probably destined to the temple of Jerusalem.[19] The inconvenient is that the 160 denarii, found in two buried pots next to the ancient synagogue of Isfiya, were again accompanying a much larger amount of Tyrian currency, around 4,400 shekels and half-shekels, significantly dated from 40/39 BC to AD 53/54, the bulk of them from AD 23 to 53.[20]

For the publisher of the Isfiya hoard, the proportion of 160 denarii in 3,400 shekels and 1,000 half-shekels is no accident. According to the Mishnah (Shek. 1:6–7), the temple tax of half the Tyrian tetradrachm for each (male) Jew over the age of twenty included an interest of 4 to 8 percent when it was individually paid. The precision is odd but it likely responds to the material aspect of the smaller coins, worn due to overuse, to a practical reason, i.e., the reckoning and distribution of the temple's treasury, or to the big demand for this type of coin. If two people together paid the tax spending one single shekel, as the passage of the didrachma in Matt 17:24–27 adumbrates, then no interest was added.[21] 160 denarii are equal to 80 half-shekels, and 80 half-shekels are precisely the 8 percent of the 1,000 half-shekels present in the hoard. The proportion of 160 denarii in the hoard seems thus to be

17. De Vaux, "Fouilles de Khirbet Qumrân," 567–69.

18. Lönnqvist, *Amman Lots of the Qumran*, 3, 24–27, 32.

19. Udoh, *To Caesar What Is Caesar's*, 234–35.

20. Kadman, "Temple Dues and Currency," 69.

21. M. Shek. 1:6 establishes an additional coin for the payment of two people together. Rabbi Meir says that if the payment is for one single person giving one shekel and receiving half a shekel (in exchange), he must pay two surcharges (one for the first coin given and a second one for coin received in exchange). But m. Shek. 1:7 says that if someone pays the shekel for a poor, his neighbor, or a fellow citizen, is exempt. That must be the case of Peter and Jesus, who apparently were considered neighbors or fellow citizens from Capernaum in Matt 17:24–27. According to Rabbi Meir's opinion in m. Shek. 1:7, the charge was one *maa* (the twenty-fourth part or 4 percent of a shekel, equal to 8 percent of a half-shekel), but according to the sages it was half a *maa* (2 percent of a shekel or 4 percent of a half-shekel).

part of a big Syrian or Phoenician whip-round for the temple representing 7,800 people, or what is the same 3,400 double payments plus 1,000 single payments. The latest shekels are dated in AD 53/54, strengthening the hypothesis that the treasure was concealed in ancient Isfiya before the temple's destruction, most probably when the Romans locked the road to Jerusalem through Megiddo soon afterwards the outset of the revolt, in AD 67.[22]

The tribute in denarii before AD 70 in Judaea must be after this argumentation, solid in some points and weak in others, taken cautiously. It appears probable that the Roman denarii circulated to an undetermined degree in Palestine during Jesus' lifetime. Jews traveling to the feasts from Rome were in need of high silver denominations which the κολλυβισταί (money changers; Mark 11:15) turned into small coins or into the silver standard for the temple's services. Thence, the petition of the Roman coin in Mark 12:14–15 could be a choice of Jesus in support of his theological position to the Jewish problem on taxes by means of a physical sign, in a similar way to Mark 9:33–37 where Jesus put an end to the argument about who was the greatest summoning his disciples and taking a child to the middle. The Tyrian currency, albeit it was expectedly much more frequent in Judaea before AD 70, would not have been as suited as the Roman denarius for Jesus' reply (Mark 12:15).

Unfortunately, the other two Marcan occurrences of the Roman coin in the first miracle of the breads (Mark 6:37) and in the anointing of Jesus at Bethany (Mark 14:5) don't grant security to the previous hypothesis. The two are direct speech reports in contexts where the common Galilean coin is expected as far as the disciples mention the denarius when they need to express assumpted high economic quantities. In the first occurrence the disciples complain two hundred denarii of breads (δηναρίων διακοσίων ἄρτους) do not suffice for the multitude, while in the second a disciple, Judas Iscariot for John 12:4–5, remonstrates with the ointment the woman poured over Jesus' head, priced three hundred denarii (δηναρίων τριακοσίων). In full view of the pre-AD 70 context it is more coherent to attribute these two other occurrences of δηνάριον to the narrator: Galileans were closer to the Tyrian mint and less influenced by Roman administration under Antipas (though yet to some extent) than Judaeans. But if this is more plausible than the opposite, the researcher feels likewise attracted by the attribution of the prophetic lesson of Jesus taking the Roman coin to shut up the Pharisees and Herodians in Mark 12:13–17 to the Marcan redactional stage, and not to the report-source stage.

22. Kadman, "Temple Dues and Currency," 71–73.

The Tyrian shekel and half-shekel bore a laureate head of Melqart on the obverse and an eagle with the legend ΤΥΡΟΥ ΙΕΡΑΣ ΚΑΙ ΑΣΥΛΟΥ (*of Tyre the holy and inviolable*) on the reverse. The most common Tiberian type of denarius, smaller in size and equal to the Greek drachma, was a four-times minor denomination to the 14 g Tyrian shekel, but in grounds of iconography was in fact parallel currency, wearing on the obverse the bust of the emperor and the legend TI CAESAR DIVI AVG F AVGVSTVS (*Tiberius, Caesar Augustus, Son of the Divine Augustus*), and on the reverse a sacerdotal figure with PONTIF MAX (High Priest).[23] In Mark 12:16 Jesus asks for the image (εἰκών) and inscription (ἐπιγραφή) of the Roman denarius. Even if it is not possible to exclude the Roman coin in pre-AD 70 Jerusalem, nothing opposes Mark 12:13–17 to be a redactional adaptation of an original Tyrian shekel episode.

Latin Transliterations and Code-Switching

The loans *κοδράντης*, *κῆνσος*, and *δηνάριον* reflect Mark's redactional stage. Besides, *κοδράντης* merited commentary to the audience of the gospel, being legitimate to adjudicate, at least these three Latin loans to the intended hearers' context and to the time of the narrator. Form criticism has here to some extent, one mine to burrow. As long as the context of the three loans is Roman, research must answer if, in accordance with the Papias-Clement tradition, they belong to the situation in Rome during the mid 60s, or if they should be assigned to the Semitic east where Latin loans are equally registered. Latin words are unusual in pre-AD 70 Palestinian inscriptions. Nevertheless, the accumulated evidence of Latin influence on the Greek of the Early Roman Period of Palestine and the increasing evidence from the last third of I AD onwards provide proof of Latin usage in religious, military, and administrative epigraphical contexts before and after the First Jewish Revolt (AD 66–70).[24]

In the religious sphere, funerary examples from Jerusalem show that the capital was chosen for cemetery of Jews familiarized with Latin names,

23. Hendin, *Guide to Biblical Coins*, 444–49.

24. The inscriptions including complete or acronym Latin words in pre-AD 70 Palestine, beyond Jerusalem and Herodian and procuratorial coins, are: (a) in Joppa: CIIP 2173 (honorary Greek dedication with Latin names and imperial Latin title, AD 41–54); 2189 (funerary Greek inscription with Latin name, AD 3–6); (b) in Yavneh: CIIP 2268 (funerary Latin inscription with names, imperial, and administrative acronym titles [*l* of *liberti*; *proc* of *procuratoris*], AD 14–37); (c) in Ascalon: CIIP 2335 (honorary Greek inscription with Latin names and Latin loan [*λεγιῶνος*], before AD 65); (d) in Gaza: CIIP 2593 (Greek inscribed weight with Latin imperial title, AD 52).

perhaps those who visited Jerusalem during the feasts, the best opportunity to carry the Roman tribute of the Diaspora mentioned by Philo.[25] On the other hand, the Italian dominance made Latin a language of prestige in the eastern provinces and it is also presumable that the pre-AD 70 tomb inscriptions of Jerusalem with Latin names belonged to Palestinian Jews of medium or high status, allowing to think that Barsabbas, surnamed Justus in Acts 1:23, and our John Mark in Acts 12:12,25 were not the unique to adopt a Latin epithet or second name in the early Palestinian church.[26] We even have one chiseled limestone slab mentioning a Jewish priest and leader of synagogue with Latin patronymic recovered in the Ophel apparently from the late Second Temple period, overly meaningful to consider Latinisms were unheard in the heart of Jewish practice.[27]

25. Philo, *Embassy* 156: ἠπίστατο καὶ χρήματα συνάγοντας ἀπὸ τῶν ἀπαρχῶν ἱερὰ καὶ πέμποντας εἰς Ἱεροσόλυμα διὰ τῶν τὰς θυσίας ἀναξόντῶν (he (Octavian) knew that (the Roman Jews) collected offerings of the first-portions sending them to Jerusalem by those who raised the sacrifices).

26. The pre-AD 70 Jerusalem tomb inscriptions with Latin marks are: CIIP 28 (Greek inscribed ossuary fragment of [N]iger, a common Latin cognomen, 1 BC–AD 1); 40 (ossuary with Latin name, Johana, 1 BC–AD 1); 171 (ossuary with Latin name, [Se]cunda, 1 BC–AD 1); 222 (Greek inscribed ossuary with Latin name, Verutarion, 1 BC–AD 1); 385 (Greek inscribed ossuary with Latin name, Rufus, AD 1–70); 416 (Greek inscribed ossuary with Latin name, Africanus, 1 BC–AD 1); 421 (Aramaic-Greek inscribed ossuary fragments with Latin name, Africanus, 1 BC–AD 1); 423–24 (Greek inscribed lip of ossuary and ossuary with Latin name, Furia Africana, 1 BC–AD 1); 427 (Greek inscribed ossuary with Latin name, Justus, 1 BC–AD 1); 507 (Hebrew-Greek inscribed ossuary with Latin name, Tertia, 1 BC–AD 1); 554–55 (ossuaries with Latin name, Iulia, 1 BC–AD 1); 559 (ossuary with Latin name, Klodi[o]s, 1 BC–AD 1); 570 (ossuary with name in Latin, Marion, 1 BC–AD 1); 582 (Greek inscribed ossuary lid fragment with Latin gentilicium, Furinius, 1 BC–AD 1); 583 (Greek inscribed ossuary with possible Latin name, Popilius, 1 BC–AD 1).

27. CIIP 9 (first half): Θεόδοτος Οὐεττήνου, ἱερεὺς καὶ | ἀρχισυνάγωγος, υἱὸς ἀρχισυν[αγώ] | γου, υἱωνὸς ἀρχισυν[α]γώγου, ᾠκο | δόμησε τὴν συναγωγὴν εἰσ ἀνά[γ] νω | σ[ι]ν νόμου (Theodotos (son) of Vettenus, priest and archisynagogos, son of archisynagogos, grandson of archisynagogos, built the synagogue for the reading of the Law; limestone slab with frame 41 centimeters high, 75 centimeters wide, 1 BC–AD 1). After examining the available bibliography on Theodotos, the reasons in favor of the Herodian date have been established by Kloppenborg, "Dating Theodotos," 259–76: (a) the datable debris of an associated stratum are not later than AD 70; (b) the Latin letter *v* was commonly rendered by ου before the II AD, whereas the same letter was rendered by β in the III–IV AD (Vettenus for Οὐεττήνος instead of Βεττήνος); (c) the calligraphic tokens in the letters α, δ, ε, μ by the inscriber suggest the I AD though the paleographic criterion must not be strictly considered. Kloppenborg points out that Theodotus (son) of Vettenus doesn't seem the name of a manumitted slave since it bears a patronymic and thence CIIP 9 (= CIJ II 1404) should not be identified with the συναγωγὴ ἡ λεγόμενη Λιβερτίνων of Acts 6:9; albeit the inscription, sole archaeological vestige of a synagogue in Jerusalem in I AD, continues in my opinion to feed the evidence for the synagogues in general mentioned by Paul in Acts 24:12.

Excluding the Egyptian papyri, the extant Latinisms in the Greek of the Roman era in the Levant pertain chiefly to inscriptions and coins that have assimilated Latin titles, names, and technical vocabulary related to Roman institutions.[28] Sometimes, a Latinism can represent a specific Roman reality with no Greek equivalent, but for the most part, when the Greek equivalent was available, the higher status of Latin in an eastern Romanized territory made recommendable the inclusion of Latin terminology to underscore the Romanness of a provincial town or civilian.[29] A provincial soldier who wanted to present himself in a Greek environment as Romanized did not, for instance, necessarily have to manage the Latin language except for a family of words related to the context where he wanted his Romanness to be recognized.[30] As it has been noticed, the adopted loans by the second language frequently enjoy special connection to the culture of the first language.[31] The higher status of the imperial language recommended or

28. For the Latin influence on Egypt during the Roman period see Adam, *Bilingualism and the Latin Language*, 527–641.

29. Mason, *Greek Terms for Roman Institutions*, 19–100 brings a complete lexicon of about 1,200 Greek terms with their loci that were employed for Roman institutions. I have extracted a full secondary list comprising thirty-one Latinisms from the I–II AD Roman eastern epigraphy. A more detailed list can even be obtained checking Mason exhaustively (Latinisms studied here elsewhere and literary sources are excluded): αἰράριον (aerarium; Ancyra); ἀκκῆσσος (accensus; Lycia); ἄλη (ala; Bithynia); ἀννῶνα (annona; Apamea); ἀρουάλις (arvalis; Pergamum); αὐγουστάλις (augustalis; Ephesus); δεκέμουιρος (Xvir; Eleusis); δεκουρία (decuria; Attalia); δεκουρίων (decurio; Lydia); δίβος (divus; Lebedus); καλενδάριον (calendarium; Iconium of Laodicea); κανδιδάτος (candidatus; Ancyra); καστρῆσις (castrensis; Phrygia); κολλήγιον (collegium; Cyprus); κουαίστωρ (quaestor; Ephesus); κουρατορεύω (curator esse; Tralles); κουράτωρ (curator; Egypt); κωδικίλλος (codicillus; Ancyra); λιβράριος (librarius; Egypt); μιλιάριος (miliarius; Lydia); μονητάλις (monetalis; Megara); μουνικίπιον (municipium; Ephesus); οὐετρανός (veteranus; Ephesus); οὐῖκος (vicus; Smyrna); οὐρβανός (urbanus; Ancyra); πατρίκιος (patricius; Ephesus); σάλιος (salius; Samos); σιγγυλάρις (singularis; Alabanda); σκρεῖβα (scriba; Ephesus); τριβουνίκιος (tribunicius; Ephesus); τριουμφάλιος (triumphalis; Ephesus).

30. *CIL* III *pars prior*/5.125 has for our case an interesting Greek inscription on sarcophagus of Izra in the Syrian Hauran. It belongs to a soldier with Latin name of the III Cirenaica, the legion sited in Bostra after the creation of the Arabian province in AD 106. The translation is problematic and I prefer to break it: ΚΛ ΚΛΑΥΔΙ | ΑΝΟϹ ΟΥΕΤ | ΘΕΟΦΑΝΟΥ | LEG PP EX LEG III | Κ | ΕΠΟΙΗϹΕΝ | ΤΗΝ ϹΤΗΛΗΝ | ΙΔΙΑΙϹ ΑΥΤΟΥ | ΔΑΜΑΝΑΙϹ (*Claudius Claudianos veteran.* (*Coffin*) *of Theophanes legate for governor of the Legio III Cyrenaica. Made the funerary monument at his own expenses*). See also Adam, *Bilingualism and the Latin Language*, 299.

31. Adam, *Bilingualism and the Latin Language*, 297–305 explains the penetration of one language into another or code-switching by four compatible purposes: (a) establishment of a relationship with the addressee, i.e., solidarity, dominance, or distance; (b) expression of cultural identity; (c) belief in the superiority of a foreign language in a given context; (d) creation of a more evocative language.

obligated thus to adopt loans for memorials, epitaphs, statues, or building dedications whenever a person or town wanted to express Roman identity, even when the language to read the loans for the multitude was Koine and not Latin.

The transliterations of the second gospel are Latin constructions rendered into Greek that bear strange grammatical shape. The best recognized are the following five: (a) *δοθῆναι αὐτῇ φαγεῖν* (be given her to eat; Mark 5:43) can be the Latin *dari illi manducare* (give her to eat), though the construction has been additionally vindicated Semitic;[32] (b) *ῥαπίσμασιν αὐτὸν ἔλαβον* (with slaps they received him; Mark 14:65) may be *verberibus recipere* (received him with blows); (c) *συνβούλιον ποιήσαντες* (having made a council; Mark 15:1) can be *consilium facere* (make a council), despite that again it is not utterly odd to the LXX;[33] (d) *βουλόμενος τῷ ὄχλῳ τὸ ἱκανὸν ποιῆσαι* (wanting to do the sufficient for the crowd; Mark 15:15) may be

32. The complete clause is *καὶ εἶπεν δοθῆναι αὐτῇ φαγεῖν*. Moulton and Howard, *Grammar of New Testament Greek*, 2:448–50 pointed out that the infinitive after *εἶπεν* is not set forth in Greek Koine but appears in the LXX, where it substitutes the Hebrew construction אָמַר (say/command) + ל (to/for) + inf. MT 2 Chr 29:27: וַיֹּאמֶר חִזְקִיָּהוּ לְהַעֲלוֹת הָעֹלָה; (and Hezekiah commanded to offer the burnt offering); LXX: *καὶ εἶπεν Ἑζεκίας ἀνενέγκαι τὴν ὁλοκαύτωσιν* (and Hezekiah commanded to offer the holocaust); 2 Chr 31:11: *καὶ εἶπεν Ἑζεκίας ἑτοιμάσαι παστοφόρια* (and Hezekiah commanded to prepare the offering room). LXX Esth 1:10–11 has the construction with two present infinites, two aorist infinitives, and one asyndeton: *ὁ βασιλεύς εἶπεν τῷ Αμαν . . . εἰσαγαγεῖν τὴν βασίλισσαν πρὸς αὐτὸν βασιλεύειν αὐτὴν καὶ περιθεῖναι αὐτῇ τὸ διάδημα καὶ δεῖξαι αὐτὴν πᾶσιν τοῖς ἄρχουσιν . . . τὸ κάλλος αὐτῆς* (and the king told Aman . . . to bring the queen to him (and) to made her reign and put around her the diadem and to show her to all the chiefs . . . her beauty). More instances: 1 Chr 21:17; 2 Chr 1:18; 14:3; 29:21,30; 31:4; 35:21; Esth 6:1; Dan 2:3 (with *εἶπεν* and *θέλω*). A similar example to Mark 5:43 appears in the second miracle of the breads, Mark 8:7: *καὶ εὐλογήσας αὐτὰ εἶπεν καὶ ταῦτα παρατιθέναι* (and he blessed them and commanded to distribute them). In Mark 5:43 we find the aorist passive infinitive *δοθῆναι* with the aorist infinitive *φαγεῖν*. Mark has the infinitive *φαγεῖν* as the direct object in other turns, some with forms of *δίδωμι* (Mark 2:26; 3:20 with passive infinitive *δύνασθαι*; 6:31,37 with imperative *δότε*).

33. In Mark 3:6 we have *συνβούλιον ἐδίδουν κατ' αὐτοῦ* (gave counsel against him). According to Pryke, *Redactional Style*, 88, it can be retraced to Aramaic regardless that he doesn't afford any example. Matt 27:1 and 12:14 have *συνβούλιον ἔλαβον* (took council). In the Greek OT I have found three cases of *βουλή* with forms of *ποιέω*. In Isa 29:15: *ἐν κρυφῇ βουλὴν ποιοῦντες* (making a counsel in secrecy) for לַסְתִּר עֵצָה (to conceal a counsel); Isa 30:1 is very alike to Mark 15:1: *ἐποιήσατε βουλήν* (made a counsel); Prov 1:25: *ἐποιεῖτε βουλάς* (made counsels).

volens turba satisfacere (wanting to satisfy the crowd);[34] (e) τιθέντες τὰ γόνατα (placing the knees; Mark 15:19) may be *ponentes genua* (putting the knees).[35]

Several possible sources of latinization give the reason for the Marcan loans and transliterations. First, they can be yielded by a Greek learner whose first language is Latin and for whom the second language is still not mastered. Mark's linguistic skill is lower than, for instance 1 Peter and Hebrews, and lower too than the competence Paul displays in the epistles, but does manage an intermediate level of Greek, superior to the author of the fourth gospel and complex enough to discard a beginner. Another possible source would be a Greek learned in a heavily Latin influenced milieu. Greek communities in Rome could influence in that way over a learner, but in this possibility, as in the first one, an additional grammar impinge on Mark beyond the extant Latin loans and transliterations should be noted. On the other hand, the Semitic interference in Mark excludes Latin as the major influence under the surface of the Greek of the document: we can be confident that Mark learned his Greek in a Semitized milieu or from a heavily Semitized source like the LXX.

A third likely origin of the Latin loans and transliterations would be therefore the limited Latin impact over a Greek milieu. A Roman colony in the east, the enrollment of provincial auxiliaries in the Roman army, or the working engagement cheek by jowl with Roman administration, borrowing some expressions and loans as a result of Roman dependency or with the intention to emphasize the aspiration to Roman status but preserving the general first language grammar different from Latin, illustrates this possibility. The number of loans and transliterations would be notorious, but not massive as they should be in the first two options and as the Semitic interference is over the second gospel. Finally, the fourth possibility, that in many

34. Incigneri, *Gospel to the Romans*, 102 meritoriously explains Mark 15:15 from the division of *satisfacere* in two components—*satis*, translated ἱκανός, and *facere*, ποιῆσαι—which Mark would have been compelled to settle on because there is not a single Greek word for a literal translation of *satisfacere*. In Mark 15:1–15 there are two alleged Latin transliterations—συνβούλιον ποιήσαντες (Mark 15:1; see foregoing note for a very akin expression in Isa 30:1) and τὸ ἱκανὸν ποιῆσαι (Mark 15:15)—using the verb ποιέω, but the high frequence of forms of this verb in the section suggests that the author had not been forced in its selection: ποιήσαντες (15:1), πεποιήκεισαν (15:7), ἐποίει (15:8), ποιήσω (15:12), ἐποίησεν (15:14), ποιῆσαι (15:15).

35. Kneeling before Jesus suggests a theological motif of the second gospel. Mark 3:10: ἐπιπίπτειν αὐτῷ; 3:11: προσέπιπτον αὐτῷ; 5:6: προσεκύνησεν αὐτῷ; 5:22: πίπτει πρὸς τοὺς πόδας αὐτοῦ; 5:33: προσέπεσεν αὐτῷ; 7:25: προσέπεσεν πρὸς τοὺς πόδας αὐτοῦ; 10:17: γονυπετήσας αὐτὸν; 14:35: ἔπιπτεν τῆς γῆς (Jesus before God). Seeing this variance, τιθέντες τὰ γόνατα in Mark 15:39 as Latin transliteration calls for prudence.

aspects must be considered variant of the third, is the intention more or less conscious of a Greek speaker to sound Romanized towards his audience.

If the lists of Latin loans and transliterations are compared, it becomes overt that four of the twelve loans (φραγελλόω, πραιτώριον, κεντυρίων, αἰτία) share with three of the alleged five transliterations (Mark 15:1.15.19) the occurrence during the contact of Jesus with the Romans[36]. Another significant fact is that the loan-words, maybe with the exception of κράββατος, belong to the military and administrative fields (discussed anew in next chapter). This must not be a coincidence in view of the penetration Latin has toiled in the Greek inscriptions of the Roman East along the I–II centuries AD.[37] It has been stated that the Latinims in Mark should be better explained by the Greek learned in Rome and not in another milieu of the empire.[38] But if the utterance is correct, we should expect loan-words from wider spectrum of semantic fields, including food, dress, or domestic customs, not from two single related groups. Considering that in some eastern territories, two of the major tasks of Roman administration were the levying of taxes and the policy, the two semantic fields of the Marcan Latin words must be, not an indication of the Greek learned in Rome, but of the Greek influenced by the Roman army and administration out of Italy.[39] Yet, it is possible to carry the research further.

Alleged Latin Style. Parataxis

The Marcan overuse of *καί* in the level of sentence syntax can, theoretically be matched with ancient colloquial Latin where several linked clauses by conjunctions must have expressed a quick motion of thought. Though the registry varies and the construction stresses there the intention to sound evocative, the chain of coordinate clauses somewhat comparable with the oral speech at the base of any language have been registered by the Roman poets and will be illustrated with three unadorned translated examples, two from Ovid (43 BC–AD 18) and one from Propertius (50 BC–AD 2) where the use of the conjunctions *et*/*-que* (and) for coordination predominates.[40]

36. This was noted by Turner, "Style of Mark," 235.

37. See some notes above.

38. Brown and Meier, *Antioch and Rome*, 196–97; Incigneri, *Gospel to the Romans*, 101–3; Taylor, *St. Mark*, 32, 45.

39. Similarly Marcus, "Sitz im Leben of Mark," 443–45.

40. Roman poets and comedians might bring more instances oddly noticed in modern versions as far as superfluous words tend to be avoided or altered to stress similar beauty or effect in the translation level. I only take here some few additional from the aforementioned authors (see Lindsay, *Syntax of Plautus*, 128 for some more

Propertius, Elegiarum 1.5:15–17: et tremulus maestis orietur fletibus horror, et timor informem ducet in ore notam, et quaecumque voles fugient tibi verba querenti (and the trembling horror will be born with sorrowful tears, and the formed fear will (be) mold(ed) on the marked face, and whatever complaining words you will desire (to say) will flee from you). Ovid, Metamorphoses 2.429–30: ridet et audit, et sibi praeferri se gaudet et oscula iungit (laughs and listens, and rejoys himself for being preferred, and unites the kisses); 7.202–6: nubilaque induco, ventos abogoque vocoque, vipereas rumpo verbis et carmine fauces, vivaque saxa sua convulsaque robora terra, et silvas moveo iubeoque tremescere montis, et mugire solum manesque exiri sepulcris! (and the clouds I drive, and the winds I expel and convene, the vipers' throat I break with (my) words and poem, and the living rocks and the plucked oaks from their earth, and I move the forests and I order the mount to tremble, and bellow to the ground and to the Manes come out from the tombs!).[41]

For comparison with Mark, we take hither but two examples of paratactic καί, one short and one long. Mark 8:22: Καὶ ἔρχονται εἰς Βηθσαϊδάν. Καὶ φέρουσιν αὐτῷ τυφλὸν καὶ παρακαλοῦσιν αὐτὸν ἵνα αὐτοῦ ἅψηται (And they come to Bethsaida. And they bring him a blind man and they beg him that he would touch him). Mark 10:33–34: καὶ ὁ υἱὸς τοῦ ἀνθρώπου παραδοθήσεται τοῖς ἀρχιερεῦσιν καὶ τοῖς γραμματεῦσιν, καὶ κατακρινοῦσιν αὐτὸν θανάτῳ καὶ παραδώσουσιν αὐτὸν τοῖς ἔθνεσιν καὶ ἐμπαίξουσιν αὐτῷ καὶ ἐμπτύσουσιν

---

instances in Plautus). Paratactic *et* (and)/*nec* (and not, neither)/*-que* (and): Propertius, *Elegiarum* 1.1:4–7: 2:11–14; 8:24–26,31–36; 13:27–29; 14:3–5; 2.5:21–24; 10:2–4; 13:19–22; 31:10–12; 3.5:3–6; Ovid, *Metam.* 2.669–72; 758–59. The idiom is close to the repetitive syndetic *et/nec*, though there its function is not the coordination of clauses but the link of nouns or noun phrases (see also notes below). It doesn't match, thus, the category of parataxis, but inasmuch it includes repetition of the conjunction we bring here too some examples: Ovid, *Metam.* 4.503: *et scelus et lacrimas rabiemque et caedis amorem* (and crime and tears and furor and from the carnage the love); Propertius, *Elegiarum* 1.1:23; 2.12:23–24; 28:53–54. Mixed examples: Ovid, *Metam.* 3.217–26 (seven syndetic *et*, seven syndetic *-que*, plus four coordinating *et*, one coordinating *-que*, and one coordinating *nec*); 8.302–17 (eight syndetic *et*, thirteen syndetic *-que*, plus four coordinating *et*, two coordinating *-que*, and one coordinating *nec*). In Mark, repetition of pure syndetic *καί* in long sequence is found only in 3:16–19. Greek authors know the idiom. Very illustrative: Periplus Maris Erythraei (AD 40–70) 6,8,24,28,29,48,49,56, etc. Others: Diodorus, *Bibl. Hist.* 1.12:6; 87:6; 96:2; 2.2:3; Strabo, *Geog.* 1.1:1,10,16; 2:6,14,18; 15.3:18, etc.

41. Since the verb is lacking, it's difficult to determine the syntactical function of the enclitic *-que* in the verse *vivaque saxa sua convulsaque robora terra*. *Viva* is the plural of *vivum* (living) and *convulsa* an adjectival participle (plucking), concording with the neuter *robora* (oaks). The first more than the second *-que* seems to introduce a coordinate clause, but unless we provide at least one verb, for instance *facio* (I make), it remains suspended and dependent on the next verb. See also below.

αὐτῷ καὶ μαστιγώσουσιν αὐτὸν καὶ ἀποκτενοῦσιν, καὶ μετὰ τρεῖς ἡμέρας ἀναστήσεται (and the Son of the Man will be delivered to the chief priests and to the scribes, and they will condemn him to death and will deliver him to the Gentiles and will mock him and will spit upon him and will beat him and will kill him, and after three days he will rise).[42]

One preliminary consideration for discernment, is that if the Marcan paratactic καί were the effect of Latin influence, we should expect more tokens in this grammatical direction in the western family of ancient mss.[43] In Codex Bezae, for example, that has a parallel Latin text *d* in the opposite sheet to the Greek D, the frequency of simple parataxis with καί from the scribe's milieu into the second gospel should be expected larger than in the critical WH edition that gives prominence to two oriental mss, B and א.[44] But occasionally D has parataxis in Mark whereas Westcott–Hort has not along with *d*, and other times D uses subordinate particles where WH parataxis.[45] The correlation between simple parataxis in D and Latin influence from *d* is difficult to establish, all the more when the editor of D underscored notorious Latin inflections over D.[46] Consequently, the paratactic style in

42. In the clause καὶ ὁ υἱὸς τοῦ ἀνθρώπου παραδοθήσεται τοῖς ἀρχιερεῦσιν καὶ τοῖς γραμματεῦσιν, the first καί (and) coordinates this clause with the previous one, but the second καί (and), non-paratactic, joins two noun phrases (τοῖς ἀρχιερεῦσιν and τοῖς γραμματεῦσιν).

43. In this paragraph and in the paragraph devoted to the Marcan Sower (4:3–9) I will take and further develop the brilliant insights of Black, *Aramaic Approach to the Gospels*, 67–69.

44. Examples of D parataxis where WH has hypotaxis, mainly with participle (from Black, *Aramaic Approach to the Gospels*, 68–69; parentheses mine): Mark 2:12 (WH λέγοντας); 2:16 (WH ἰδόντες); 4:36 (WH ἀφέντες); 6:45 (WH ἕως); 7:6 (WH ὡς); 8:10 (WH ἐμβάς); 8:26 (WH λέγων); 10:16 (WH τιθείς); 10:22 (WH στυγνάσας); 12:20 (ἀποθνήσκων); 14:4 (WH one less καί); 14:22 (WH εὐλογήσας); 14:57 (WH λέγοντες); 16:4 (WH ἀναβλέψασαι). Striking are the D cases of καί after a subordinating participle and before the verb of the main action. Appreciably superfluous or ungrammatical, we are here perhaps before scribal errors: Mark 11:2 (WH λύσατε); 14:63 (WH lacks καί); 15:46 (WH begins a new sentence). It must be added, before the hypotactic participle Mark 1:13 (WH lacks καί); also Mark 15:1, where D has understood a new clause; 15:2 (WH δέ postpositive); 15:23 (WH ὅς).

45. καί is almost always a coordinating conjunction (= and), but as a conjunction can introduce coordinate and subordinate clauses alike. This last usage resembles the subordinating καί we analyzed in the Semitic section, but differs notably in that subordinating καί has there a hypotactic function by itself, whereas in a subordinate clause introduced by καί, the hypotactic function rests on another word, be it another conjunction specific of subordination or a participle (underlined in the first set of D examples below, next to following note).

46. The Bezaean textual order ascribes the codex to the western family, Matthew, John, Luke, Mark, Catholic Epistles (only a fragment of 3 John is extant), and Acts. Besides, many recognizable forms entered D from the scribe's milieu, proposed to be Gaul

D Mark mustn't be seen as a Latinism because when we find the paratactic construction in the WH Mark we should, accordingly, expect its presence in D, and when we find a parataxis in *d* Mark along with non-western mss, it should again be found in D and WH.[47]

But stronger is the argument hailed from the LXX comparison where καί renders the Hebrew clause beginning with *waw*/ו consecutive. The style of the second gospel is so akin to the Septuagint that the hypothesis of possible Latin oral influence over the Marcan paratactic καί would be defensible only if OT literature is ignored. The first thousand words of the second gospel (Mark 1:1—2:17) have fifty-one independent clauses beginning with καί while δέ postpositive only occurs five times in the same usage. In the middle of the gospel, Mark has fifty-four clauses beginning with καί for eight δέ (Mark 8:1—9:21). The last thousand words of the gospel (Mark 14:6b—16:8) raises the rate, but its proportion still is close to 2/1 with forty-one καί for twenty-six δέ. Similar rates appear in LXX literature, with fifty-one independent clauses beginning with καί for zero with δέ in the first thousand words of the story of David (1 Sam 16:1—17:37), forty-nine

by the editor, where the Cantabrigiensis was created around the end of the V century from a Greek original that was copied into D, translated into Latin d, and arranged by parallel verses, D against d, in opposite folios. Western particularities in calligraphy apart, we have visible Latinisms in letters and terminations entering the Greek words: τυbλοί (Matt 11:5); ἀπέσταlκεν (John 5:38); MAPCON (Fol. 296b title); gαζοφυλάκιον (Mark 12:43); APOST (Fol. 469b title); θηνσαυρός from *thensaurus* (Matt 2:11; 13:44); σαμαριτανῶν from *samaritanorun* (Matt 10:5); δανιήλου from *danielum* (Matt 24:15); λεπρωσοῦ from *leprosi* (Matt 26:6); λεγειώνης from *legiones* (Matt 26:53); φλαγελλώσας from *flagir caesus* (Matt 27:26; Mark 15:15); πέτρους from *petrus* (John 13:24); ἔχετες from *habetis* (Mark 6:38); γραββάτοις from *grabattis* (Mark 6:55); the symbol * instead of δηναρίων (Mark 14:5); βασιλεούς (Mark 15:26); κρῆτης καὶ ἄραβοι from *cretenses et arabi* (Acts 2:11); τοὺς ἀκούοντες (Acts 5:11); ἀκούσαντες from *audientes* (Acts 17:8). For a full discussion see Scrivener, *Bezae Codex*, xviii–xliv.

47. Examples of D hypotaxis with WH parataxis are Mark 1:37: καὶ <u>ὅτε</u> εὗρον αὐτὸν λέγουσιν αὐτῷ (and <u>when</u> they found him they tell him; D); καὶ εὗρον αὐτὸν <u>καὶ</u> λέγουσιν αὐτῷ (WH); 6:13: καὶ <u>ἀλείψαντες</u> ἐλέῳ πολλοὺσ ἀρρωστοὺς ἐθεράπευον (and <u>having anointed</u> with oil cured many sick (people); D; ἐλέῳ = ἐλαίῳ); καὶ ἤλειφον ἐλαίῳ πολλοὺς ἀρρωστοὺς <u>καὶ</u> ἐθεράπευον (and anointed with oil <u>and</u> cured many sick (people); WH); 11:4: καὶ <u>ἀπέλθοντες</u> εὗρον πῶλλον δεδεμένον (and <u>having gone</u> they found a colt tied; D); καὶ ἀπῆλθον <u>καὶ</u> εὗρον πῶλλον δεδεμένον (and they went <u>and</u> they found a colt tied; WH). More instances in the list of Black, *Aramaic Approach to the Gospels*, 67–69: Mark 2:15; 4:38; 5:28; 6:7,22,34; 7:28; 8:25,33; 14:13; 15:24. Additionally, I found the same pattern in Mark 4:38; 5:21,38; 6:26,50,55; 11:17; 14:54. Finally, WH cases of paratactic καί absent in D are: Mark 2:6 (D δέ postpositive); 2:7 (D δέ postpositive); 5:5,26; 8:14; 9:5; 10:30,41; 11:14,33; 14:26 (D τότε); 14:54,67,69 (= D 14:68); 15:24. After the scrutiny of D and WH, I must correct Black, *Aramaic Approach to the Gospels*, 67. WH paratactic incidence in Mark is not much smaller than D, but the contrary. D parataxis absent in WH: twenty-one cases. WH parataxis absent in D: thirty-seven.

initial καί for one δέ in the cycle of Elisha (2 Kgs 2:19—4:8), or forty-seven καί for three δέ for the same length in Judges (1:1—2:2). Lesser paratactic LXX literature but yet high can be found in Ruth (1:1—2:22) with forty-one καί for seven δέ, the story of Abraham (Gen 12:1—14:9), twenty-one καί for fifteen δέ, and in the section 1 Macc 14:1–44, twenty-five καί for three δέ. The average καί/δέ for chapters 1–4, 6, and 39 of Genesis—taken for good Koine and therefore ruling out lack of idiomatic expertise on the part of the narrator, has been found in 6/1.

Random sections of non-paratactic Jewish authors bear very low rates for similar lengths, two καί for eleven δέ in one thousand words of Paul to the Romans (3:1—5:10), one for thirteen in Philo (*Embassy* 197–215), and one for sixteen in Josephus (*B.J.* 2.1—2.2). Contemporary Hellenistic authors show identical low rates in random sections of one thousand words with four καί for twenty δέ in Diodorus (*Bibl. Hist.* 5.1:1—5.5:4), three for twenty-four in Strabo (*Geog.* 3.1:1–6), and four for twenty-two in Plutarch (*Alex.* 10.1—14.3). Other reckonings of καί/δέ throw averages of 0.5/1 in Paul and 0.36/1 in Josephus, and of 0.24/1, 0.6/1, and 0.44/1 in Plutarch, Polybius, and Epictetus. Shepherd (Sim. 25.1—30.2) is not the exception, with four independent clauses beginning with καί for ten δέ postpositive; Roman production, it yet remains far off from Mark. Herm. Sim. 25.1—30.2 resembles the middle and final parts of the fourth gospel, where we find five καί for thirteen δέ in John 10:1—11:20, and nine καί for twelve δέ in 19:23—20:31, though the first part of John is tangibly paratactic, with twenty-one καί for ten δέ in one thousand words in John 1:19—2:24. In the NT only Revelation approaches Mark and the LXX with thirty-one καί for zero δέ in one thousand words in the first third (4:1—6:14), thirty καί for zero δέ in the middle section (13:1—15:1), and thirty-one καί for one δέ at the end (20:14—22:17). In sum, the peering of the Marcan simple parataxis leads to a diaphanous conclusion: the overuse of καί in the second gospel is not a Latinism, nor Hellenistic Greek. It is a Semitism, whose better Greek antecedent is LXX literature and its most akin NT partner Revelation.[48]

Notwithstanding, that the best correlation to the most prominent Semitism in Mark comes from LXX literature doesn't constrain to cease research, believing Mark is always following LXX style whenever we find any Semitic feature. Indeed, one burning question, extremely arduous, grazed by the present study but beyond its aim, is the discernment of the Semitic influence that has entered Mark from the imitation of LXX and Hebrew literature, which degree comes off from the I AD oral Aramaic that can be attributed to the author of the second gospel, and which to the primitive

48. The counts are mine. For the averages I rely on Maloney, *Semitic Interference*, 67.

tradition on Jesus he works with. To this respect, it is noteworthy that consistent parataxis in Jesus' parables, i.e., parataxis predominance over hypotaxis in non-independent clauses, only appears in Mark among the synoptics whereas Matthew and Luke develop more literary style from the point of view of subordinate construction.[49]

In the Sower (Mark 4:3–9), for instance, Mark lacks any hypotactic aorist participle, plenty in other sections, to express an action before the main verb.[50] On the contrary, the Matthean parallel has one absolute genitive with aorist participle, ἡλίου δὲ ἀνατείλαντος ἐκαυματίσθη (having the sun risen, they were burnt; Matt 13:6), where Mark 4:6 has the less cultured but yet correct ὅτε ἀνέτειλεν ὁ ἥλιος ἐκαυματίσθη (when the sun raised, they were burnt), whereas Luke has three subordinating aorists in three verses, φυὲν ἐξηράνθη (having grown, it was dried; Luke 8:6), συμφυεῖσαι αἱ ἄκανθαι ἀπέπνιξαν αὐτό (having grown with, the thorn plants choked it; Luke 8:7), and φυὲν ἐποίησεν καρπὸν (having grown, it produced fruit; Luke 8:8). In the Sower, Marks prefers current subordination with ὅπου (where; Mark 4:5); διά (because of; Mark 4:5,6); ὅτε (when—cited above; Mark 4:6); and the less clear implicit paratactic imperative ἀκουέτω (let him listen; Mark 4:9). Against the

49. Pure Semitic style would tend to refrain from subordinating participles since the idiom is rare in Hebrew and Aramaic. For sections of the same length, the statistics in Martin, *Semitic Sources in Greek Documents*, 34–35 give one adverbial participle in translation Greek (LXX and Θ´) against at least three hypotactic participles in original Greek authors (Plutarch's *Lives*; Polybius, books 1–2; Epictetus, books 3–4; Josephus, *C. Ap./A.J.*, and Egyptian papyri). The difference heightens to one hypotactic participle in LXX 1 Kgs 17 and in the LXX version over Aramaic sections of Ezra for every ten in original Greek, or to one in LXX 1 Sam 3; 4; 22, and the LXX translation over Hebrew Dan and Ezra for four in non-translation Greek.

50. Just before the Sower we can bring the next hypotactic aorist participles: Mark 3:5: καὶ περιβλεψάμενος αὐτοὺς μετ' ὀργῆς . . . λέγει (and having looked around them with anger . . . he told); Mark 3:21: καὶ ἀκούσαντες οἱ παρ' αὐτοῦ ἐξῆλθον (and having those around him heard (about him) they went out = when those around him heard); Mark 3:23 καὶ προσκαλεσάμενος αὐτοὺς ἐν παραβολαῖς ἔλεγεν αὐτοῖς (and having called them, he told them in parables = when he called them). More examples in the previous section: Mark 3:6 (ἐξελθόντες); 3:27 (εἰσελθών); 3:31 (στήκοντες); 3:33 (ἀποκριθείς); 3:34 (περιβλεψάμενος). It should be observed that the Sower is perfectly convertible using the hypotactic participle, especially the coordinated simple aorist ἔπεσεν (it fell; Mark 4:4,5,7,8) for πεσόν (having it fallen = when it fell). The Marcan hypotactic aorist participle cases can be amply multiplied. I only give two for each of the resting chapters: Mark 1:21 (εἰσελθών) 1:35 (ἀναστάς); 2:1 (εἰσελθών); 2:16 (ἰδόντες); 4:18 (ἀκούσαντες); 4:39 (διεγερθείς); 5:2 (ἐξελθόντος); 5:6 (ἰδών); 6:46 (ἀποταξάμενος); 6:48 (ἰδών) 7:2 (ἰδόντες); 7:14 (προσκαλεσάμενος); 8:23 (πτύσας, ἐπιθείς); 8:34 (προσκαλεσάμενος); 9:14 (ἐλθόντες); 9:25 (ἰδών); 10:1 (ἀναστάς); 10:41 (ἀκούσαντες); 11:11 (περιβλεψάμενος); 11:12 (ἐξελθόντων); 12:41 (καθίσας); 12:43 (προσκαλεσάμενος); 13:13 (ὑπομείνας); 13:43 (ἐλθών); 14:3 (συντρίψασα); 14:26 (ὑμνήσαντες); 15:1 (ποιήσαντες); 15:35 (ἀκούσαντες); 16:1 (διαγενομένου); 16:2 (ἀνατείλαντος).

Matthean and Lucan parallels, here the less literary Marcan Sower sidestepping the aorist participle draws near the direct translation from Aramaic.[51]

Beyond the Sower, the Aramaic original substratum of Mark may have included sayings, other parables, and a collection of events, this last more or less chronologically organized though perhaps not yet out of the oral tradition. But in regards to the task of gleaning from the grammatical imprints which exact sections correspond in Mark to the primitive Aramaic substratum he works over, and which to his redactional stage, the Marcan Sower and perhaps some few more examples could be pearls in the sand. Beyond parataxis and dismissing doubtful cases, the remaining categories of Semitism studied in our second chapter give 121 instances to the narrative parts of Mark for 89 in direct speech, being all the categories except pleonastic ἤρξατο/ἤρξαντο (he/they began to) represented in Jesus and the narrator alike.[52]

The equally concentrated Semitic interference in narrative sections and in direct speech stiffens the impossibility to ascertain, uniquely upon this criterion, if the second gospel is a Greek edition from a Semitic original. Hints to find the Aramaic substratum in Mark like bizarre Greek terms or even whole clauses which become intelligible or more evocative when retranslated into Aramaic uncover the presence of the primitive tradition and the job of Mark as Greek translator, but the real extension of this pre-Marcan substratum solely in base of Aramaic compatibility, despite the method's great intuition, will result misleading.[53] To discriminate in this level the

51. Black, *Aramaic Approach to the Gospels*, 63–64. Although the Marcan Sower seems to reflect Semitic style, the implicit paratactic ἀκουέτω in Mark 4:9, similarly to Mark 2:11 ἔγειρε ἆρον (wake up, take) and Mark 4:39 σιώπα, πεφίμωσο (be silent, silence), is not necessarily Semitic (Taylor, *St. Mark*, 57–58).

52. (A) Subordinating καί: narrator 2, Jesus 2. (B) Asyndeta: narrator 15, Jesus 28, others 9. (C) Parallel and redundant speech: narrator 10, Jesus 15, others 3. (D) Pleonastic ἤρξατο/ἤρξαντο + inf.: narrator 26, Jesus 0. (E) καὶ ἐγένετο + circumstantial complement: narrator 3, Jesus 1. (F) Redundant pronouns and personal pronouns following casus pendens: narrator 4, Jesus 7, others 1. (G) Prepositions (repetition in a series, instrumental ἐν, imperative and epexegetical ἵνα): narrator 28, Jesus 6, others 6. (H) Adjectives, numerals, distributives, and adverbials: narrator 10, Jesus 5. (I) ὁ υἱὸς τοῦ ἀνθρώπου: narrator 3, Jesus 11. (J) Other Semitic expressions: narrator 20, Jesus 3, others 2. Totals of Semitic interference: evangelist 89, Jesus 68, other characters 21.

53. It is not here the occasion to dive deep into the problem disclosed by the agreements of Matthew and Luke against Mark in the parallels to the three. Burkett, *Rethinking the Gospel Sources*, 7–42 studies numerous Marcan favorite terms (πολύς, πάλιν, ἴδε, ἔφη, ἐναγκαλισάμενος, ἦν/ἦσαν + participle, περιβλέπομαι, forms of διδάσκω, ἀναστάς, etc.) absent each time in both Matthew and Luke when they follow the common source to Mark. Being impossible that Matthew and Luke agreed in the omission of the same words each time if the two depended on canonical Mark, a pre-Marcan source must be admitted (proto-Mark), or an epitome (deutero-Mark) of canonical Mark which fell

pre-Marcan materials from the final editor, to be Aramaic oral witness behind or/and possible lesser Aramaic pre-written units of the Jesus tradition, the Aramaic compatibility will result the necessary diagnostic criterion only when collated with ancillary resources, like the synoptic comparison or the identification of literary devices employed to sew single episodes into longer sections, but even in these circumstances will not always be totally reliable.[54]

---

in their hands (Burkett, *Rethinking the Gospel Sources*, 133–42). The first option, the pre-Marcan source, obligates to defer the retranslation into Aramaic to a second filter since the Aramaic-compatible sections of canonical Mark may contain elements of pre-Marcan material and of secondary edition by the Semitized narrator likewise. Aramaic compatibility alone is not thus an infallible criterion to reach the original gospel (see further discussion in next note). On the other hand, it appears more plausible in my view that a pre-Marcan source already gospel-fashioned existed than the possibility of Matthew and Luke working over the resume of canonical Mark. It is improbable (though still possible) that the author of the pre-Marcan source acted against the general rule of all times and didn't return any more to his work. Under this assumption, Mark would have edited conservatively—again in my view—the common source, namely, the first edition of his own gospel, whereas Matthew and Luke, occupied with the inclusion of Q, the enarrations of infancy, more elaborated accounts of resurrection, other materials, and the worry for more underscoring the divine image of Jesus, would have left the pre-Marcan source in the primitive shape oftentimes, and modified it divergently from canonical Mark others (like the episode of Gerasa/Gadara with two demoniacs in Matt 8:28–34 stressing the divine power of Jesus instead of one in Mark 5:1–20, or the stunning earthquake in Matt 28:2 absent in Mark 16:4). Burkett, *Rethinking the Gospel Sources*, 60–132 defends canonical Mark conflating two earlier versions—proto-Mark A, common to Matthew, and proto-Mark B, common to Luke—that will explain the many duplicates of information in Mark, who would have preserved the divergences of proto-A and proto-B. However, some of the minor Marcan duplicates might result in cases of Semitic redundancy or emphatic style; but the double account of the Miracle of the Breads (Mark 6:30–44;8:1–10) asks for another reason. The proto-Mark theory, which must turn true after exhaustive synoptic contrast, not aimed at the present monograph, has driven me to spare the ultimate precision on Mark's gospel date for a next encounter with the reader.

54. Doudna, *Greek of the Gospel of Mark*, 128–36 admitted that translation Greek is not the necessary hypothesis, though he finally concluded Semitic interference was constant enough in Mark to consider translation hand under the whole gospel including narrative parts. The impossibility to unravel here this riddle doesn't inhibit me from conceding to the reader one expression in Mark 3:20–21 as a random prototype for the problem on Aramaic reconstruction of the gospel. Mark 3:20–21 fits well the task since the passage is originally Marcan, for which there is no synoptic parallel: Καὶ ἔρχεται *εἰς οἶκον· καὶ συνέρχεται πάλιν ὁ ὄχλος, ὥστε μὴ δύνασθαι αὐτοὺς μηδὲ ἄρτον φαγεῖν. καὶ ἀκούσαντες* <u>*οἱ παρ' αὐτοῦ*</u> *ἐξῆλθον κρατῆσαι αὐτόν* (And he comes to home: and a crowd comes together again so that they were not able to eat, not even bread. And having heard (it) <u>those of him</u> went out to hold him). Here Casey, *Aramaic Sources of Mark*, 150–51 suggests that the original Aramaic term under *οἱ παρ' αὐτοῦ* (those of him = his family), אֲחוּהִי (his kinsmen), explains its occurrence at the expense of other possible Greek words. According to him, the notion of Jesus being seized by his mother and brothers, given by the context of verse 21, would have inclined Mark in the rendering of

It is not totally out of time to remember that examining some Marcan hallmarks not yet considered since they usually fall out of Semitic categories, εὐθύς (immediately), γάρ explanatory (for/because), and πάλιν (again), we attain but the same uncertainty insofar they are regularly present in redactional verses as much as they are in source verses.[55]

Women's Rights to Divorce and Ban of Remarriage in Mark 10:12

Beyond the general grammar of the second gospel doesn't pinpoint Italian provenance, more on the contrary a Semitic milieu, the Roman roots of the second gospel author continue to have in the Latin loans a stronghold, further underpinned by the passages where the Roman reading appears to be the most suitable, one of which is found in the second part of the Marcan

---

אֱחוּהִי towards the expression οἱ παρ' αὐτοῦ instead of the expected οἱ ἀδελφοὶ αὐτοῦ (his brethren/kinsmen), which, despite being the direct rendering of אֱחוּהִי, didn't include his mother, further commented in Mark 3:31–35, only his brothers. At first sight, the retranslated term under the expression οἱ παρ' αὐτοῦ added to the context supplies the reason for the expression. Notwithstanding, the sole conversion to Aramaic, despite its congruence, doesn't prove to be the original. At least in the verses where no synoptic parallel is at hand, Mark could be writing in Greek without any Aramaic document before his eyes. Moreover, אֱחוּהִי is not an indispensable step to arrive at the expression οἱ παρ' αὐτοῦ. The Greek level of Mark is advanced enough to conceive, directly, the expression because bilingual speakers don't always think beforehand of what they are to say in their mother tongue and then render it into the language of the target culture. Grammatical structures and vices stemming from the native language interference stand in the mental matrix of the second language until it is perfectly mastered, but soon the bilingual speaker is able to compose directly from his own mental baggage concepts and creations in the second language. In conclusion, the existence of an Aramaic document behind Mark in this particular is one possibility, but he could had also been working with mental remembrances of the primitive tradition, with oral reports from fellow Christians present in the room where Mark composed the gospel, or simply producing his own Greek version of the facts from incomplete traditional reports.

55. I assume the brainy study of Pryke, *Redactional Style*, 32–135, glimpsing here from his handy lists a small heap of distinctive Marcan usages in apparent pure traditional materials: (a) εὐθύς (immediately): Mark 4:5,15,16,17,29 (parables and Jesus teaching); 11:3 (saying); (b) πάλιν (again): Mark 11:3 (saying); 12:4 (parable); (c) impersonal verb subject: Mark 13:9,11 (prophecy); (d) ὥστε + inf. (in order that): Mark 2:28 (saying); 4:32 (parable); 10:8 (teaching); (e) two or more participles before or after the main verb: Mark 13:34 (parable); (f) γάρ explanatory (for/because): Mark 4:22,25 (parable and saying); 7:10,21,27 (teaching); 8:35,36,37,38 (teaching); 9:39,40 (teaching and saying); 10:14 (saying); 10:27 (teaching); 12:14 (Herodians/Pharisees); 12:23 (Sadducees); 12:25,44 (teaching); 13:19,33,35 (prediction, warning, and parable); 14:5 (one in Simon the Leper's house); 14:7 (teaching); 14:70 (bystanders in the chief priest's palace).

teaching on divorce (10:11–12). Mark 10:12 bans the possibility of a woman remarrying after divorcing her consort, seemingly assuming therefore the existence of women's rights to divorce. The suspicion of editorial material in Mark 10:12 is levied because the possibility of women divorcing their husbands is not contemplated in the synoptic parallels (Matt 5:32; 19:9; Luke 19:18): *καὶ ἐὰν αὐτὴ ἀπολύσασα τὸν ἄνδρα αὐτῆς γαμήσῃ ἄλλον μοιχᾶται* (and if she, having divorced her husband marries another, commits adultery). Further, the practice hinted by Mark 10:12 sharply contrasts with the general Jewish custom of the I AD, allowing straightforwardly to suppose, the editorial warning of the second gospel author (through the words of Jesus) towards a Romanized audience.

Justin's *2 Apo.* 2.1–20 reports the first extant account of Christian martyrdom outside the NT, disgracefully triggered—against her will—by a Christian Roman woman who gave the bill of divorce (*ῥεπούδιον*) to her husband, remediless perverted in Alexandria. The conceited husband, contra-denounced her but was unable to win over the woman's defense, so he then lashed out against one Ptolemy, who had introduced the woman into the Christian faith. Ptolemy was taken to the prefect of Rome. Urbicus I (AD 146–50), with all likelihood instigated by a centurion, friend of the perverted husband, sentenced Ptolemy, who was accompanied to death by two other confessed Christians that protested against the unjust Urbicus, one of them named Lucius. Despite the Christian woman in Justin is not said to wed again, Mark 10:12 can be read against the report, assuring the ground for the hypothesis that Roman women's rights to divorce didn't disappear forthwith in the early church of Rome.[56]

56. Lampe, *From Paul to Valentinus*, 237–40, 296–97 suggests this woman is Flora, addressee of the Letter of Ptolemy, Valentinian of the II century, also to be identified with the teacher in Justin, *2 Apol.* 2. The Letter to Flora, entirely preserved in Epiphanius, *Pan.* 33.3–7, describes the doctrine of the Gnostic Ptolemy in private teaching. Carefully written, in it Ptolemy sees the Pentateuch divided in three partitions upon the scheme of the divine essence emanations: the pure Law of the Ten Commandments bestowed by the pure good God, Father of Jesus, other Mosaic laws corresponding to the Demiurge, and the commandments the Jewish elders later introduced in the Scriptures. Besides the platonic furnishing, the Letter to Flora witnesses the NT usage by Ptolemy. Direct quotations: *Pan.* 33.3:5//Matt 12:15; 4:4//Matt 19:6,8; 4:12 + 5:7//Matt 15:4–9; 5:15//1 Cor 5:7; 6:2–3//Matt 5:38–39; 6:6//Rom 7:12. Allusions: *Pan.* 33.3:6//John 1:1,3; 3:7//John 1:18; 6:6//Eph 2:15; 7:5//Matt 19:17. In the letter we have thus four direct Matthean quotations (Matt 5:38–39; 12:25; 15:4–9; 19:6,8) plus one Matthean paraphrase (Matt 19:17). Of the five, four have Marcan parallels: Matt 12:25// Mark 3:24–25; Matt 15:4–5//Mark 7:10–12; Matt 19:6,8//Mark 10:5–6,8; Matt 19:17// Mark 10:18; but the form in the letter agrees in the four with Matthew against a Marcan source. The absence of Mark in the Letter to Flora would be an extra proof of the low esteem and perhaps unemployment of the second gospel in the mid-II AD city of Rome. For the Gnostic Ptolemy see also Irenaeus, *Haer.* 1.11:3; 12:1.

Roman marriage was bilateral, requiring the consent of the paterfamilias if he was alive, but divorce was unilateral, and neither of the two needed documentary proof. In practice, then as now, it was less difficult to divorce than to marry. By the I century AD, it seems that either the wife or the husband under Roman law could seek divorce without any external authorization, usually sending a simple notification (*repudium mittere*) to the spouse often by a freedman.[57] From the late Republic downwards, fluctuations of political interests made the divorce one of the most common phenomena in leisured women. High rate of men mortality added to the divorce anticipated at least two marriages during the fertile period, not infrequently some more in the consular elites.[58]

Women divorcing their husbands was such a common practice in the I AD, that lifted the complaint of Seneca the Younger (4 BC–AD 65): *Numquid iam ulla repudio erubescit, postquam illustres quaedam ac nobiles feminae non consulum numero sed maritorum annos suos conputant et exeunt matrimonii causa, nubunt repudii?* (Is there now any that ashames with the divorce, after some illustrious and noble women not by the number of the consuls but of their husbands reckon the years and go out of the marriage, (and) marry (again) with the pretext of divorce?; *Ben.* 3.16:2).[59]

It appears hence tenable that Mark 10:12 envisages an Italian audience, but it will be too naive to dispatch the question on Jewish women divorce kicking out the Palestinian Talmud which records some circumstances the Jewish women could exploit to force the divorce (y.Ketubot 5.10; 7.7,10–11). Despite the PT belongs to the IV AD, two of the four mishnayot holding the rights of women to separate from their husbands come from Rabban Simeon ben Gamliel and Rebbi Meïr, sages of the fourth Tannaitic generation, or in other words commentators of the Mishnah in the II century.[60] The teaching could be looking to earlier times considering that Jewish

57. Treggiari, "Divorce Roman Style," 31–46.

58. Bradley, "Upper-Class Roman Family," 79–98.

59. Juvenal, *Satirae* 6.229–30 on the frivolity of the early-II AD Roman upper-class lady: *sic fiunt octo mariti quinque per autumnos* (thus, eight husbands succeed per five autumns).

60. Y. Ketubot 7.10 (translation of Guggenheimer, *Talmud First Order*, 15–16; parentheses mine): "Rabban Simeon ben Gamliel says, if it was a major defect, e.g., blind in one eye, amputated of one of his hands, lame in one of his legs, immediately he shall divorce and pay the ketubah" (upon the wife's request); 7.11: "For all these (impediments) says Rebbi Meïr that, even if he contracted with her (= he informed her of his impediment before the marriage), she can say "I thought that I could stand it, now I cannot stand it." The other two mishnayot belong to the fifth Amoraitic generation (AD 350–375), emphasize more the will of the wife to divorce upon her criteria, accusing the husband physical impediments or not. Y. Ketubot 5.10: "Rebbi Yose said: Those

ketubot including female rights to divorce were documented among the well preserved Elephantine papyri from the V century BC.[61]

In last place, the colophon to the discussion whether Jesus in Mark 10:12 is describing a Jewish worry or whether we are before Marcan redactionism, must weigh up Roman women had to claim divorce in Hellenistic centers in the edge of Palestine, sheltering Jewish neighborhoods from ancient times. Thence had to emerge a non-disgusting matter of discussion for the Pharisees of the I AD taking further in minds that Palestine was under Roman influence and that the Jewish upper classes traveled around and imitated the Roman customs. This was plain in the marriage of Antipas, the ruler of Galilee, with Herodias, which required she divorced first Antipas' half-brother Philip.[62] According to the collation of Josephus *A.J.* 18.116–19 with Mark 6:16–28, Antipas' scandal splashed out to the Jewish lower classes and made roll the Baptist's head.[63] It had to provoke some commentary on the part of Jesus and it could have provided the Pharisees

who write (in the ketubah): "If he hates, is she hates; that is a monetary condition (for the unilateral divorce) and these conditions are valid"; 7.7: "Rebbi Mana said to them, bring the ketubah that we may read it. They brought the ketubah and found written in it: If this X marries this Y as her husband and should no longer desire his company, she shall take half the ketubah sum."

61. Cowley, *Aramaic Papyri* 15:22–26 (441 BC) decoded: "Tomorrow or another day (if) Miphtahiah should stand up in the congregation and say, I divorce Ashor my husband, the price of divorce (shall be) on her head; she shall return to the scales and weigh out to Ashor the sum of 7 shekels 2 R and all that I have put into her hand she shall give up, both shred (?) and thread, and she shall go away whither she will, without suit or process"; also Kraeling, *Brooklyn Museum*, 2:9–10 (449 BC); 7:24–25 (420 BC). Friedman, "Upon the Wife's Request," 36–46 translated the next and other three similar examples from the Geniza documents of the X–XI centuries AD, suggesting that the formula for female rights to divorce of y. Ketub. 7.7 and the Elephantine papyri was continued for centuries: "And if this Maliha hates this Sa'id, her husband, and desires to go out from his house, she will lose her ketubba money and will take nothing except that which she brought from her fathers' house, that alone, and she will go out with the permission of the court and on the authority of our lords the rabbis."

62. Josephus, *A.J.* 18.5: Ἡρωδίας ἐπὶ συγχύσει φρονήσασα τῶν πατρίων Ἡρώδῃ γαμεῖται (Herodias married Herod deciding on the violation of the laws of the country).

63. According to Mark 6:19–20, Herodias wanted to kill the Baptist but was hindered from it by the fact that Antipas feared (ἐφοβεῖτο) John because he was righteous and holy (δίκαιον καὶ ἅγιον). Josephus, *A.J.* 18.116–19 gives the political reason for his murder in the fortress of Machaerus. It was consequence of his popularity: Antipas feared the increasing size of the Baptist's movement, as suggested by Matt 14:5. John's intrusion in Antipas' marital life once the scandal was unavoidable in the territory of the sovereign where John preached probably was the final excuse to eliminate John. Mark 6:20 also utters that Antipas heard John gladly (ἡδέως). The precision, avoided in Matt 14:5, can be an editorial supposition of Mark, but it can be a *lectio difficilior* holding historical data from the early stage of John the Baptist's mission.

the excuse to trample him. Paul, addressing Corinthian converts seems to testify that women's rights to divorce attracted the attention of Jesus the teacher (1 Cor: 7:10–11): *τοῖς δὲ γεγαμηκόσιν παραγγέλλω, οὐκ ἐγὼ ἀλλὰ ὁ κύριος, γυναῖκα ἀπὸ ἀνδρὸς μὴ χωρισθῆναι* (but to those (who) have married I command, not me but the Lord, (that the) woman from (the) husband doesn't separate). Was then the ban of women's divorce an original Jesus' input into Christian tradition?

In this sense the Marcan question on divorce (10:2–12) is a discussion with the Pharisees whose conclusion is deeper teaching to Jesus' disciples (10:10–12), as we see in the twofolded narrative frame for the teaching on purity (7:1–13 and 7:17–23, if we excuse 7:14–15). The story-telling thread of Mark 10:2–12 is analogous to Mark 7:1–23, but in Mark 10:2–12 the wording marks for obtaining the independent narrative unit are more on view or have been worse disguised. Indeed, the Marcan question on divorce bears signs of a displaced pericope. Mark 10:1 places the scene in Judaea or Peraea, whilst the conclusion in Mark 10:11 at all lights occurs again in the house (*εἰς τὴν οἰκίαν πάλιν*) of Capernaum mentioned in Mark 9:33. The sayings on divorce can belong to the primitive Palestinian tradition, but the whole hides editorial hand, becoming factible at least three alternatives after plucking up all the foregoing elements: (a) women's rights to divorce in Mark 10:12 pertain to Jesus' lifespan and milieu, i.e., Palestine; (b) they belong to the narrator and to the Italian context; (c) they belong to the narrator's time, but to the same eastern context as Jesus'.[64]

Mark 15: Pilate the Prefect and His Centurion's Faith Confession

Another attempt towards the search of the Italian print is the analysis of the Roman characters during the trial of Jesus, Pilate and the soldiers, and of more possible clues of Roman influence over the text. If Mark really was written in Rome as tradition asserts, and if the Italian pressure was strong enough to introduce a number of Latinisms, it could be expected also some kind of influence over the narrative dealing with the Roman characters. Peter's death under Nero reported by Tertullian points to a persecution burst against the Christians around AD 66–67, close upheaval to the date when,

64. Mark 9:33: Καὶ ἦλθον εἰς Καφαρναούμ. Καὶ ἐν τῇ οἰκίᾳ γενόμενος ἐπηρώτα αὐτούς (And they came to Capernaum. And being he in the house asked them). Mark 10:1: Καὶ ἐκεῖθεν ἀναστὰς ἔρχεται εἰς τὰ ὅρια τῆς Ἰουδαίας καὶ πέραν τοῦ Ἰορδάνου (And having departed from there he comes to the territories of Judaea and beyond the Jordan). Mark 10:10: Καὶ εἰς τὴν οἰκίαν πάλιν οἱ μαθηταὶ περὶ τούτου ἐπηρώτων αὐτόν (And in the house again the disciples asked him concerning this).

depending on the Papias-Clement tradition the gospel of Mark was written down. If Mark was fixed under Roman context just after Nero's savage persecution, then it should be possible to pull the rope and find anti-Roman tones along the gospel.

It is a matter of fact that Mark among the four gospels is the least charitable in the put on scene of Pilate, the major Roman character, whereas Luke is probably not by chance, the most bountiful. Seemingly, the treatment of Pilate and the several persecution forecastings in Mark could be interpreted from an Italian context, but there are intrinsic reasons to the gospel and the serious external one of the First Jewish War (AD 66–70) against Rome in Palestinian territory to refuse the hypothesis, or if it can not be driven out, to lower its credibility. Influenced by the liturgical proclamation of John's gospel on the Good Friday, the Catholic obedience has accidentaly spread the belief in the south-occidental countries that Pilate wanted to release Jesus during the trial and that it only was under strain of the chief priests that he was compelled to appeased them condemning Jesus to the cross. On the contrary, careful reading of Pilate's allocutions in Mark 15 challenges this view, suggesting Pilate wanted to condemn Jesus, and that his intention to release Jesus was not pure at all.

The four gospels show it was customary in Jerusalem the liberation of a prisoner on the Passover (Matt 27:15–17; Mark 15:6–9; Luke 23:18–19; John 18:38b–40). In the four, Pilate apparently exploits the excuse to persuade the Jews of the convenience to release Jesus. The motif is plain in Matthew, Luke, and John, and from them the reading of Mark can be misunderstood. But doing the opposite, first approaching Mark and making therefrom the collation of the other three, a divergent profile of Pilate emerges. Matthew, Luke, and John develop the motif to highlight Jesus' innocence, widen the guilt of the chief priests and, it could be, diminish the responsibility of Pilate for the crucifixion of Jesus. In Mark, the way Pilate speaks of Jesus to the crowd, using twice the incisive epithet βασιλεὺς τῶν Ἰουδαίων (king of the Jews; Mark 15:9,12) knowing it was on account of envy of the chief priests (διὰ φθόνον; Mark 15:10) that Jesus had been delivered, seems ironic, and the manners Pilate deals with the mob and the elders shadow his intention to acquit Jesus. By contrary, the defense of Jesus is reduced to one indirect allocution in Mark (Mark 15:14), and the single verse where the inclinations of Pilate are specified reveals he was liable to satisfy the crowd (βουλόμενος τῷ ὄχλῳ τὸ ἱκανὸν ποιῆσαι; Mark 15:15), not to set Jesus free.[65]

65. Matthew follows Mark (or proto-Mark) for the passion trial, but as usual in the parallel sections, different niceties are found. In this sense Matt 27:23 parallels Mark 15:14, but counterbalances the slight defense of Jesus' innocence in Mark, introducing the dream of Pilate's wife (Matt 27:19), the washing of hands (Matt 27:24), and the

The role Josephus displays of Pilate is ambiguous, melting the dialogue with the Jews, i.e., the pacific denouement of the imperial ensign scandal, and the relentless methods to quench tumults, i.e., the killing of Samaritans and the barbarous extinction of a riot in Jerusalem, club in hand.[66] For certain, Josephus points out the fierce personality of Pilate when his soldiers staved to death dissident Jews who were protesting for the misappropriation Pilate made of the temple's treasury to fund an aqueduct, or when his henchmen heartlessly chastised innocent Samaritan villagers along with those suspicious of rebellion in Mount Gerizim.[67] But contrasted against

crowd's self-declaration of guilt upon Jesus' death (Matt 27:25), a last motif better understandable if read from a post-AD 70 perspective. John, with Mark 15:2–4 and Matt 27:11–13, draws attention to the harsh personality of the Roman governor in the first conversation with Jesus (John 18:33–35). Notwithstanding, he adds one more interview with the prefect and the tension possibly is felt more in the second interview than in the first one (John 19:9–11). John, going beyond Mark and Matthew, underlines that Pilate considered Jesus innocent of the charges he was accused of with three allocutions in direct speech (John 18:38; 19:4,6) and makes explicit once more that the Roman wanted to release Jesus when he comments on the actions of Pilate (ἐζήτει ἀπολῦσαι αὐτόν; John 19:12). John's treatment of Pilate's personality is, in accordance with Matthew, more polarized than Mark's. John's benefic treatment of Pilate, thus, must be seen next to the humiliation by the cohort in the praetorium (John 19:1–3, an episode common to Matt 27:27–31 and Mark 15:16–20), and to Jesus' exposure wearing the crown of thorns and the purple robe (John 19:5,14, absent from the other gospels). Luke shares with John the confession of Jesus' innocence by Pilate and the explicit intention to set Jesus free, but adds one allocution to the three of John and two declarations of his will to release Jesus to the single one of John. In Luke, the Roman governor twice states he doesn't find any of the charges Jesus had been accused of (οὐδὲν εὑρίσκω αἴτιον; Luke 23:4; οὐθὲν εὗρον . . . αἴτιον; Luke 23:14), and another two there is nothing worthy of death in Jesus (οὐδὲν ἄξιον θανάτου ἐστὶν αὐτῷ; Luke 23:15; οὐδὲν αἴτιον θανάτου εὗρον; Luke 23:22). Equal to John, Luke says once in reported speech that Pilate wanted to release Jesus (Luke 23:20), but has two in direct not present in John, Mark, or Matthew (Luke 23:16,22). In the third gospel Pilate doesn't threaten Jesus or impose authority when he interrogates him (Luke 23:1–5), and neither does Pilate berate Jesus in the following verses. The prefect neither insists in the title of Messiah (Χριστός; Matt 27:17,22) or in the title King of the Jews when he speaks to the crowd. After the profile of Pilate has been likened between the four gospels, the benign treatment of Luke emanates. The intervention of Pilate in Luke is unique, where the bad personality elements have disappeared. The conclusion crystalizes if the focus highlights the way the soldiers interact with Jesus. The Lucan troop is not as bountiful as Pilate's because the soldiers mock Jesus hanging on the cross (Luke 23:36), but the big scorn in the praetorium—Jesus dressed in purple and saluted as king by the Roman cohort—doesn't appear (Matt 27:27–31; Mark 15:16–20; John 19:1–3). On the contrary, the Lucan scene of the robe occurs in the palace of Herod Antipas (Luke 23:7–11), and it was Herod and his guard who despised Jesus with the purple (Luke 23:11), not the Roman soldiers.

66. Josephus, *A.J.* 18.55–62.85–87; *B.J.* 2.169–81.

67. This is the last certain happening in the life of Pilate, AD 36/37: before Vitellius, at that time governor of the Syrian province, the council of the Samaritans accused

Mark, as a whole, Pilate's profile in Josephus yields a not incompatible outcome. In the episode of the imperial images that Pilate introduced in Jerusalem, albeit finally he threatened the Jews with the capital punishment if they didn't cease in their supplication, no blood was poured and Josephus shows Pilate hearing the Jewish delegation for six days. This means that the simple, harsh, and ironic treatment of Pilate in Mark, playing two cards with the mob and the chief priests but finally dooming Jesus to crucifixion is historically plausible and that the Roman setting for the second gospel is expendable to explain how the intervention of Pilate has been related.

Curiously, we find the Roman governor's relentless character in the Lucan report of the Galileans whose blood Pilate mingled with the sacrifices they were offering (Luke 13:1–3), perhaps a lost reference to the episode of the aqueduct. It is worth noting that the episode of the Galileans only known to Luke crashes with the soft Pilate during the Lucan trial of Jesus, excepting the fact that in the four gospels Roman authority crucified Jesus, something that cannot be alleged as lenient treat (Matt 27:26; Mark 15:15; Luke 23:24; John 19:16). To a degree Mark neither fails to this contrast, but the difference has more to do in the second evangelist with one middle rank officer of Pilate's soldiers than with the Roman governor.

Following the humiliation in the praetorium by the troop, once Jesus has been led to the Golgotha, Mark reports a faith confession of the centurion custodying the cross. This surprising confession, considering that from the reader's standpoint this centurion presumably witnessed (if not provoked!) the scene of the praetorium, comes after Jesus' last breath: ἀληθῶς οὗτος ὁ ἄνθρωπος υἱὸς θεοῦ ἦν (truly this man was Son of God; Mark 15:39). Exegesis mostly elucidates the confession from the messianic secret, particular to the second gospel. Mark 15:39 is the last of the confessional series (Mark 1:11,24; 3:11; 5:7; 8:29; 9:7; 10:48) and the culmination of the messianic tension that has nailed Jesus to the cross.[68] The tension increases

Pilate of murdering guiltless peasants, and Pilate was commissioned to Rome to account for the matter, but Emperor Tiberius died before Pontius arrived (Josephus, *A.J.* 18.88–89). Henceforth, Pilate's fate is uncertain.

68. The rest of the confessions in Mark, seven in number, ensure the Mark 15:39 translation above instead of the less messianic *truly this man was a son of God*. Mark 1:11 (speaks God): ὁ υἱός μου ὁ ἀγαπήτος (my beloved Son); Mark 1:24 (a demoniac): ὁ ἅγιος τοῦ θεοῦ (the Saint of God); Mark 3:11 (an unclean spirit): ὁ υἱὸς τοῦ θεοῦ (the Son of God); Mark 5:7 (the Gerasene demoniac): υἱὲ τοῦ θεοῦ ὑψίστου (Son of God the Most High); Mark 8:29 (Peter): ὁ χριστός (the Christ); Mark 9:7 (God): ὁ υἱός μου ὁ ἀγαπήτος (my Son, the Beloved One); Mark 10:48 (Bartimaeus): υἱὲ Δαυίδ (son of David). In indirect speech, Mark 1:1 can be added in representation of the narrator's faith: 'Ιησοῦ Χριστοῦ [υἱοῦ θεοῦ] (Jesus Christ Son of God; being the words in brackets doubtfully original due to the strong support of the short reading 'Ιησοῦ Χριστοῦ in B, D, and W; Metzger, *Greek New Testament*, 73); and Mark 16:19 of the long ending as

to a maximum during the trial of Jesus. He is seven times addressed by messianic titles, most ironic from the position of the narrative characters and towards which Mark 15:39 is staked as antithetic conclusion (Mark 14:61; 15:2,9,12,18,26,32).[69]

Taking into account that one soldier of Pilate confesses Jesus in the cross, not a disciple or one of the Galilean women, it becomes reasonable to suppose Mark 15:39 conceals a reference to the Gentile members of Mark's community, represented anywhere else by the translation of Semitic words, the explaining of Jewish customs, and in some degree by Latinisms. Besides, the inference that the first Gentile converts around AD 40 are related to a member amidst the military personnel under the Roman governor for Judaea in Caesarea (Acts 10:34—11:18), the household of Cornelius the centurion (Acts 10:1–33), is very remarkable, and it is to a similar extent that they were introduced into the faith by (the gospel of) Peter because according to Paul, Peter was entrusted with the ministry for the circumcised, not for the uncircumcised (Gal 2:8).[70]

well: Ὁ . . . κύριος Ἰησοῦς (The . . . Lord Jesus; most probably being the long ending a later addition, absent in א and B; Metzger, *Greek New Testament*, 122–26).

69. Iverson, "Centurion's Confession," 334–36 underscores that nothing proves Mark 15:39 to be ironic, and that aside from the adverb ἀληθῶς, unambiguous in the second gospel (Mark 12:14; 14:70), the centurion's confession lacks the usual Marcan commentary to clarify an ironic meaning of the direct speech. In Mark 14:66–72, for example, the command to prophecy the Jewish guard give Jesus is described as part of a mockery, and it similarly occurs in Mark 15:16–20 when the Roman troop salutes Jesus as king, or in Mark 15:29–32, where the title King of Israel serves to insult Jesus.

70. For Álvarez, "Centurion's Statement," 149–59, Mark 15:39 would be a *restitutio memoriae* in service of Gentile Christians tempted to see a failed Son of God on the cross. The inconvenience to this supposition is that moving Mark over OT references the parallel between Jesus' death and the *damnatio memoriae* of Nero, Galba, and Vitellius before Vespasian's reign doesn't sound convincing. On the other hand, the resurrection announcement restituted Jesus' memory in the 30s and the Christian community was not in need of an urgent *restitutio* at the time Mark was written. To a lesser degree, but yet out of historical ground, is the suggestion of Álvarez, "Centurion's Statement," 157 that Jesus' miracles present him surpassing Vespasian's deified power. A Hellenistic literary tradition benefiting the comprehension of the divine Jesus is expected in the eastern Mediterranean basin. Despite this, the second gospel miracle motif moves on the OT and Mark's readers are invited to partake in Jewish categories. Yarbro, "Mark and His Readers," 100 admits υἱὸς θεοῦ at first expressed a messianic conviction but, owing much to an assumed standpoint in her foregoing dissertation, doesn't develop the inference. The traditions on Asclepius and Demeter deserve careful study but the OT directly parallels Jesus' baptism, the transfiguration, and healings, theophanies and miracles Yarbro, "Mark and His Readers," 87–95 discusses (LXX Exod 19:9,11; 34:29–35; 40:34; 1 Kgs 17:8–24; 19:11–18; 2 Kgs 2:19–24; 4:8–10,32–37,42–44; 5:8–14; 6:33). As Yarbro states, Christians of Gentile origin would have been inclined to understand Mark in terms of their own cultural context, but we don't know to what extent their scheme would have remained intact after the baptismal catechesis.

In Acts 10:1, the cohort to which Cornelius belongs is called Italian (σπείρης τῆς καλουμένης Ἰταλικῆς), plausibly a real one. An epitaph at Carnuntum in Austria, dated to AD 69–70, records the seven years service of the archer Proculus Rabili of Philadelphia in the army of Syria under the *cohors II Italica civium Romanorum.*[71] The patronymic, Rabi'a, is Nabataean, permitting to identify Philadelphia with Amman-Philadelphia, less than one hundred kilometers from Jerusalem through the pass of Jericho. Noteworthy, the inscription reveals that the vexillation of Proculus was part of the II Italian Cohort belonging to the Syrian army. Syria was governed by an imperial legate, Petronius (AD 39–41/42) in times of Cornelius. The prefect of Caesarea directly depended for bigger things in the Syrian legate and in strict sense until Judaea acquired the status of procuratorial province (AD 70), for replacements the Caesarean detachments had to be considered part of the Syrian army.[72] It is quite possible thus, that the Judaean regiments occasionally or in a permanent way shared units with the Syrian army, and that on Cornelius the centurion of the cohort called Italian lodged in Caesarea rest historical data.[73]

Legion, the Evil Spirit of Mark 5:1–20

Scholarship has thrown into relief that the long pericope of the Gerasene (Mark 5:1–20) evocates an anti-Roman conflict going back to the First Jewish Revolt (AD 66–70) and that tradition could have elaborated from the model of a Christian exorcism. The interest Mark has devoted to the making up of the passage is patent in the description of the possessed, maniac

71. ILS 9168 (given in minuscule): *Proculus | Rabili f. Col. | Philadel., mil. | optio coh. II | Italic. c. R. 7 Fa[us]tini, ex. vexil. sa | git. exer. Syriaci, stip. VII, vixit an. | XXVI, | Apuleius frater | f.c.*, dated in AD 69/70 from the locus Tacitus, *Historiae* 2.83 mentioning the shipment of Syrian troops to Italy in support of Vespasian's candidature.

72. The stone of Pilate, a fragment of limestone slab measuring 82 centimeters high, 66 centimeters wide, 21 centimeters deep, found by the Italian mission in the theater of Caesarea in 1961, possibly dedicates a building that bears the emperor's name. Dated to AD 31–36, it proves that before Claudius (AD 41–54) the head of the Judaean province held the title of prefect, not procurator: [---]S TIBERIEUM | [-PO]NTIUS PILATUS | [PRAEF]ECTUS IUDA[EA]E | [-----ʹ----] (Lehmann–Holum, *Joint Expedition to Caesarea*, 67–70).

73. Broughton, *Beginning of Christianity*, 5:441–43. In the ten years Pilate governed over Judaea (AD 26–36), the bulk of Roman forces probably consisted in three thousand auxiliary recruits, divided into infantry cohorts (σπεῖραι) and cavalry wings (εἴλαι), possibly the same five Syrians (of Caesarea) and Samaritan regiments inherited by Agrippa I (AD 41/42–44), according to Josephus, *A.J.* 19.9 (Speidel, "Roman Army in Judaea," 233–37). For a discussion of the Roman military presence in Judaea AD 6–130 see Zeichmann, "Military Forces in Judaea," 86–120.

dwelling in the sepulchers that no one could subdue even stringing him with chains and fetters, a tormented demoniac who cried out in the mountains and cuts himself against the rocks that with three verses is the most dramatized character of the second gospel (Mark 5:3–5). The name of the evil spirit, λεγιὼν ὄνομά μοι, ὅτι πολλοί ἐσμεν (Legion is my name, because we are many; Mark 5:9), the fact that the spirits before being cast out begged Jesus to be sent to the pigs that were pasturing (Mark 5:12), the round number of two thousand swines rushed into the sea (ὡς δισχίλιοι; Mark 5:13), and the extension of the episode, all denotes a hidden motif in the composition of the pericope.[74]

The passage, already discussed, is located on the oriental shore of the sea of Galilee, territory highly reminiscent of the First Jewish War. Gadara, Gamala, and their surroundings east of the lake underwent painstaking combats in AD 67 between the insurgents and the Roman troops. Many Jews were sword-passed, villages burnt up, and the survivors enslaved, scene extensible to Jotapata north of Sepphoris in Middle Galilee and to Tarichae-Magdala on the western shore of the lake.[75] For the primitive Judeo-Christian believer it should not have been difficult to spot in Mark 5:1–20 the emotive blend of the pig, shameful creature for Judaism, and the λεγιών, name for the demons that couldn't pass unaware after the burst of the Roman squadrons.[76] The inference is reinforced once more by the recent exegetical heritage considering that one of the three legions that razed the oriental territories to the sea of Galilee was *Legio X Fretensis*, Roman elite unit whose vexillum exhibited the emblem of the wild boar.[77]

74. There are four episodes portraying exorcisms with some detail in the second gospel, the Gerasene being the longest with twenty verses (Mark 5:1–20). Then it comes the Healing of a Boy with a Spirit, fifteen verses (Mark 9:14–29); the Syrophoenician's Daughter, six verses (Mark 7:24–30); and the Man with an Unclean Spirit, five verses (Mark 1:23–28). Aside, Mark has six or seven reports/commentaries on exorcisms, all along the Galilean part of the gospel: 1:32–34; 3:11–12; 3:15; 3:22–27; 6:7,13; 9:38–41.

75. Josephus, *B.J.* 3.141–306.316–91.462–511.522–31; 4.1–83. Josephus, commander of the Galilean insurgents, will surrender to Vespasian after the future emperor besieged Jotapata the summer of AD 67 (*B.J.* 3.392.)

76. The evocation of the Roman army by means of the name λεγιών can be taken as unmistakable, though the many ramifications Dormandy, "Expulsion of Legion," 335–37 and Garroway, "Mustard Seed," 70–73 extract from the antinomy Jesus (God)-legion (Roman Empire) belong to the speculative sphere (less ambitious is Boring, *Mark*, 147–55). Garroway, "Mustard Seed," 70–75 slightly forces Scripture reading the conclusion to the demoniac's healing, i.e., the spread of the miracle through the Decapolis (Mark 5:19–20), from the increase of the mustard seed (Mark 4:30–32), i.e., the kingdom of God growing from the small.

77. See for instance Dąbrowa, *Legio X Fretensis*, 318–20. Previous military feats granted the Xth legion maritime insignias, the galley, the dolphin, and the god Neptune,

The anti-Roman coloring of the Gerasene, points out an audience of Jewish origin. Since the anti-Roman taste fits Nero's persecution too, we could inquire whether the suggested audience is not a Roman community of Judeo-Christian origin. However, the persecution of Nero must be seen as the private business of the emperor and the Praetorian Guard. The likely exclusion of the war legions as such during Nero's persecution and the unquestionable Palestinian orientation of the pericope make the conciliation with the Gerasene in the stage of composition scarcely more consistent than a mirage. At any event the recognizable anti-Roman flavor of the Gerasene clashes with the pro-Roman elements of the second gospel, i.e., the use of Latin words (the official language of the Roman legions), transliterations, and the centurion's faith confession in Mark 15:39; altogether, hinder the reduction of the exegetical perspective. Perhaps, the solution to the problem springing from confronted parts of the second gospel rests on a middle position, i.e., a historical ground that ensures the transmission of different provenance traditions arranged in the narration under the form of pericopes, without reaching the unquestionable driving thread the scholar is enticed to find.

A Roman Reading for Mark 13:9–13

One further attempt to solve the enigma of the second gospel composition place in favor of its Italian origin, supported by the Latinims and the reliability of the Papias-Clement tradition, can be raised from passages where persecution to Christians is announced (Mark 4:17; 8:34–35; 10:29–31; 10:38–39; 13:9–13). The composition *terminus post quem* for these passages would ideally be from AD 64 to 67, the severe persecution of Nero ensuing the fires in Rome, when Peter feated the crown of martyrdom according to tradition, or scant years thereafter. Even if the Roman milieu is not considered the foremost composition hub for the Marcan persecution announcements, the Roman hermeneutics remains feasible and can't be ruled out.[78]

but its main icon in the I AD was the wild boar, standing from left to right, usually represented on brick stamps and coins (Barag, "Stamp-Impressions of the Legio X," 245–64). In spite of the strong reminiscences, the biggest difficulty Zeichmann, "Military Forces in Judaea," 99 finds to relate Mark 5:1–20 and Legio X Fretensis comes from the reference to Gerasa, where during the Jewish War it never was stationed, but the difficulty easily disappears admitting the geographical error of Gerasa for Gadara in Mark 5:1, shown by the already discussed corrected verse, Matt 8:28.

78. In the saying on renouncement (Mark 10:29–30), Jesus promises a hundredfold reward (ἑκατονταπλασίονα) and foreshadows persecutions (μετὰ διωγμῶν). The Roman reading is possible because the particular can be understood in the general, but the inverse, to account for the verses by means of the persecution under Nero, forces the text. In Mark 10:29–30 Jesus answers Peter's question on missionary disinterestedness (Mark

Nevertheless, a brief return to Mark 13:9–13, the most obvious persecution prediction, demonstrates that the Roman orientation of the text must be partial to be successful.[79]

The emerging Christian mission embraced territories to the north and west of Palestine, wherein individuals who opposed the new faith could deliver the followers of Jesus to Roman authorities. Among the persecutions the early church underwent, that of Nero appears the fiercest and in the first exegetical check could be fitting context for Mark 13:9–13.[80] It's certain

---

10:28). The mission foreseen in Mark 10:28–30 comprises Rome in the 60s (and all the missions), but since the Christian mission began in the 30s and the persecution the same, it is inessential to see there exclusively the persecution under Nero. The author of the second gospel could have it in mind, but the text doesn't prove it. The parallel Donahue, "Windows and Mirrors," 15–16 finds on the occurrence of persecution (διωγμός) in Mark 4:17 (the explaining for 4:5–6) and 10:30 is ingenious, but the lecture of the seed that falls in rocky ground—easily growing but suddenly scorched (4:5–6)—from Peter's eagerness to follow Jesus to the cross but ending in failure (14:29–30,66–72) neither accounts for the text. We have again the particular read from the general. The Sower (4:3–9) and its explanation (4:13–20), moves all time in common experiences. Rather, the position of 4:5–6 next to agricultural teachings (4:26–32) doesn't allow the reading from Peter's denying.

79. The Roman context as the unquestionable key to many of the Marcan passages, including Mark 13:9–1,3 is systematically adopted by Brian J. Incigneri, who is served by form criticism to such an extent that builds in some matters over increasingly debatable floors. For instance: Incigneri, *Gospel to the Romans*, 78–82, a bold extension of the author's thesis, for whom the request to leave houses (οἰχίαν) and fields (ἀγρούς) in Mark 10:29 must preferablly be understood from the Roman environment, forgetting that a semi-urban landscape was the rule in Palestinian towns; and judging unnecessary the scene of the Cyrenee (Mark 15:21), who for him perhaps represents those coming into Rome from the countryside. Incigneri, 108–14, dispensing with the historic plausibility of Jesus in the Judaean desert and the parallel John the Baptist-Jesus (Mark 1:1–13), abruptly considers Mark 1:13, Jesus with the animals in the wilderness, a reference to the beasts of the Roman circus where Christians are called to find Jesus in their martyrdom. Incigneri, 194–202 reads Mark 12:13–17, the question on paying taxes, from an Italian position, obviating the theological problem on taxes to the empire was in Palestine at least from Judas the Galilee in AD 6; Incigneri, 225–28 considers Mark 4:11–12, the kingdom of God hidden to strangers, and itself a parallel to Isa 6:9–10, as referring to Roman persecutions wherein it was imperative to keep the faith in secret; Incigneri, 241–47 reads the trial of Jesus in terms of a story Rome-modeled where the praetorium and the soldiers' procedures shall be elements taken from what Mark knew of Rome, emptying Mark of historical interest in Jesus and making inconceivable why would he resort to this archetype destined to Christians who could verify the truth by asking believers who had traveled to or resided in Jerusalem, or even the more long-lived who knew the crucifixion of Jesus by experience.

80. Tacitus, *Annals* 15.44 describes the severe punishment Nero wrecked against the Christians to appease the social indignation after the two fires that destroyed Rome in AD 64 (15.38–43), eaten by dogs and burned alive at nightfall like human torches for the public spectacle. A multitude of Christians were persecuted, convicted, and executed more for hatred of them than for being suspicious of the arson *(multitudo*

that for Mark 13:10, before the persecution comes, the gospel must face the universal mission and be preached to all the nations (καὶ εἰς πάντα τὰ ἔθνε πρῶτον δεῖ κηρυχθῆναι τὸ εὐαγγέλιον), apparently setting hence the persecution of Mark 13:9 in a late date that harmonizes well with Nero's reign. All the same, the chosen terms don't express geographical preference. Mark 13:9 lists two institutions to which the Christians shall be delivered, συνέδρια (local councils) and συναγωγαί (synagogues), and two ruling authorities that shall hear their witness, ἡγεμόνες (governors) and βασιλεῖς (kings), which recall the persecution in Palestinian or nearby territories.[81] Moreover, the preference for προσευχή (house of prayer) instead of συναγωγή in contemporary references of the Jewish assemblies in the city of Rome questions the Italian composition of the forecast.[82]

Matthew himself, who parallels the persecution by the nations (Matt 24:9), incorporates the replica of Mark 13:9–13 to the mission commandment (Matt 10:17–22) and narrows its scope to the towns of Israel (Matt 10:5–6,23), and even the residual form in John 16:2 envisages the conflict chiefly with Judaism. The shift of context Matthew has operated is possible as far as Mark 13:9–13 describes the general items during public harassment: afraid relatives of civil authorities accusing one another to safeguard their lives and belongings, and the general hatred from the mob, who wants to hush whoever questions their mores, especially if the provocation

ingens haud perinde in crimine incendii quam odio humani generis convicti sunt). A similar scene is depicted in Mark 13:9–13, especially verse 13: καὶ ἔσεσθε μισούμενοι ὑπὸ πάντων διὰ τὸ ὄνομά μου (and you will be hated by all for my name), but the use of the recurrent term for hate (*odio*) in Tacitus rejects the strict dependence (for instance 13.19; 14.31,61,62; 15.21,28,48,64). Mark 13:13 can be inspired in the experience of aversion to the just (Ps 7,1–6; 35:19–20; 69:4–5), in the life of Jesus (ulteriorly developed in John 15:18; 1 John 3:13) or Paul, or in the social tensions of the First Jewish War (AD 66–70).

81. Jöris, "More than Family Dispute," 365, in view of the use of συνέδριον in Mark 14:55; 15:1, wisely suggests that συνέδρια in Mark 13:9 more likely represents the Jewish councils since the disciples would not have been flogged (δαρήσεσθε; Mark 13:19) in the synagogues by Gentiles. For Mann, *Mark*, 516–17 the expression ἐπὶ ἡγεμόνων (before rulers) refers to Roman provincial governors, like Felix (Acts 23:24) and Festus (Acts 24:27), but the inaccurate term βασιλέων and the Jewish framework of Mark 13 makes superfluous for him the setting out of Palestine.

82. Zeichmann, "Loanwords or Code-Switching?," 64. Philo, *Embassy* 132,134,137,138,148,152,165 uses προσευχή/προσευχαί for the Alexandrian synagogues, a term kept in 156–57 for the Jewish Roman meeting houses. Philo has a plural neuter συναγώγια for the meeting houses in Asia (311) and again προσευχή/προσευχαί for synagogues in general (346,371). As Zeichmann points, the term had to be widespread in Rome, since in the first half of II AD Juvenal, *Satirae* 3.295 has the Graecism *proseucha*.

touches moral, political, or religious beliefs.[83] The persecution forecast of Mark 13:9–13 accepts the Italian reading, in the sense that the particular is comprised in the general, but even beyond what has been stated it is not necessary to leave the Scriptures to spot sources of inspiration for the text (Isa 19:2; Jer 12:6; Mic 7:6) and persecutions before Nero and out of Italy.[84]

83. Jöris, "More than Family Dispute," 368–74 reads Mark 13:12–13 from Isa 66:1–5 to enlighten the familiar conflicts of the first Christians with their Jewish relatives, seeing there a dividing line between the true believers in the Jewish God (those who accepted the Christian faith) against the false ones (those who refused conversion). The parallel Isa 66:1–5 fulfills the task, though it is a bit oblique next to the classical Mic 7:6 and Isa 19:2, which Jöris, "More than Family Dispute," 360–63 comments before.

84. Notoriously in Acts: 4:1–21 (Jerusalem); 5:17–40 (Jerusalem); 6:8—7:60 (Jerusalem); 8:1–3 (Jerusalem); 9:23–25 (Damascus); 9:28–29 (Jerusalem); 12:1–4 (Jerusalem); 13:42–50 (Antioch of Pisidia); 14:1–5 (Iconium); 14:19 (Lystra); 16:16–24 (Philippi); 17:1–9 (Thessalonica); 17:13 (Beroea); 18:12–17 (Corinth); 19:23–41 (Ephesus); 21:27—23:22 (Jerusalem); 24:1–21 (Caesarea); 24:13—26:29 (Caesarea); others loci: Phil 1:12 if not attributed to Rome (Ephesus? Caesarea?); 2 Tim 3:11 (Antioch, Iconium, Lystra); 3:12 (universal persecution); 1 Pet 1:6–7; 4:12; 5:9–10 (general distress, apparently Anatolia); Rev 2:8–10 (Smyrna); 2:12–13 (Pergamum). But see Heb 10:32–34; 13:3, mentioning Christian prisoners (τοῖς δεσμίοις), mistreated (κακουχουμένων) and suffering expropriation (ἁρπαγή) in Italy (accepting the location of Heb 13:24).

4

Conclusion and Proposal

Tradition and Scripture

Scripture, on one hand, registers the link between Paul and Mark in several stages (Acts 12:12; 13:5,13; 15:37–39; Col 4:10; Phlm 24; 2 Tim 4:11) and, on the other hand, the less-attested partnership of Mark and Peter (Acts 12:1–12; 1 Pet 5:13). As we have examined, the tradition on the origin of the second gospel is solidly interwoven with the Roman Petrine tradition. It's hard to determine which of the two fundamentals came first. After the full revision of all available sources from the I to the early III AD, the sole secure scriptural source to place Peter in Rome before his connection with Mark, pointed out by Papias (ca. AD 130), is the Roman reading for Babylon in 1 Pet 5:13, but whose first known extant attestation is indeed (for Eusebius) the same Papias along with Clement Alexandrinus (*Hist. Eccl.* 2.15:2). The best support outside Scripture, in my view, to 1 Pet 5:13 is Ignatius, *Rom.* 4.3 (AD 107–20), wherein Petrine traditionalists with critical aspirations can fix their gaze like the eyes of the pilot sailing at night do to the lighthouse on the horizon. In this case paleography is not of great help: the first witnesses to 1 Peter are P^{72} and P^{125} in the first half of III AD.[1]

1. P^{7}2 (= P.Oxy 4394) is a Egyptian codex joining the entirety of 1 Peter, 2 Peter, Jude, and several apocryphal works, seemingly owing to several phases of compilation. The text of 1–2 Peter doesn't surpass the III AD, but altogether guess discrepancies between 1 Peter—clearly cognate with B—2 Peter, and to greater degree Jude, whose text-type is more licentious. The more fragmentary exemplar of 1 Peter, P^{12}5 (= P.Bodmer VII–VIII), first half of III AD, is more of the same, agreeing for the major part with P^{72},

In the IV century, Eusebius found three different traditions of Peter in Rome he deemed worth mentioning: (1) Peter's persecution of Simon Magus, apocryphal romance. Coming from Justin and Irenaeus gave Eusebius the motif for Peter's travel to Rome from Palestine under Claudius (*Hist. Eccl.* 2.13:1—15:1).[2] (2) The delivering of the gospel through Mark his interpreter to the Roman community when Peter was missioning there, taken from Clement Alexandrinus (to a minor extent from Irenaeus) and the Roman reading of 1 Pet 5:13 (*Hist. Eccl.* 2.15:1–2). (3) Peter's martyrdom in Rome (under Nero), attested by Gaius the Presbyter and Dionysius, bishop of Corinth, the former additionally reporting the funerary monument of Peter in the imperial see (*Hist. Eccl.* 2.25:5–7).

The nonexistence of conclusive proofs, if not fastened to definite contrary ones, doesn't carry by force the impossibility of a tradition. Nonetheless, inasmuch as Peter's voyage to Rome when Claudius was emperor (AD 41–54) depends on the romance of Simon Magus—and this in the confused interpretation of the Latin stele in the Tiber Island (*CIL* VI,567)—and in Justin's tendency to connect the current phenomena of pagan society with Scripture under the ancient principle that the older of two similar facts should provide the reason for the later (*1 Apol.* 59)—whence the link of the heresy of Menander the Samaritan with Simon Magus reported in Acts 8:9–25—Peter's sojourn in Rome hardly could endure the company of modern conventions for historicity.[3] The author of Acts knew the Roman church

ℵ, A, and B (Comfort and Barrett, *Earliest NT Manuscripts*, 1:446; Comfort, *Earliest NT Manuscripts*, 2:183, 349, 350, 354). Similar colophons in the nativity of Mary and 1–2 Peter (εἰρήνη τῷ γράψαντι καὶ τῷ ἀναγινώσκοντι; peace to the writer and to the reader) make Wasserman, "Papyrus 72," 145–54 think 1–2 Peter (and Jude) belonged to a first collection then subsumed in the codex not before AD 300 alongside Melito's homily on the passion (late II AD, Sardis in Minor Asia), writing with some Petrine parallels that would explain the coalition to the former documents: On Pascha 12: ὡς ἀμνοῦ ἀμῶνου καὶ ἀσπίλου (like defectless and blemishless lamb)//1 Pet 1:19; 68: ἐκ σκότους εἰς φῶς (out of darkness to light)//1 Pet 2:9 (but see Acts 26:18); 68: ἱεράτευμα καινόν (new priesthood)//1 Pet 2:9.

2. I only give here the key words, but the passage in full is longer: παρὰ πόδας γοῦν ἐπὶ τῆς αὐτῆς Κλαυδίου βασιλείας ἡ πανάγαθος καὶ φιλανθρωποτάτη τῶν ὅλων πρόνοια τὸν καρτερὸν καὶ μέγαν τῶν ἀποστόλων, τὸν ἀρητῆς ἕνεκα τῶν λοιπῶν ἁπάντων προήγορον, Πέτρον, ἐπὶ τὴν Ῥώμην ὡς ἐπὶ τηλικοῦτον λυμεῶνα βίου χειραγωγεῖ (certainly, at the moment, in the reign itself of Claudius, the completely good and most philanthropic Providence of all, carries by the hand to Rome the firm and great of the apostles, for the sake of virtue the first among all the others, Peter, as against so large destructing life (= Simon Magus); Eusebius, *Hist. Eccl.* 2.14:6).

3. The Christian Platonist Justin saw in the older Jewish prophets the outset of Greek philosophy and pagan mythology. The demons would have heard the prophets announce the coming of Christ and in order to delude the humans, created the heathen myths, so that the Gentiles would confuse Christ in his coming with one more

in the 50s (28:14–31), Peter's silence about Rome being conspicuous in his address to the council of AD 50 (15:6–9). Meaningful for the author of Acts was too the preservation of Peter's previous notice in Caesarea (10:48) and Jerusalem (12:17), and Peter's oblivion after the council (15:7–11), since he appears no more in the work. As for the third Roman Petrine tradition, the death of Peter in Rome based in the Vatican cenotaph, it belongs with certainty to the second half of the II AD, and to earlier dates solely in degree of possibility (first half of II AD). Hence, Peter's cenotaph is subjected too to possible contrary conclusions if pushed beyond its secure date.

If we had to rely purely on Scripture, the tradition of Peter in Rome with Mark hangs on 1 Pet 5:13, though John Mark in Rome by means of Paul is possible attributing the letters of captivity to the Roman context, where Mark is listed among Paul's trusted companions (Col 4:10; Phlm 24), or even solely under the supposition that the commission to Timothy in his second epistle to take Mark with him to Rome was accomplished (2 Tim 4:11), or both. Indeed, the best cross-reference in support of the Papias-Clement tradition is the intricate merging of Col 4:10; 2 Tim 1:17; 4:11; Phlm 24; and 1 Pet 5:13: Mark would have alleviated Paul's captivity (Col 4:10; Phlm 24), at some time been dispatched, and stayed afterwards in the Aegean basin, possibly in Philippi (Phil 1:19; 2 Tim 4:13), then went or returned with Timothy to Rome (2 Tim 4:11), remained with Peter (1 Pet 5:13), and finally wrote the gospel as Peter's interpreter for the Roman community, either while Peter was still living (Papias, Clement Alexandrinus) or after his death (Irenaeus).

Beyond all the objections taken against the convoluted harmonization that looms up from Colossians, 2 Timothy, and Philemon, 1 Pet 5:13 results necessarily polemic if we make it the earliest angular stone for the Roman Petrine tradition. The epistle seems deutero-Pauline in composition, and

---

of their myths (*1 Apol.* 54; 56; 64). For Justin, even the demons would have delivered the Mithraic mysteries to the Gentiles to be performed in imitation of the Eucharist (*1 Apol.* 66.18–22). For Justin, this plagiarism would account for the diabolic component in false philosophies like the heresy of Simon Magus and Menander, men the demons aroused (*1 Apol.* 56.1–8). The creative character of Justin in finding nexuses is plain in the forced link of Plato with the biblical story of the brass serpent (Num 21:4–9) and with Jesus' crucifixion: Plato borrowed from the biblical account of the serpent pole in the wilderness (Num 21:8–9) the idea that the universe was created under the form of the letter chi/χ (*Timaeus* 8), but the similarity of the pole with the chi comes from the form of Jesus' cross, who would be the recognizable form of the serpent pole shaped by Moses (*1 Apol.* 60.1–17). Justin himself confesses this Christian interpretation of Plato, to which he gave credibility, was common among uncultured Christians (*1 Apol.* 60.28–31), a stratum of popular Roman Christianity where we also should look for Justin's source of connection between the stele in the Tiber Island dedicated to the pagan god of contracts, Semo Sancus (CIL VI,567), and Simon Magus.

the sender appears to have reached the faith by knowledge of Scripture, not from prolonged witness of Jesus in the flesh, and so he, against what is expected of the apostle Peter, is bereft of definite personal references to Jesus' life (geographical, temporal, and personal data) out of the traditional mainstream. Further, his interest in a very large spectrum of Anatolian communities, the social disturbances at the epistle's backdrop, and the very probable post-AD 70 date for the metaphor of Babylon for Rome in 1 Pet 5:13 (four certain post-AD 70 occurrences for one possible pre-AD 70) matches better Anatolia in AD 85–90 than Rome in AD 60s.[4]

Omitting 1 Pet 5:13 there is no NT mention of Peter in Rome. Scripture halts in the role of Peter in Jerusalem (Acts 1–5; 11:1–4; 12:1–19; Gal 1:18; 2:9), and in his mission to the Palestinian coastal plain (Acts 9:32—10:48; 11:5–18); it further mentions Peter in Antioch (Gal 2:11–14), and in relation to Corinth (1 Cor 1:12; 3:22; 16:12), and attests his martyrdom in the fourth gospel (John 21:18–19), likely relying on Ephesian tradition. Scripture links Peter with military personnel in Caesarea, Cornelius the centurion and his household (Acts 10). Cornelius served in an Italian company (Acts 10:1) and is in Caesarea, where for the first time Gentiles were given the repentance that leads to life (Acts 11:18; 15:7–9). The verses 2 Pet 1:1; 3:1 appeal for Petrine authority and build over the existence of 1 Peter. According to Eusebius the ancient presbyters refuted 2 Peter's authenticity even though some deemed it useful for study (*Hist. Eccl.* 3.1,4). Viewed from one side, 2 Peter's disfavor champions 1 Peter's authenticity, but conversely manifests that Petrine pseudonymity existed in the early church.

Multiple loci for the Petrine authorship of 1 Peter are found in the *Miscellanies* of Clement Alexandrinus towards the third quarter of the II or beginning of the III century (3.11:75; 18:110; 4.7:46–47; 20:129; 6.15:128). Before the Alexandrine, Clement Romanus, *Ad Corinthios* (*Prae.*; 7.4; 30.2; 49.5; 57.1; 59.2) and Polycarp, *Ad Philippenses* (1.3; 2.1–2; 8.1; 10.2) could know the letter, the latter in western Anatolia, though none of the two mention Petrine authorship. Ignatius, *Ad Romanos*, writing from Smyrna

4. The biased exegesis is a sort of circular reasoning based in two components: (a) Apologetics, i.e., the defense of previous assumptions in the fields of theology, authority, or morals, reading from this original gaze the sources, especially those ambiguous and subjected to interpretation, which end to say what the exegete has projected into them. The projected belief presents the advantage to extract what is compatible in the sources, as if it were a magnet, but the price to be paid is overlooking the remaining elements (see for instance Ray, *Upon This Rock*, 5–6, 11–19, 58–59, who approaches early Petrine tradition from the modern controversy on religious authority). (b) The retroactive effect within the referent vital group to which the exegete belongs. The outcome of circular positions is almost always self-confirmation, defense, and identity reinforcement.

(10.1), says Peter made recommendations to the Romans (4.3), suggesting the context of Ignatius' words rather strongly that Peter made the recommendations before his death but not directly declaring this Ignatius.

The partnership of Paul and Peter, linearly considered in Clement Romanus and Ignatius, allows the early association of the two great pillars of the church in their death and with the city of Rome. Unfortunately *Ad Corinthios* 5.4 and *Ad Romanos* 4.3, and despite the latter's stronger suggestion, cannot escape from uncertainty. The opening of *Ad Romanos* 4.1, ἐγὼ γράφω πάσαις ταῖς ἐκκλησίαις καὶ ἐντέλλομαι πᾶσιν (I write to all the churches and give commands to all), restated by οὐχ ὡς Πέτρος καὶ Παῦλος διατάσσομαι ὑμῖν (I don't give instructions to you like Peter and Paul), and the tradition of Peter admonishing the Roman Jews in Jerusalem available to the author of Acts (2:10,41), who certainly knew the Roman church (28:16,30) and the lives of Peter and Paul better than modern commentators, retains Ignatius, *Ad Romanos* 4.3 in the orbit of ambiguity. Canon Muratori, an allegedly II-century Roman list of NT writings, stingingly for Roman traditionalists doesn't include 1 Peter.

It must be noted, Secunda Clementis, mid II AD, in the eastern part of the Roman Empire shows up many points of contact with 1 Peter as to exclude that the author borrowed from it or from a common source (1.1–2; 5.1–4; 11.2; 14.4; 16.1; 17.3.5). Strikingly 2 Clem. seems to paraphrase Mark 4:28 (11.3), shows preference with two occurrences (7.6; 18.5) for Isa 66:24 only found in Mark 9:48 among the synoptics, and in appearance uses LXX Deut 6:5, resembling the second gospel more than Matthew or Luke (3.4). Assuredly, Justin, around the same date, knows in Rome with security Mark 3:14 (*Dial.* 106.16–19), and some more Marcan materials of difficult assessment (*1 Apol.* 16.22–25; 45.15–16; *Dial.* 76.41–43; 100.16–18). Justin and the aforementioned Muratori ignore 1 Peter, whereas 2 Clem. and perhaps Papias have notice of both Mark and 1 Peter, around mid II AD in the Roman East.

The first unquestioned author to acknowledge 1 Peter's authorship will be Irenaeus, AD 180 (*Haer.* 4.9:2; 16:5; 5.7:2). This last put us behind the hint that the second gospel and 1 Pet 5:13 seem not to have been associated in the primitive documentary level in the Roman west, and if the Papias-Clement tradition were correct, the foreseeable situation had to be their indisputable possession by the Roman church, copy, and distribution, by Justin and inexcusably by Clement of Rome. Against tradition, we have that 1 Clem. doesn't resort to the second gospel, a document tradition later assigned to the personal interpreter of Clement's predecessor in the Roman episcopacy! The very fact that the first verbalized commentary on Mark's gospel and of 1 Peter's authorship in the case Eusebius, *Hist. Eccl.* 2.15:2 and

3.39:15 are reporting the truth, befalls in one Anataloian bishop, Papias of Hierapolis, alerts the eyes of the researcher.

Some more consistency surrounds the first fundamental of the second gospel, Mark the interpreter of Peter (without reporting location). In this sense it must be inferred that Papias, from whom most probably this assignment was handed into the stream of tradition, granted credibility to the testimony of John the Elder, who nevertheless underscores again the early Asian reception of the tradition. The titles *εὐαγγέλιον κατὰ Ἰωάννην* (gospel according to John) in P^{6}6 and *κατὰ μαθ'θαῖον* (according to Matthew) in P4 substantiate the circulation of entitled gospels in the second half of II AD, making credible the attribution of authorship to the gospel of Mark (and Matthew's) by Papias. Most likely, the gospel authorship was backed up by oral stories accompanying the titles and that gave reason for the creation, motifs, and place of composition of each gospel found within each codex in hand of the local churches. All in all, the exhaustive scrutiny of the external evidence on the second gospel origin sets Mark as the private person responsible for the document, at best in the early first half of II AD. Going beyond to former dates in dependence on external sources requires faith, but from Papias onwards Mark is undisputed by the traditional chain of witnesses.

Semitisms and Latinisms

Internal analysis affords four forceful props to tradition: (1) Mark is a Petrine gospel with up to twenty-six references of Peter, which describes an episode that occurred in Peter's house in Capernaum where probably Jesus was lodged, and that has been neatly checked by modern archaeology. The gospel bears vivid narratives in small physical spaces where it is natural to see in Peter the pivot of the Galilean tradition. (2) The second gospel is fraught with Semitisms, standing at the forefront is simple parataxis in the field of syntax, pervasive and most likely yielded as a consequence of biblical style imitation; the pleonastic ἤρξατο/ἤρξαντο (he/they began to) accompanying an infinitive to which it adds very little meaning in the field of semantics; and the presence of Aramaic words in the narrative order.[5] (3)

5. Baum, "Mark's Paratactic *Καί*," 1–26 has summarized all the relevant material for Marcan parataxis drawing the same inference: Marcan parataxis is unparalleled out of biblical Greek. Worthy to be considered among Baum's comparisons is the use of *καί* as introductory particle characteristic of Marcan sections as well as of LXX pericopes, rendering there as a rule the Hebrew *waw*/ו, which the biblical authors used even to open the first paragraph of the sacred books (Lev 1:1; Num 1:1; Josh 1:1; Judg 1:1; Ruth 1:1; 2 Sam 1:1; 1 Kgs 1;1; 2 Kgs 1:1, etc.). Mark seems to have copied the biblical paratactic style possibly because the Jewish rolls were his learning books for writing,

Mark takes pains to make more accessible some of the Aramaic words and some of the Jewish customs reported in his gospel to the intended audience, who seems partially to be not Judeo-Christian. (4) Mark has a remarkable number of Latinisms, especially loans.

The four internal features appeal for a Judeo-Christian author and a Gentile-Christian audience, it being debatable whether the Latinisms belong only to the author's milieu, i.e., the Greek of the author was affected by Latin due to his position in society; whether they also belong to the intended audience, i.e., the Latinisms were part of the social milieu of the addressees too; whether they were willful, i.e., the author wanting to sound Romanized towards his audience; or less probably unintentional, i.e., the author was not aware of the Greek equivalents for his Latin loans. Among the Latinisms, the mainstay for the Italian provenance of the second gospel Gentile audience is *κοδράντης* (Mark 12:42), a western coin extremely rare in the east. But even *κοδράντης* is not exclusively Marcan. Matthew's gospel, linked according to extant sources to Ignatius of Antioch, employs the word in an independent saying (Matt 5:26).

Against the Italian provenance, the strongest support for a Roman center in the east is the concentration of Latinisms which fall into the administrative/military area: *λεγιών* (Mark 5:9,15), *σπεκουλάτωρ* (Mark 6:27), *δηνάριον* (Mark 6:37; 12:15; 14:5), *κῆνσος* (Mark 12:14), *φραγελλόω* (Mark 15:15), *πραιτώριον* (Mark 15:16), *κεντυρίων* (Mark 15:39,44), and *αἰτία* (Mark 15:26). *Λεγιών*, *κῆνσος*, and *δηνάριον* point better the post-AD 70 scenario. We don't have Latinism coming from dress, the religious sphere, or nourishment. *Κράββατος* (Mark 2:4,9,11–12; 6:55), *μόδιος* (Mark 4:21), and *ξέσται* (Mark 7:4) fall into the home-type Latinism, but the list as a whole drags the two last to the business, taxes, and customs fields in the sense that despite they are meant by Mark as domestic holders they indeed represent metric measures at the expense of other possible Greek terms; and the first of the three to the military (despite what has been stated). The cognate *Ἡρῳδιανοί* (Mark 3:6; 12:13), accepting Latin background, may have been used in popular strata, but fits closely the first category where it should have been born.

Eastern archaeology and epigraphy demonstrate the existence of Latinisms in Anatolian, Syrian, Egyptian, and Palestinian Greek. In pre-AD 70 Palestine, the fan of instances goes from coin legends (Roman prefects'

and because he wanted to portray Jesus in biblical style (for the similitude between some Marcan miracles and the cycles of Elijah and Elisha, see next to next note). However, the lesser frequency of conjunctive *καί* in the last chapters of Mark, though still high, could point to an increasing conscience of the self-style and perhaps the revision of the foundational purpose of biblical imitation.

prutot and Herodian large copper denominations), to Latin personal names (CIIP 28,40,171,222,385,416,421,423–24,427,507,554–55,559,570,582–83,2189), imperial titles in public dedications (CIIP 2268,2335,2593), and names of towns and buildings (Caesarea, Tiberias, Julias, Fort Antonia; the Tiberieum). The NT knows Latin names in the Palestinian members of the church: Barsabbas surnamed Justus (Acts 1:23), and our John surnamed Mark (Acts 12:12,25). In the second gospel properly we have Rufus, son of Simon of Cyrene (Mark 15:21), a name attested in Paul to the Romans (16:13) and in a Jewish tomb in Jerusalem as well (CIIP 385).

Geographical errors (Mark 5:1; 6:45–53; 11:1; cross-reference 9:33; 10:1,10), corrected or avoided by Matthew (8:28; 14:22; 21:1; to the foregoing cross-reference 18:1; 19:1; and 19:10), displace preferably the Judeo-Christian author of the second gospel from Galilee or Jerusalem. This would alienate him from John Mark, Paul's and Barnabas' companion, who, traveling from Jerusalem, where his mother (Acts 12:12) lived and probably himself, to Antioch (Acts 12:25—13:1), should manage the Palestinian geography. The argument taken alone is, notwithstanding, not wholly conclusive: the setting of Jerash and even Gadara in the Lake of Galilee is hardly passable in the cultured Jew from Jerusalem (enough to compose in Greek) even if it is admitted he was forced to sew incomplete reports into longer narrative units, but the confusion at the point of Bethphage and Bethany in the arrival of the road from Jericho to East Jerusalem is not grave. The semantics of the Latin loans, checked against archaeology, as well as the Semitic interference, points to a Roman center in the east wherein the narrator of Mark learned Greek, in possible combined dependence on oral Aramaic, LXX literature, and to the partly Romanized social milieu.

Strikingly, in the gospel of Mark there is a faith confession of one centurion depending on Caesarea (15:39), the gospel bearing an anti-Roman pericope (5:1–20) crushing against the spirit of its pro-Roman elements, i.e., the Latin loans. Lastly, the Roman reading for Mark 13:9–13 is feasible insofar as the particular situation is comprised in the general statement. The circumstances of the forecast have been read in Palestinian sense by the first gospel (Matt 10:5–6,23). Against the use of *συναγωγαί* (synagogues) in Mark 13:9, the name for the Roman Jewish meetings would preferably be according to Juvenal (*Satirae* 3.295) and Philo (*Embassy* 156–57) προσευχαί (houses of prayer), the same usage employed for the Jewish meetings in Alexandria (*Embassy* 132,134,137,138,148,152,165).

The Caesarean Frame. Christian Communities on the Western Shore

Against the resource to primitive vivid Galilean traditions, some plainly elaborated pericopes (Mark 5:1–20; 6:45–52; 9:2–8; 13:1–37; 16:1–8) and post-AD 70 markers (λεγιών, Mark 5:9,15; δηνάριον, Mark 6:37; 12:15; 14:5; κῆνσος, Mark 12:14) make reluctant the attribution of the gospel to John Mark (Acts 12:12,25) or to any second-generation Christian who, still in touch with surviving witnesses of Jesus in the flesh, were not yet so much in need of theological literary dressing. Howbeit, two obscure pieces of data approach John Mark to the second gospel. First: Acts suggests this John was preferably known by his second Roman name: Ἰωάννου τοῦ ἐπικαλουμένου Μάρκου (John, surnamed Mark; Acts 12:12); Ἰωάννην τὸν ἐπικληθέντα Μᾶρκον (John, who was surnamed Mark; Acts 12:25). As far as Roman names were not uncommon in Jerusalem's I AD funerary register (see above), it may be granted that John Mark had accepted the pro-Roman social fashion of the big Palestinian towns, making viable the remote hypothesis, otherwise unprovable, that Mark was related to Roman administration, further elucidating his assistance in the first Pauline mission (Acts 12:25; 13:4–5). Second: Mark's debut (Acts 12:12) follows Peter's release from prison. Once the angel sets Peter free, he hastens to Mark's mother's home. Then Peter leaves Jerusalem and goes to another place (ἐξελθὼν ἐπορεύθη εἰς ἕτερον τόπον; Acts 12:17).

The cryptic expression εἰς ἕτερον τόπον opens the door to diverse hipotheses: the coastal plain, Samaria, Galilee, Antioch, Corinth, and Rome—all of them crop up from scriptural and traditional references. Anyhow, the author of Acts has set silence between Peter's exit from Jerusalem in around AD 44 and Peter's last apparition in the council of AD 50, possibly because from then onwards Peter's role was for the same author less extraordinary than Paul's. For our case, Peter's flight to the northern Sharon plain strengthens the link with the recently founded Christian community in Caesarea, represented elsewhere by Philip and Cornelius (Acts 8:40; 10:44–48; 21:8), whilst is at odds considering that if Peter fled to Caesarea, he could be seized again because the city was then under Agrippa I, but this was less possible southwards.[6]

6. The expression in Acts 12:19 καὶ κατελθὼν ἀπὸ τῆς Ἰουδαίας εἰς Καισάρειαν διέτριβεν (and he went down from Judaea to Caesarea (where he) remained) considered alone finds some grammatical ground for attributing it to Peter (αὐτόν), but the implicit subject for the verbs κατελθών and διέτριβεν in 12:19 is taken again in 12:20 to begin Herod's misfortunes in Caesarea, excluding Peter.

It is noticeable that the section on Cornelius follows two episodes resembling Mark, the healing of Aeneas the paralytic in Lydda (Acts 9:32–35) and the resurrection of Tabitha in Joppa (Acts 9:36–43), the two in the southern Sharon plain. The style of miracle depicted, raising the deceased by the hand and using a direct call that returns Tabitha to life and stands up Aeneas, is preluded in the third gospel (Luke 5:18–26; 8:49–56). A pair of clues—*κράβαττος* (cot) in Acts 9:33, whereas the word is absent in Luke, and the similarity between the Semitisms *ταλιθα* (טְלִיתָה, little girl) in Mark 5:41 and *Ταβιθά* (טְבִיתָא, Gazelle) in Acts 9:36,40—nonetheless point to Marcan or proto-Marcan sources to which the Aeneas and Tabitha episodes (Mark 2:1–12; Mark 5:21–24,35–43) are reminiscent.[7]

For the author of Acts, Caesarea was the first Gentile-Christian audience, and to the gospel of Peter. It is striking that a Petrine gospel sets forth one centurion confessing Jesus before the cross in AD 33 (Mark 15:39), and that in Lucan tradition a centurion receives the gospel of Peter in AD 40 (Acts 10:44–48). Since even the standing Roman detachments in Jerusalem depended on Caesarea's headquarters and the Roman prefects moved therefrom to Jerusalem on occasion of the feasts, both centurions are directly or indirectly related to Caesarea and belong virtually to the same period. Another apparent agreement is that Jewish purity is the subject of the custom the narrator of the second gospel more extensively explains (Mark 7:2–4), the same topic that is theologically addressed in the dream of Peter before meeting the emissaries of Cornelius (Acts 10:9–17,27–28). Conspicuously Matt 15:1–20 and partially Luke 11:37–41 restate Mark 7:1–23, but don't

7. Luke 8:54 lacks the Semitism *ταλιθα* too, and prefers *ἡ παῖς, ἔγειρε* (child, wake up!). It should be noted the twin set *κλιναρίον* (small bed) and *κράβαττος* (mat) in Acts 5:15. The Aramaic טְבִיתָא is the feminine of טַבְיָא, deer, gazelle, a cognate of the Hebrew צְבִי and its feminine צְבִיָּה, both rendered by the feminine *δόρκας* in the LXX (2 Sam 2:18; Song 2:9; 4:5; 7:4; 8:14; an exception is *τῷ δόρκωνι* in Song 2:17; Davidson, *Hebrew and Chaldee Scriptures*, 690; Sokoloff, *Jewish Palestinian Aramaic*, 220). In Acts 9:32–35 and 9:36–43 the author is more evoking a known Marcan source than paralleling it. Interestingly, Martin, *Semitic Sources in Greek Documents*, 101–8 included Acts 9:32–35 among the possible translation Greek sections from a Semitic source of the first part of the book of Acts (1:1—15:35). The Semitic markers in Acts 9:32–35 for such conclusion are four *καί* (I correct to six, including *καί* beginning sentence and simple coordination: 9:32,34,34,34,35,35) for two *δέ* postpositive (9:32,33), only one subordinating participle (*διερχόμενον*; 9:32), and six unseparate articles from their substantive (*τοὺς ἁγίους τοὺς κατοικοῦντας*; 9:32; *ὁ Πέτρος*; 9:34; *οἱ κατοικοῦντες, τὸν Σαρῶνα, τὸν κύριον*; 9:35). Haenchen, *Acts of the Apostles*, 339–40 finds the proto-Marcan source of Talitha's miracle in LXX 1 Kgs 17:17–24 and 2 Kgs 4:32–37: *ἡ δὲ ἤνοιξεν τοὺς ὀφθαλμοὺς αὐτῆς* (and she opened her eyes; Acts 9:40) covers *καὶ ἤνοιξεν τὸ παιδάριον τοὺς ὀφθαλμοὺς αὐτοῦ* (and the child opened his eyes; LXX 2 Kgs 4:35). Indeed, we can overlap some Marcan episodes (Mark 1:12–13; 1:40–45; 5:35–43; 6:30–44) with the cycles of Elijah (1 Kgs 17:2–24) and Elisha (2 Kgs 4:1—6:7).

merit commentary, suggesting the topic could be of greater interest in Mark's addressees than in the intended audiences of the first and third gospels.

In the event this particular supposition of mine is rooted in firm historical ground, it would have to arise from two factors the least, which would have minimized the Christian interest in Jewish purity rules in the recipients of Matthew and Luke in comparison with the audience of Mark, namely, the general withdrawal of the Gentile mission from the Jewish Christianity during the second to the third Christian generation, and the oftentimes neglected question about the dwindling in domestic purity rules as a consequence of the fall of Jewish nationalism after AD 70. This second factor would have affected converts still depending on Jewish Christianity, who would have been less pressured by Judaizing Christians—each time decreasing in number and less accredited, as a result of the destruction of the temple and the rebuff towards traditional Pharisees, to attach themselves to purity concerns.[8]

It is widely admitted that from Herod the Great's reign to the First Jewish Revolt the stone vessel industry in Palestine was at its apex, to some rate as an effect of the economic public stone industry hook associated with subsidiary private businesses, those involved in rock-cut and façade tombs, in constructions of *mikva'ot* for ritual washing, and in the domestic vessel market.[9] But the great decay of imported clay wares, particularly Eastern Sigillata A (onwards ESA) in comparison with the Hellenistic Period, and its substitution within Jewish contexts by stone vessels for food-table service and clay pots locally made for cooking, must be explained alike by the reinforcement of Jewish ethnicity and the step up of the religious attention to Pharisaic-rabbinic rules which considered stone among the scant materials incapable to admit impurity and to convey it afterwards to other people, to cuisine materials and others, and to water (m. Kelim 10:1; m. Oholoth 5:5).[10]

8. Regardless of the fact that the alert on purity of the former period had to be reduced by the disaster of Jewish nationalism after the Jewish revolts (AD 70–135), the gradual depletion of stone vessel fragments in the archaeological level from AD 70 onwards must not be fathomed from the disappearance of Jewish purity worry. Miller, "Stone Vessel Finds," 408–17 challenges in this sense the opinion that the use of stone wares decayed in Palestine because they had lost in the eyes of the rabbis the properties for preventing contamination of food or water (by means of contact with a source of impurity). He is aided by several examples from the Tannaitic and Amoraitic eras, but in my view it only brings consistency Rabbi's opinion (AD 200–220) and that of the sages in Tosefta Shab 16,11, where the (pure) water in stone vessels retains the property to convert by contact profane water into pure. T. Shab 16,11 is indeed the perpetuation of the earlier opinion of Shammai and Hillel in Betzah 2:3.

9. For this assertion and the next one I rely on Berlin, "Jewish Life before the Revolt," 429–62; Reed, *Archaeology and the Galilean Jesus*, 44–51.

10. Cattle dung, stone, and unbaked clay vessels form in the Mishnah a category of vessels unsusceptible to transmitting uncleanness. The above entries offer the clearest

The ethnocentric character in the choice of simple wares locally made and wares made of stone against imported ones seems without doubt in the Palestine of the Early Roman Period (63 BC–AD 135; onwards ERP), since the ESA continue to be present during the same time in all the peripheral Gentile centers, Caesarea on the Golan, Tel Anafa, Samaria, Tyre, Pella, etc.[11] In Sepphoris, for instance—whose situation can be considered typological because the town was not razed in the First Revolt—stone vessels for domestic purposes, to judge from the number of recovered fragments after excavation, the same as in Capernaum, reached the highest point during the ERP and decreased severely in the Middle and Late Roman Periods, exactly the same pattern observed in other indications of ethnicity and austerity like the aniconic Herodian lamps which came to be supplanted by floral and animal-ornamented lamps after the ERP, as were supplanted too in the sphere of tablewares, the stone vessels by the return of imported ESA.[12]

All these factors contribute to the assumption that the ERP of Palestine to which the traditions in Mark 7:1–23 and in Acts 10:9–17,27–28 are attributed was an outstanding situation for Pharisaic-rabbinic discussions about purity rules (see Matt 23:25–26; Luke 11:37–41) and for the growth of social concern on the Jewish identity, reinforced by political nationalism. The Jewish Christianity represented in Palestine by James the Just and Peter in the middle part of the ERP necessarily had to feel resistance to the aperture to Gentile Christianity if it resulted at the price of questioning fidelity to Jewish ethnicity (Acts 11:2–3; 15:20,29; Gal 2:11–14), making more intelligible the outset of the tradition on Peter's worry on Jewish purity matters before accepting Cornelius to the Christian faith in the Palestinian church of the ERP than anywhere else. For the same reason, the Gentile converts

declaration of their protection against contamination. A useful note in Berlin, "Jewish Life before the Revolt," 429 has also m. Kelim 6:2; m. Parah 5:5; m. Yadayim 1:2.

11. Berlin,"Jewish Life before the Revolt," 445–46; Reed, "Stone Vessels," 383–85.

12. Reed, "Stone Vessels," 386–87 registers in Sepphoris sixty fragments of stone vessels in the Early Roman stratum, ten in the Early to Middle Roman, and less than ten in the Late Roman. Some twenty had been dumped into a cistern with Middle Roman debris, but here the MR pottery brought to light numerous wholly restorable pots against the non-restorable fragments of stone vessels, revealing that the stone pieces had probably been dumped into the cistern from a more ancient mound of detritus. Regards the imported Eastern Terra Sigillata A (ETSA o simply ESA) tablewares, they present red fine slips tending to external absence of grain and roughness. ESA can be subdivided into three types: Roman, North African, and Cypriot. The sacred room in the so-called House of Peter in Capernaum sets forth two ESA sherds in the Hellenistic Period and four more fragments from the Early Roman Period in associated loci. Then on, the ESA appears represented in one half-plate from the first half of the II AD, and after a period of abandonment, then by another plate a little wider in the third quarter of the V AD (Loffreda, *Cafarnao*, 2:117, 166–67).

depending on the Jewish Christian mission of the ERP, were still under the influence of Jewish interests, placing Mark 7:3–4, the long commentary devoted to the Jewish custom of cleaning pots and washing of hands, not too far from the Palestinian church's area of influence, though perhaps not within an unalloyed Jewish environment, where, the Jewish customs being practiced in the foreground, the commentary would have sounded superfluous to the Marcan audience.[13]

If we accept the sequence of Acts, the gospel aperture to Gentile Christians stemmed from Peter's mission in Caesarea, the Roman garrison for Palestine (Acts 11:1–18), where the problem concerning the presence of the Holy Spirit beyond the folk of Israel was solved for the first time (Acts 10:44–48).[14] For the author of Acts, Peter led the entry of Gentiles to the

13. See for instance Mark 7:3, perfectly contextualized in m. Yadayim 2:3 (translation of Danby, *Mishnah*, 779–80): "The hands are susceptible to uncleanness, and they are rendered clean (by the pouring over them of water) up to the wrist. Thus if a man had poured the first water up to the wrist and the second water beyond the wrist, and the water flowed back to the hand, the hand becomes clean; but if he poured both the first water and the second beyond the wrist, and the water flowed back to the hand, the hand remains unclean."

14. Compare the Gentile Christian mission in Caesarea depending on Peter in Acts 10:1–48, in the case we were driven to understand that from the conversion of Cornelius' household, with Acts 13:44—14:28, where soon later (AD 40–41), as a result of the Jewish contempt towards the Christian announce the Pauline Gentile mission was branded in Antioch of Pisidia, Iconium, Lystra, and Derbe in southern central Anatolia. Haenchen, *Acts of the Apostles*, 346–63 bets that the theological reading of the episode at Caesarea (Acts 10:1—11:18) is the unique approach resistant to criticism. Hence Haenchen, *Acts of the Apostles*, 360 belittles too easily the historical plausibility of the Petrine mission for the reason that Luke-Acts is only delivering an edification tale hardly sustained in historical deeds traceable to the apostolic era. I will correct him focusing on three points: (a) The argument that no Roman troops were stationed in Caesarea in times of Cornelius because then the army was under Agrippa I (AD 41/42–44) is a complete supposition. Josephus says the great part of Caesarean troops were of Samaritan and indigenous origin. But he also utters that they were under Roman service for the successor of Agrippa I, the prefect Fadus, was eventually commanded to send them to the Pontus to conclude their duty there (*A.J.* 19.365). Additionally, it is unconceivable Rome properly was not represented among commanders at Caesarea (see the incident with the Jews in the neighboring Phoenician Dora intervening the Roman centurion Proculus Vitellius, AD 39; *A.J.* 19.299–398) (b) Stating it is improbable that the early church handed down, for purposes of edification, the conversion stories of men of rank because it was an apocalyptic church is a second but not minor risky utterance. The early church wasn't centered on the end of the present world to the point to eclipse the Christian mission based on the evangelical ethics. Moreover, the second arrival of Jesus made urgent the call to conversion in imitation of John the Baptist and Jesus. (c) Finally, that the centurion (ἑκατοντάρχης) in Luke 7:2–10 is anonymous doesn't infer the name Cornelius is invented. It is not necessary to exceed familiar or local level to acknowledge how oral tradition assures worldwide the transmission of historical data through generations.

good news, even if later Peter adjusted himself again to the ritual standards of James' party in Antioch (Gal 2:11–14) or was ascribed by the church's requirements to the mission to the circumcised (Gal 2:7–9). In spite of the precedents, the connection of Cornelius and Mark 15:39 only can be sustained on hypothetical grounds. A cohort held five centurions with the result of thirty centurions under Pilate for the Judaean province (see note 73 in chapter 3). The amount and time lag (from AD 33 to 40) does not allow any identification, but the proximity of the canonical Acts of Peter towards a possible Marcan source awakes to the question of dependence.[15]

The two related semantic fields, administrative and military, holding almost all the Marcan Latin loans we have studied, may represent the evangelist's *Sitz im Leben*. A close orientation, i.e., occupational, towards a Gentile audience involved in Roman administration, would explain the interest in rendering Aramaic words and Jewish customs, and simultaneously gives reason for the Latin imprint that through his daily vocation could have entered the Greek of the second gospel author, otherwise Semitized in greater extent than Latinized. Fitting this context, a Judeo-Christian in touch with the Caesarean administration is not necessarily impossible. In Philippians, Paul mentions that his imprisonment for the sake of the gospel has been widely known in the praetorium and quotes believers within the governmental staff (Phil 1:13; 4:22; see Phlm 2). This letter, Ephesians, Colossians, and Philemon are usually ascribed to Paul's captivity in Rome or Ephesus, but the hypothesis that they were sent from Caesarea's prison in view of the two-year period of Paul's captivity there remains acceptable,[16]

15. Mason, *Greek Terms for Roman Institutions*, 60 has five epigraphic occurrences of *κεντυρίων* in the expected military contexts, two in Egypt (32–30 BC; AD 41), one in Lydia (11–12 AD), and two uncertainly dated in Thracia and Crimea. The nearest to Palestine is *CIG* 4963 (= I,1057), an Alexandrine centurion's dedicatory under the prefecture of Vitrasius Pollio Junior (AD 38–41). Haphazardly, the date overlaps the service of Cornelius: ΕΤΟΥC Δ [Γ . . .] | ΚΑΙCΑΡΟC | ΑΥΤΟΚΡΑΤΟΡΟC | CΕΒΑCΤΟΥ ΕΠΙ | ΟΥΙΤΡΑCΙΟΥ | ΠΩΛΙΩΝΟC | ΗΓΕΜΟΝΟC | ΡΑΓΩΝΙΟΥ ΚΕΛΕΡΟC | ΕΠΙCΤΡΑΤΗΓΟΥ | ΛΟΓΓΙΝΟC ΚΕΝΤΥΡΙ[ΩΝ] (Year 4 of [Gaius] Caesar Autokrator Augustus, over Vitrasius Polio governor, Ragonius Celeris epistrategos, (writes) Longuinus centurion). Note that I have somewhat adventurously assigned the title *ἡγεμών* (governor) to the prefect. Otherwise, the name of the epistrategos is missing.

16. Phil 1:13: *τοὺς δεσμούς μου φανεροὺς ἐν Χριστῷ γενέσθαι ἐν ὅλῳ τῷ πραιτωρίῳ* (my chains manifested in Christ have been known in all the praetorium); Phil 4:22: *ἀσπάζονται ὑμᾶς πάντες οἱ ἅγιοι, μάλιστα δὲ οἱ ἐκ τῆς Καίσαρος οἰκίας* (greet you all the saints, especially those of the Caesar's house). Even if Philippians is ascribed to Rome or Ephesus, the presence of Christians visiting Paul in the prison of Caesarea is tenable: (Felix the governor) *διαταξάμενος τῷ ἑκατοντάρχῃ τηρεῖσθαι αὐτὸν ἔχειν τε ἄνεσιν καὶ μηδένα κωλύειν τῶν ἰδίων αὐτοῦ ὑπηρετεῖν αὐτῷ* (having ordered the centurion to keep him and to have a loosening (imprisonment) and to forbid no one of his own to look after him; Acts 24:23). Are we here to understand the local Christians to which Philip the Evangelist belongs visiting

and if accepted, Mark is not with Paul in Rome or Ephesus but in Caesarea: Ἀσπάζεται ὑμᾶς Ἀρίσταρχος ὁ συναιχμάλωτός μου καὶ Μᾶρκος ὁ ἀνεψιὸς Βαρναβᾶ (Aristarchus my co-prisoner greets you and Mark the cousin of Barnabas; Col 4:10 authenticity accepted; see Phlm 24). Aristarchus is said in Acts 27:2–3 to have joined Paul in Caesarea before leaving the ship for Sidon on the way to Rome. Though unprovable, we should thus not delete too fast the possible link of John Mark with Roman Caesarea.[17]

But there exists yet a second alternative if the circumstances did not force the Greek of Mark to include Latinisms. The considerable amount of Latinisms, preferably, would result in this second conjecture from the voluntary choice to sound Romanized before an audience involved in Roman administration in the east. The first and second hypotheses are built over Romanized audiences and a Judeo-Christian author, but in the latter the author doesn't forcedly belong to the social milieu of his addressees but makes his gospel sound as such to provoke more favorable reception. The deceptive mention of the four night watches in Mark 13:35 confirms, in congruence with this hypothesis, that our author is not entirely Romanized because in the fourfold Greco-Roman scheme the ἀλεκτοροφωνία (cockcrow), listed by the second evangelist in third place, actually belongs, and seems it cannot be otherwise, to the fourth watch, which ends at dawn.

Mark 6:48 puts Jesus walking on the Lake of Galilee around the fourth night watch (περὶ τετάρτην φυλακὴν τῆς νυκτός), from where it turns very

Paul (Acts 21:8–10), Christians of the outside, or the two things?

17. In a study still current, Abbott, *Ephesians and Colossians*, l–lix refuted any and all the drawbacks against Pauline authorship in Colossians, acknowledged from Muratori and Irenaeus, *Haer.* 3.14:1. Even against my argumentative line, I will take one case from him, turned about, to raise up the possibility of pseudonymity. From eight diagnostic Pauline terms absent in Colossians, argues Abbott—δίκαιος (righteous) and cognates, σωτηρία (salvation), ἀποκάλυψις (revelation), πιστεύειν (to believe), ὑπακοή (obedience), κοινωνία (communion), νόμος (law), δοκιμάζειν (to test)—many are in fact missing in the undisputed Pauline epistles too. Three are absent in 1 Corinthians (σωτηρία, ὑπακοή, δίκαιος), three in 1 Thessalonians (δίκαιος, ἀποκάλυψις, ὑπακοή), two in Galatians (σωτηρία, ὑπακοή), and two in Philippians (ἀποκάλυψις, ὑπακοή). Besides, 1 Corinthians has δικαιοσύνη once (1:30), and 2 Corinthians mentions σώζω only twice (12:1,7) and πιστεύειν once (4:13). So the argument that Colossians lacks Pauline terminology is defective for Abbott since the undisputed epistles also lack the same terminology. But this counterargument is badly founded because the correlation must be between Colossians and each of the undisputed alone. If this is made, we have: 8/8 absences in Colossians for 3/8 in 1 Corinthians, 2/8 in 2 Corinthians (in the best choice; 0/8 in rigor), 2/8 in Galatians, and 2/8 in Philippians. After returning several times to Colossians, I have achieved but a taste of uncertainty. They are not insurmountable barriers, but the angelology under Col 1:16, the worry on social order in 3:18—4:1, and the exchange of letters between Colossians and Laodiceans in Col 4:16 justify the tardy date, as I have stated elsewhere.

odd that Mark 13:35 names the third night watch ἀλεκτοροφωνία, unless he displaced the fourth watch forward to the third, because the rooster marked for Romans and Greeks the closing of the night and the beginning of the day (Josephus, *B.J.* 3.87; Pliny the Elder, *Nat. Hist.* 10.24.46; Strabo, *Geog.* 7.35). The confusion could come from the inclusion of πρωΐ in Mark 13:45 in the stretch of night vigils. From πρωΐ in Mark 1:35 and 16:2 we know πρωΐ in Mark 14:25 corresponds either to the ultimate moment of the night or already to the sunrise. πρωΐ has been set by Mark 13:35 in the fourth place of the list, provoking the odd displacement of the last watch of the night, the rooster crow, which in fact is quite similar to the usage of πρωΐ in Mark 1:35, to the third position.[18]

In the second option, a Semitic author using Roman concepts for a Romanized audience, but not himself totally Romanized—albeit to some length he necessarily is insofar as his Greek denotes the choice for imperial tones plausibly at the expense of available equivalent Greek terms—the Latin imprints in the vocabulary would unveil the Romanness of some receptors, but not unavoidably the Roman precedence of the author himself. Geographical inaccuracies concerning Palestine along with copious Semitic idioms fit the hypothesis of a Judeo-Christian of Phoenician or Syrian origin, but it doesn't underpin a definite Caesarean origin of the author. Notwithstanding, the coastal Romanized cities from Caesarea to Antioch on the Orontes supply the literary, epigraphic, and archaeological matrix for the

18. I am gratefully indebted to Martin, "Watch during the Watches," 685–701 for marshalling the sources and his deep gaze at this matter, wherefrom the above insight and what follows in the note have drunk. Notwithstanding, I have emended one point of his commentary. In the Parable on Watchfulness, Mark 13:35 reads: γρηγορεῖτε οὖν· οὐκ οἴδατε γὰρ πότε ὁ κύριος τῆς οἰκίας ἔρχεται, ἢ ὀψὲ ἢ μεσονύκτιον ἢ ἀλεκτοροφωνίας ἢ πρωΐ (be alert then: for you do not know when the master of the house comes, either at evening, or at midnight, or at roostercrow, or at early morning). In accordance with Pliny the Elder, the Roman working day was divided into three-hour periods, calling the farmyard cocks to labor before sunrise at the fourth camp watch (*Nat. Hist.* 10.24.46: *quartaque castrensi vigilia*). Ἀλεκτοροφωνίας in Mark 13:35 must equal then the last hour of the night or ἐσχάτην φυλακήν in Josephus, *B.J.* 3.319 (τετάρτην φυλακήν in *A.J.* 18.356), but πρωΐ in Mark 13:35 to the ἑωθινῇ φυλακῇ (seer hour) in Diodorus, *Bibl. Hist.* 15.84:1; 19.93:2; 95:3 and Josephus, *B.J.* 3.251 (see τὴν ἕω in 3.87). Luke 12:38 parallels Mark 13:35 solely with the second and third watches (τῇ δευτέρᾳ κἂν τῇ τρίτῃ φυλακῇ). Luke seems here—in opposition to Mark following the Roman custom introduced in the Levant from Pompey (63 BC)—to preserve the native reckoning of the Jews, that can be deduced from Jub 49:10 paraphrasing the commandment in Exod 12:6 to eat the Passover between the (two) evenings (בֵּין הָעַרְבָּיִם), distinguishing day and night in three watches each (translation of Charles, *Book of Jubilees*, 254–55): "Let the children of Israel come and observe the Passover on the day of its fixed time, on the fourteenth of the first month, between the evenings, from the third part of the day to the third part of the night, for two portions of the day are given to the light, and a third part to the evening."

second gospel grammar, including syntactical and semantic features as well, through which the position of the second evangelist in relation to his work and audience can be better explained.

Pliny the Elder records that Vespasian settled a Roman colony in Caesarea and granted thereto the title Prima Flavia, attested by coins and inscriptions.[19] The status of Roman colony was granted to honor the city's fidelity to Vespasian during the First Jewish War. The colony used Latin in official issues and thrived from AD 70 forward. Certainly, most of the eighty-four recovered Caesarean Latin inscriptions are assigned to this period, especially to the II–III centuries, and hardly a few, the Stone of Pilate aside, to the I century on calligraphic criterion. Thus, according to inscriptions, the Marcan Latinisms parallel better the post-AD 70 milieu, matching the formerly noted Latin markers λεγιών, δηνάριον, and κῆνσος. Nonetheless, it is inconceivable that the Latin presence in Caesarea before AD 70 didn't overcome the numerical extant of inscriptions.[20] In estimation of the corpus' compiler, the inscriptions still in existence represent less than 10 percent of the original, and surely the Roman imprint at the head of the Judaean province had to be felt in Caesarea before the town was rewarded.[21]

Not afar we have one Roman colony for the resettlement of V Macedonian and VIII Gallican Augustan veterans after the battle of Actium in 31 BC: ancient Berytus, 160 kilometers north of Caesarea, albeit the evidence substantiates a lag for the bulk of the colony, 15/14 BC, still persuasive for

19. Pliny the Elder, *Nat. Hist.* 5.14. At the outset, the colonization must be seen more as the Latinization of politics than as the massive resettlement of civilians, especially focused in the introduction of duumviri and decuriones replacing the Hellenistic council, and pontifices (Lehmann and Holum, *Joint Expedition to Caesarea*, 6; further comments in next note). The Caesarean mint shifted from Greek to Latin legends from Domitian issues (AD 83–93) onwards, though the coinage bearing the legend COL PRI FL AVG CAESARENSIS or similar abbreviated forms is only attested from the early II century and ends during Herennius Etruscus in the mid III century AD (Evans, *Joint Expedition to Caesarea*, 110–15). They are all bronze or any copper alloys, represented in the II century by one issue of Trajan (AD 114–17; 9 g), three of Hadrian (AD 117–38; 4, 6, and 11 g), and one of Aurelius (AD 161–89; 12 g).

20. Lehmann and Holum, *Joint Expedition to Caesarea*, 20 estimate the Roman staff in Caesarea through the I to the III century in one hundred men, comprising legates in command of the legions, finance *procuratores Augusti*, an *officium* of men including priests, *tabularies* or *comentarii*, and *beneficiarii*, *primus pilus*, *stratores*, and several centurions. The next Latin inscription on a marble pedestal from the I to the III centuries, publicly funded, and honoring a priest holding a probable Judaean surname, testifies the cultural mixture in ancient Caesarea (given in minuscule): *M(arcum) Fl(avium) Agrippam pontif(icem) | II viral(em) | col(oniae) I Fl(aviae) Aug(ustae) Caesareae oratorem | ex dec(reto) dec(urionum) pec(unia) publ(ica)* (n.4, Lehmann and Holum, *Joint Expedition to Caesarea*, 36–37).

21. Lehmann and Holum, *Joint Expedition to Caesarea*, 6, 10.

our case.[22] Caesarea, even if it was not granted the colonial status as Berytus was before AD 70, it was too the object of the Herodian interest for the embellishment of towns in the will to maintain the Roman approval to which the Herodian dynasty owed her power. According to Josephus, Caesarea was endowed by Herod the Great (37–34 BC) with theaters and amphitheaters, public baths, and a temple for Rome and Augustus. The same installations were provided or restored by Herod the Great, his grandson Agrippa I (AD 41/42–44), and his great-grandson Agrippa II (AD 50–92) for the Roman colony of Berytus.

The archaeological evidence recovered under modern Beirut falls within Hellenistic typology and doesn't assure the existence of specific Roman architecture during the Herodian period. In spite of this, the gladiatorial games Agrippa I organized in its amphitheater corroborate the introduction of Roman diversions and permits the possibility that Caesarea, provided of similar civil structures and where Herod the Great and Agrippa I also funded games in honor of the emperor, was like Berytus a town prepared for a Roman-fashioned audience a long time before the Jewish War.[23]

This presumably pro-Roman or pro-Latin staff of Caesarea before AD 70 would have encompassed military and civil personnel in touch with a Greek and Semitic population of Jewish, Samaritan, Judeo-Syrian, and Syrian pagan origin alike, part of which were merchants engaged in maritime trade with the west. Pitifully, coin scan from the period of the prefects in Caesarea has not given birth to western coins, while Jewish prutot in

22. Strabo, *Geog.* 16.2.19; Josephus, *A.J.* 16.143.344; *B.J.* 7.39; Millar, *Greek World and the East*, 168.

23. Josephus, *A.J.* 15.293.339; 19.335–38; 20.211–12; *B.J.* 1.414–15.422; Jones, *Roman Berytus*, 45–85; Millar, *Greek World and the East*, 171. A providential inscription at Berytus in Latin shows the reliability of Josephus: [R]EGINA BERENICE REGIS MAGNI A[GRIPPAE FIL(IA) ET REX AGRIPPA TEMPLUM (?) | QU]OD REX HERODES PROAVOS EORUM VE[TUSTATE CORRUPTUM A SOLO RESTITUERUNT | MARBORIBUSQUE ET COLUMNIS, [S]EX [. . . EXORNAVERUNT] (Queen Berenice, daughter of the Great King Agrippa (I), and King Agrippa (II), have raised up the edifice built formerly by their ancestor King Herod (the Great) which has fallen to ruin through the ages. It is decorated by them with marble and six columns; Jones, *Roman Berytus*, 63). The monumental inscription, first poorly published in 1927, belonged to a lintel or architrave and was found scattered in six fragments, approaching three meters all together, near the Great Mosque of Beirut, where the foundations of a civil basilica were unearthed. The type of building Agrippa II and his sister Berenice restored in Berytus could be a *templum*, but it is not clear (Mouterde, *Inscriptions de Syrie*, 23–24, 31). Haensch, "Herodian Dynasty," 105–6 proposes a *balneum* within a new restored reading, coherent but in my humble opinion too elongated. For an illustrated overview of Roman Berytus, from the I to the VI centuries AD, see Jidejian, *Beirut through the Ages*, 73–130.

number preferably depict circulation towards or from Jerusalem.[24] Nonetheless, amphora stoppers from I BC to I AD in one of the warehouses in the harbor belt testify to western imports—Spanish fish products, olive oil and defrutum, wine from the Italian Campania, Apulian olive oil from southern Italy or Croatia in the Adriatic (or perhaps wine and garum), and Rhodian or Aegean wine—tracing routes of western intercourse and for early missionary enterprises.[25] All the more, Latin tituli in western wine amphorae and fish products consumed in Masada and the Herodium trace the final fringe of the maritime imports and reveal Herod the Great's trends to customary Romanization, which must also be admitted in his heirs, at least in Agrippa I and II, who according to Josephus were brought up in Rome.[26]

Josephus' estimation of the Jewish population in Caesarea was twenty thousand before the war.[27] The number could be excessive but not the notion of a large Jewish community.[28] Five thousand Jewish souls, or even less if we

24. The Judaean prutah corpus from 4 BC to AD 70 found by the twenty-four-year Joint Mission at Caesarea (1971–1995) stands as follows: thirty-one Archelaus', 0.38—2.36 g (4 BC–AD 6); fourteen Coponius' and Ambibulus', 0.65—2.81 g (AD 6–12); fifteen Gratus', 1.40—2.61 g (AD 15–24); eighteen Pilate's, 0.99—2.47 g (AD 29–31); twenty-four Agrippa I's, 0.71—3.30 g (AD 41–42); four Antonius Felix's, 1.25—2.37 g (AD 54); twenty-seven Festus', 0.37—2.89 g (AD 59); and five uncertain prefects'/procurators', 0.76—2.08 g (AD 5–58; Evans, *Joint Expedition to Caesarea*, 103–25).

25. Blakely, "Ceramics and Commerce," 35–42.

26. Haensch, "Herodian Dynasty," 104. The most interesting artifact for the transport of western fish products in Masada is a reconstructed neck of one southern Spanish amphora with a Latin-Greek inscription in six differentiable elements, datable to 30–19 BC: (1) GARUM (2) [symbol] (3) Δ[(4) BACIΛΕΩ[(5) . . . P.O. . . . [(6) A. (Lernau, Cotton, and Goren, *Fish Sauces from Masada*, 35–40). The sense is clear from 1 and 4, *Garum βασιλέως* (Garum of the King = Garum of the King Herod) or *Garum βασιλέων* (Garum of the Kings = high-quality Garum; Berdowski, "Garum of Herod the Great," 111–16); Josephus, *A.J.* 18.143; 19.360.

27. Josephus, *B.J.* 2.457.

28. Josephus, *B.J.* 2.285–92 reports one of the sparks that ignited the First Jewish Revolt: disturbances between Jewish youths and Greek workers who were building shops on the way to the Caesarean synagogue. The report matches the urban center where the need for space was bigger. This disagrees with the Jewish remains (coins not considered) archaeology recovered in the beach line north to the Crusader Fortification, quite away from the expected I AD scenario. Avi Yonah's 1956 and 1962 excavations got back promising material there associated with foundation walls: capitals with menoroth, several inscribed mosaic fragments, one quoting Isaiah, and a Greek inscribed column of one Beryllos archisynagogos. The finds and structures were tentatively attributed to a synagogue site comprising a V-strata chronology. After a massive corner foundation, apparently from the Hellenistic Period and distant from the remaining finds, Avi Yonah's II stratum from the Herodian to Roman phase was featured by a nine-by-nine-meter walled structure partly exposed, modified onwards, first by a pool or cistern in stratum III, and then by consecutive pavements of the strata IV–V. Unluckily, the finds were shoddily described, lacking the usual diagnostic chain, datable associated

are compelled to admit Paul was thither preserved from the mischievous plans of the Jerosolimite Jews (Acts 23:34—24:1–9), is still considerable to assume a bilingual Greek-Aramaic pagan population influenced by Jewish proselytism as well as by Roman tendencies, partly converted into candidates for the Christian faith. The study of the book of Acts based on scene shift, places, and persons grants lavish information regarding Caesarea and permits the isolation of the Caesarean or Jerosolimite-Caesarean tradition comprising Acts 8:5–40 (Philip's apostleship to the southwest of Jerusalem but ending in Caesarea); 9:29–30 (Paul carried to Caesarea possibly by Hellenistic Judeo-Christians from the group of the Seven); 9:32—11:18 (Peter's mission in the coastal plain, Lydda, Joppa, and Caesarea); 12:1–24 (James the Great's martyrdom and Peter's imprisonment by Agrippa I, Peter's flight from Jerusalem, and Agrippa's death at Caesarea); and 21:8–9 (Paul's stance at Philip's abode in Caesarea).[29]

Given the syntactical features of this quite extensive tradition in the form it has come down to us, statistics only acknowledges Semitic features in Acts 9:32–35 (the healing of Aeneas, see above) and 11:1–18 (Peter's discourse on Cornelius).[30] This means that the author of Acts, since his style in the second part of the book (15:36—28:31) doesn't develop Semitic coloring, is in general more resourcing his expertise when writing the Caesarean tradition than previous Semitic sources, but this doesn't prevent us from accepting oral tradition based on distant facts. The narrative context supports faithful knowledge beneath this tradition in a broad sense, at least in the cycle of Philip, for we are told the author of Acts, supposedly the owner of the voyage diary of its second part (16:10—28:16), spent some days along with Paul in the abode of Philip in Caesarea (21:8–10,16).

It is also worth noticing that this possible Caesarean source includes John Mark in relation with Peter (Acts 12:12) and the mention of Philip's

material, and exact correlation with the buildings' structures. Some twenty years later, the Joint Expedition 1982 and 1984 seasons fought for permission and undertook a clean. The work assented with Avi Yonah's IV stratigraphic level containing the lower mosaic pavements dated to IV AD and assumed a likely synagogue building from the V to the VI centuries, to which the capitals and inscribed column must be attributed. Avi Yonah's intuitions were partly confirmed, for the expedition was able to recover several lamp fragments in the dumping material and from a probe datable from I BC to II AD, but patient examination belied Avi Yonah's structures from the II–III strata that can in fact be part of the first secure datable phase of occupation, stratum IV. In short: the field north of the Crusader Fortification promises future information related to Caesarea's Jewish community if permission to dig there is obtained, but until 2005 only a small Jewish living or working area from the Byzantine Period has been ascertained (Govaars, Spiro, and White, *Joint Expedition to Caesarea*, 23–101, 124–27, 138–40).

29. Harnack, *Acts*, 162–202.

30. Martin, *Semitic Sources in Greek Documents*, 98–102, 108.

daughters (Acts 21:9), traditions we find nuanced in Papias of Hierapolis (both) and Polycrates of Ephesus (only the second).[31] This is thoroughly compatible with the fact that the author of Acts adopts an Aegean (or Roman) perspective, from where he seems to be writing (coordinates of the voyage diary), enabling the arrival of this possible Caesarean tradition into western Anatolia in the cross from the second to the third generation of believers, AD 70–90, the period to which the author of Luke-Acts ascribes himself (Luke 1:1–4).[32]

Not less important is the concept of justice underneath Cornelius' story (Acts 10:1–48), an upright (δίκαιος; 10:22), devoted (εὐσεβής; 10:2), and God-fearing man (φοβούμενος τὸν θεόν; 10:2) who pleased God for his pious deeds, doing many alms for the people (ποιῶν ἐλεημοσύνας πολλὰς τῷ λαῷ; 10:2), and continuously praying to God (καὶ δεόμενος τοῦ θεοῦ διὰ παντός; 10:2). The approval this kind of justice (δικαισύνη; 10:35) and memorial in the presence of God (μνημόσυνον ἔμπροσθεν τοῦ θεοῦ; 10:4) produced in accord with Jewish categories is attested by Peter (10:35), iconizing in Cornelius the Judeo-Christian mission converts among proselytes of the Jewish nation (10:22) during the early stage of the church. The passage assumes the Jewish concept of sanctity by means of pious deeds and borders the relationship of the synagogue institution with Gentiles in foreign cities (near Palestine), as James the Just recognizes apologizing for Peter in the Council of Jerusalem (15:7–21).[33]

The second half of Philip the Evangelist's itinerary (from Ashdod to Caesarea; 8:40), Peter's mission (from Lydda to Joppa and then on to

31. Eusebius, *Hist. Eccl.* 3.39:9.15; 5.24:2–7.

32. Conzelmann, "Lugar de Lucas," 381–91 cleverly observes there is no firm doctrine of apostolic succession in Luke-Acts as we see in 1 Clem. 42.1–5; and on the other hand the apocalyptical tension compared with Mark 13 and Phil 3:20 (see for instance Luke 19:11–27) has been debased in Luke-Acts to a church separate from Judaism which has found its place in the Roman world and in the Gentile era (see Luke 21:24), so we should date Luke-Acts accordingly at the transit of the I to II century AD.

33. Dupont, *Études sur les Actes*, 75–81. The memorial (μνημόσυνον) in the Pentateuch is materialistic, consisting in priestly offerings before the Lord (ἔναντι κυρίου) in the altar of sacrifices: redemption money (symbolically offered; Exod 30:16); incense, oil, and choice flour for first fruits offerings (Lev 2:2,9,16); the same accompanying atonement sacrifices for sin (Lev 6:8); incense in the table of breads (Lev 24:7); barley flour for marital jealousy (Num 5:15,18,26). Later, the personal prayer acquires the property to be elevated unto the Almighty (Ps 102:2–3; 141:1) and to soften God so he might remember (μνησθῇς; LXX 1 Sam 1:11) the afflicted person. The late III century BC, in the dawn of the synagogue institution, incorporates alms to prayer as pious deeds expected to be done by the righteous believer (Tob 1:3,16; 2:14; 3:16; 4:7–11,16; 11:8–9; 12:12), concept of spiritual memorial the NT inherits (Luke 1:13; Acts 10:4,31; Rev 8:3).

Caesarea; 9:32—10:24), and Paul's journey to Jerusalem before his arrest (from Tyre to Ptolemais and then to Caesarea; 21:3–8) point to six cities abounding in Jewish presence that had been evangelized and where Christian communities expectedly missioned along the Via Maris between the Palestinian coastal plain and southern Phoenician coast. We must even add a seventh, Sidon, insofar as Acts reports Paul had some friends there (27:3). Even admitting the enlargement of the Caesarean tradition by the editor of Acts in the more theological sections concerning Philip (8:30–38), Peter (10:10–22,28–29,34–43), and Cornelius (10:3–6,30–33), the remaining data are fully concordant to consider non-fictitious the attribution of the gospel Gentile aperture to the Palestinian church's maneuver towards the close west, being natural to see, once one or two generations elapsed, this historical upgrowth centered in Peter (15:7).[34]

Jerusalem (the Judeo-Christian church core and John Mark's hometown), Caesarea Maritima (the first location where the Gentiles entered the gospel of Peter), Anatolia (the first mention by Papias of the second gospel origin in regards to Peter and Mark), and Rome (the traditional setting for its composition by Mark after Peter's death) close the circle of the earliest extant sources for the making up of Mark, whereas among the four Caesarea is the one that, following the previous analysis, fits better the archaeological and syntactical correlation with the second gospel. As it has been stated above, other candidates from the Syrian Diaspora in touch with Latin language, i.e., a Judeo-Christian community including Romanized Gentile candidates for the Christian faith, shared ideally with Caesarea in the last third of the I AD the same internal and outward features required for the composition of Mark's gospel. Berytus (Beirut), Tyre (21:3–6), Ptolemais (28:7), Antioch, and large towns of Transjordan can perfectly stand at the rear of the second gospel, but we lack in them the concentration of information and extant correlation we see around Caesarea Maritima.[35]

34. The attribution of the gospel's Gentile aperture to Peter during the Jerusalem council by the author of Acts is notorious, all the more that he puts Paul's mission to Gentiles in central Anatolia (13:46—14:27) two times in second position (15:7,12,14).

35. Mack, "Spyglass and the Kaleidoscope," 181–96 claims Tyre over the argument that Mark 7:24–30 sets forth a conflict of ethnic identities which would have pushed Mark to invent the story and exemplify the conflict in Jesus' encounter with the Syrophoenician woman. However, that the context of a sole Jesus episode is guessable doesn't inescapably unearth the evangelist's *Sitz im Leben*. If it were, we would be compelled to see Mark at once in Tyre, Galilee, Jerusalem, Capernaum, the oriental shore of the Lake of Galilee, the Decapolis, and the Judaean Desert, all locations where information to rebuild the I AD context is available and where several social groups or identities are at hand in the evangelic text. Ruefully, the previous claim, and the chraracterization by Mack, "Spyglass and the Kaleidoscope," 186–205 of Jesus as noble-death mythos based in Herakles-Melqart, result from the overuse of form criticism (Bultmann-Strauss

Several sections of the Acts of Peter related to the coastal plain, at least four (Acts 9:32–35; 9:36–43; 10:9–17,28–29; 10:34—11:18), find counterparts in the gospel of Mark (Mark 2:1–12; 5:21–24,35–43; 7:2–4; 15:39). The tradition about the daughters of Philip surfaces in Acts related to Caesarea (Acts 21:8–9) and then in Papias, associated to the tradition on Mark and Peter (Eusebius, *Hist. Eccl.* 3.39:9). The scrutiny of the Marcan grammar and the Caesarean social milieu parallel both a Gentile audience in a Semitic setting influenced by Latin administration, whereas finally Peter appears as the natural center, after Jesus, of the second gospel and, added to Philip, of the plausible Caesarean tradition in Acts. From Caesarea, manufactured copies of the second gospel not afield from its composition date could have traveled to Rome, Alexandria, Ephesus, Antioch, and other parts of Palestine in the last decades of I AD or early II AD, giving support to the first receptions of the gospel in Italy, Egypt, Syria, Anatolia, and Israel.[36]

Even more, it is fully respectful to the earliest source to close this monograph by asserting it was through the track that connected Hierapolis to the Aegean by way of Miletus and Ephesus that the second gospel tradition could have reached Papias. Two strong reasons come in help. First, John the Presbyter, from whom Papias received the tradition on Mark, was said to be buried in Ephesus, which should be recalled as the center of his

school) methodology that insofar as it hedges onerous contrary reasons anterior to the projection of the interpretative model, can be depicted as soft exegesis (see still valid conspectus of inconsistencies in Habermas, *Historical Jesus*, 27–57). Space reasons constrain here to a brief refutation for the second claim: (a) The institution of the Eucharist in 1 Cor 11:23–26, paralleled in Mark 14:22–25, proves tradition related to historical words of Jesus within a Jewish context and by which we learn Jesus was betrayed one night and that while dining saw himself as human offering establishing a new covenant in his blood, already existed in AD 55–57, less than twenty-five years distant from the facts they narrate. Jesus could have been wrong, but his words are a defiant problem to mythologists. (b) In 1 Cor 15:3–9, a not-less-revulsive tradition from the same date that Paul received on Jesus' resurrection, conceive the Jewish Scriptures as the window to read the risen Jesus, experienced (which kind of experience is not now relevant) among other contemporaries by James the Just, Jerosolimite attested in AD 62 (Josephus, *A.J.* 20.200–201). (c) In 1 Thess 4:15–17, AD 51, Jesus was understood by Paul as heavenly figure. (d) Peter's discourses in Acts, dated at the latest to AD 90, understand the heavenly Jesus from Davidic (2:22–36//Ps 16:8–11; 110:1//132:11), Mosaic (3:22–23//Deut 18:15–16,18–19; Lev 23:29), and Abrahamic (3:25//Gen 2:18) categories, and Philip's speech to the Ethiopian official in the same book reads Jesus' passion from Isaiah (8:32–33//Isa 53:7–8). Long-period social contexts could have cast common Levantine religious ideas, but the first believers in the crucified-risen Jesus firmly did not read the fact from Hellenistic-Phoenician mythology.

36. Eusebius, *Hist. Eccl.* 2.16:1 collects the tradition (φασιν, they say) of the early reception of the gospel of Mark in Egypt and of Mark as the first bishop of Alexandria. This tradition could be retaining again reminiscences of the eastern origin of the second gospel.

activity.[37] Second, as it has been stated too, one of Philip's prophetess daughters was said to have lived in Hierapolis with his father, and a second daughter different from the former, according to Polycrates, was to be buried in Ephesus, reinforcing the existence of Christian exchange between Caesarea, Hierapolis, and Ephesus (represented by Philip, his two daughters, Papias, and John the Presbyter). It cannot be totally proven, but the entailment with Ephesus implies that the Marcan tradition likely was introduced into Anatolia from another coastal town, Caesarea being a superb candidate in view of its Christian link with Hierapolis and Ephesus (by way of Philip and his daughters). If the previous is accepted, it's quite cogent, therefore, to suppose that not only the tradition on the origin of the second gospel sailed to Anatolia, arriving first at Ephesus and not much later on at Hierapolis, but also the second gospel itself.[38]

As a contrast, it is fair to elude blind confidence in the proceedings of modern exegesis, bearing in mind that for history proving the possibility is not the same as proving the fact. The geographical imprecisions in the Galilean part of Mark dull the easy identification of nearby Caesarea: a Christian, Jewish by origin, in contact for sufficient time with Roman administration in the Sharon Plain so as to include a number of Latinisms, would have to manage the geography of Palestine and the Decapolis, unless

37. Eusebius, *Hist. Eccl.* 3.39:3–6.14–15; 5.24:2–24.

38. The Hellenistic city of Ἱεράπολις (the Holy City) owed its name to the sacred cave of Plutonium, a natural grotto of toxic steam blooms. Situated in the fringe of the central-western Anatolian Plateau, the ruins of Hierapolis, Pamukkale today, are sixteen kilometers north of Denizli, a town that gives name to the modern province. At more or less double the former distance from Hierapolis were located the closest towns, Laodicea to the southwest and Colossae to the southeast, which with Hierapolis formed the hub of southern Phrygia (see Col 4:13). The town measurements approximately were 1.5 kilometers in the east-west axis by 600 meters north-south, highlighting its necropolis to the north, where a slope with natural springs of calcareous water marked the northern limit of the town. The main human channels crossed to the west and south. To the northwest, a mountain passage led to Philadelphia, Sardis, and Magnesia, and from this last it was possible to arrive at Smyrna on the mid-Aegean coast. To the west, Ephesus also in the Aegean, could be reached by taking a detour from the low course of the Meander River (actual Büyuk Menderes), which died at the coast in Miletus, 60 kilometers south of Ephesus. Finally, Hierapolis connected southeastwards through Pisidia with the Mediterranean in the Pamphylian shore (D'Andria, *Hierapolis of Phrygia*, 9–26). Perga and Attalia in the last coast, visited by Paul during his first journey (Acts 13:13–14; 14:24–25), were potential spots for the penetration of Christian traditions into southern Phrygia, but the letter of Polycrates and Eusebius on Papias denote Ephesus. During Paul's captivity, the harsh winds obliged to cabotage navigation from Caesarea to the Aegean by way of Cyprus, Pamphylia, and Lycia (Acts 27:1–8), but the direct way back from Ephesus to Caesarea performed by Paul in his second journey (Acts 18:21–22) most probably shows the route that was usual in its proper season and/or with good conditions.

his interest in detail displayed in other Marcan sections is not extensible to all his document for reasons today unguessable. Insofar as the final material proof is lacking, the outcome of honest research in classical disputed issues of ancient Christianity must be crowned with the question mark, a spur for next inquiry. Other researchers will find, surely, faults in what has been stated here, more congruent hypotheses accounting for the same phenomena, and clearer answers in matters where the line of decision has been for me hard to draw. It is practically impossible that no serious question will be raised against the weakest points of this monograph. Facing this assumption, perhaps the best contribution it offers scholarship is the inclusive perspective, mulling favorable and contrary claims over the chief Marcan subjects available to study.

Bibliography

Sacred Scripture and Jewish Oral Tradition

Aland, Barbara, Kurt Aland, et al., eds. *Nestle-Aland Novum Testamentum Graece: Greek-English New Testament*. 28th ed. Stuttgart: Deutsche Bibelgesellschaft, 2013.

Biblia de Jerusalén: Nueva Edición Revisada y Aumentada. Bilbao: Desclée de Brouwer, 1998.

The Complete Hebrew-Greek Bible. Peabody, MA: Hendrickson, 2017 (= Dotan, Aron, ed. *Biblia Hebraica Leningradensia*. Tel Aviv: ADI/School of Jewish Studies, 1973; Westcott, Brooke Foss, and Fenton John Anthony Hort, eds. *The New Testament in the Original Greek: The Text Revised*. Cambridge: Macmillan, 1885).

Coogan, Michael D., ed. *The New Oxford Annotated Bible: New Revised Standard Version with the Apocrypha*. Oxford: Oxford University Press, 2018.

Danby, Herbert, trans. *The Mishnah: Translated from the Hebrew with Introduction and Brief Explanatory Notes*. London: Oxford University Press, 1949.

Del Valle, Carlos, ed. *La Misná*. Madrid: Nacional, 1981.

Guggenheimer, Heinrich W., ed. *The Jerusalem Talmud First Order: Zeraim. Tractate Berakhot*. Berlin: De Gruyter, 2000.

———, ed. *The Jerusalem Talmud Second Order: Mo'ed. Tractates Šeqalim, Sukkah, Roš Haššanah, and Yom Ṭov (Besah)*. Berlin: De Gruyter, 2014.

———, ed. *The Jerusalem Talmud Third Order: Našim. Tractate Ketubot. Sixth Order: Tahorot, Tractate Niddah*. Berlin: De Gruyter, 2006.

Nova Vulgata Bibliorum Sacrorum. Vatican City: Vaticana, 1979.

Rahlfs, Alfred, ed. *Septuaginta: Id est Vetus Testamentum Graece Iuxta LXX Interpretes I–II*. Stuttgart: Württembergische Bibelanstalt Stuttgart, 1965.

Scrivener, Frederick H., ed. *Bezae Codex Cantabrigiensis: Being an Exact Copy, in Ordinary Type, of the Celebrated Uncial Graeco-Latin Manuscript of the Four Gospels and Acts of the Apostles*. 1864. Reprint, Seattle: Scholar Select, 2015.

Church Fathers, Pseudepigrapha, and Classical Sources

Acts of Peter. *The Apocryphal*. Translated by Pick Bernhard. Chicago: Open Court, 1909.

Ascension of Isaiah. *Translated from the Ethiopic Version*. Translated by R. H. Charles. London: Adam and Charles Black, 1900.

2 Baruch. *The Apocalypse: Translated from the Syriac*. Translated by R. H. Charles. London: Adam and Charles Black, 1896.

Book of Jubilees. *Translated from the Editor's Ethiopic Text*. Translated by R. H. Charles. London: Adam and Charles Black, 1902.

Canon Muratorianus. *The Earliest Catologue of the Books of the New Testament*. Edited by Samuel P. Tregelles. 1868. Reprint, Norderstedt: Hansebooks, 2019.

Clement Alexandrinus. *Stromatéis: Memorias Gnósticas de Verdadera Filosofía*. Translated by Domingo Mayor. Burgos: Aldecoa, 1994.

———. *Stromata Buch I–VI*. Edited by Otto Stählin. Leipzig: J.C. Hinrichs, 1906.

———. *Stromata Buch VII und VIII. Excerpta ex Theodoto. Eclogae Propheticae. Quis dives Salvetur. Fragmente*. Edited by Otto Stählin. Leipzig: J. C. Hinrichs, 1909.

———. *Supplementum*. Edited by Theodor Zahn. Erlangen: Andreas Deichert, 1884.

Clement Romanus. *Ad Corinthios Epistulae Versio Latina Antiquissima*. Edited by Germanus Morin. Maredsous: Oxaniae/J. Parker, 1894.

———. *Carta a los Corintios. Homilía Anónima* [*Secunda Clementis*]. Edited by Juan José Ayán. Madrid: Ciudad Nueva, 1994.

1 Clement, 2 Clement, and Papias. In *The Apostolic Fathers*, translated by Bart D. Ehrman. 2 vols. LCL. Cambridge, MA: Harvard University Press, 2003.

Constitutiones Apostolorum. In *Dicascalia et Constitutiones Apostolorum*, edited by Franciscus Xaverius Funk. Paderborn: Libraria Ferdinandi Schoeningh, 1905.

Diodorus Siculus. *The Library of History*. Translated by C. H. Oldfather et al. 12 vols. LCL. Cambridge, MA: Harvard University Press, 1933–1967.

1 Enoch. *The Books: Complete Edition*. Translated by R. H. Charles. 1912. Reprint, Las Vegas: International Alliance, 2012.

Epiphanius. *Ancoratus und Panarion Haer. 1–33*. Edited by Karl Holl. Leipzig: J. C. Hinrich Buchhandlung, 1915.

———. *Panarion (Sects 1–46)*. Translated by Frank Williams. Leiden: Brill, 2009.

Eusebius. *The Ecclesiastical History*. Translated by Kirsopp Lake and J. E. L. Oulton. 2 vols. LCL. London: William Heinemann/Harvard University Press, 1926–1932.

Gospel of Thomas. *Coptic Text Established and Translated*. Edited and translated by A. Guillaumont et al. Leiden: Brill, 1959.

Ignatius and Polycarp. Edited by Juan José Ayán. Madrid: Ciudad Nueva, 1991.

Irenaeus. *Contre les Hérésies: Livre III/2, IV/2, V/2*. Edited by Adelin Rousseau and Louis Doutreleau. Paris: Du Cerf, 1965–2002.

Jerome. *Obras Completas: Comentario a Mateo y Otros Escritos*. Translated by Virgilio Bejarano. Madrid: BAC, 2003.

Josephus. Translated by H. St. J. Thackeray et al. 10 vols. LCL. London: Heinemann/Harvard University Press, 1926–1965.

———. *The Complete Works*. Translated by William Whiston. Green Forest, AR: New Leaf, 2008.

Justin Martyr. *Writings*. Translated by Thomas B. Falls. Washington, DC: Catholic University of America Press, 2008.

———. *Apologia Prima. Dialogus cum Tryphone Judaeo*. Edited by William Trollope. Cambridge: Macmillan/Barclay/George Bell, 1845–1847.

Juvenal. *Satirae*. Translated by G. G. Ramsay. LCL. London: Heinemann/Putnam, 1918.

Melito. *On Pascha*. Translated by Alistair C. Stewart. Yonkers, NY: St. Vladimir's Seminary Press, 2016.

Origen. *The Commentary on S. John's Gospel Vol. I.* Edited by A. E. Brooke. Cambridge: J. and C.F. Clay, 1896.

Ovid. *Metamorphoses*. Translated by Frank Justus Miller. 2 vols. LCL. Cambridge, MA: Harvard University Press/Heinemann, 1916.

Periplus Maris Erythraei. *Text with Introduction, Translation and Commentary*. Translated by Lionel Casson. Princeton, NJ: Princeton University Press, 1989.

Peter the Deacon. Edited by J.P. Migne. Patrologia Latina. 217 vols. Paris: 1844–1864.

Philo. Translated by F. H. Colson. 10 vols. LCL. Cambridge, MA: Harvard University Press, 1929–1962.

Pliny the Elder. *Natural History*. Translated by H. Rackham. 10 vols. LCL. Cambridge, MA: Harvard University Press/William Heinemann, 1938–1962.

Pliny the Younger. *Letters*. Translated by William Melmoth. 2 vols. LCL. London: Heinemann/Putnam, 1915.

Plutarch. *Lives*. Translated by Bernadotte Perrin. 11 vols. LCL. Cambridge, MA: Harvard University Press/Heinemann, 1914–1926.

Propertius. *Elegies*. Translated by H. E. Butler. LCL. London: Heinemann/Putnam, 1916.

Seneca. *Moral Essays*. Translated by John W. Basore. 3 vols. LCL. Cambridge, MA: Harvard University Press, 1928–1935.

Shepherd of Hermas. In *The Apostolic Fathers*, edited by J. B. Lightfoot and J. R. Harmer. London: Macmillan, 1893.

Sibylline Oracles. *Translated from the Greek into English Blank Verse*. Translated by Milton S. Terry. New York: Hunt & Eaton/Cranston & Stone, 1890.

Strabo. *Geography*. Translated by Horace Leonard Jones. 8 vols. LCL. London: Heinemann/Putnam, 1917–1932.

Tacitus. *Annals*. Translated by John Jackson. 2 vols. LCL. London: Heinemann/Harvard University Press, 1962.

———. *Histories*. Translated by Clifford H. Moore. 2 vols. LCL. London: Heinemann/Harvard University Press, 1962.

Tertullian. *"Prescripciones" contra Todas las Herejías*. Edited by Salvador Vicastillo. Madrid: Ciudad Nueva, 2001.

———. *A los Mártires, El Escorpión, La Huida en la Persecución*. Translated by Constantino Ánchel and José Manuel Serrano. Madrid: Ciudad Nueva, 2004.

Epigraphy and Paleography

Ameling, Walter, Cotton, Hannah M., Eck, Werner., et al., eds. *Corpus Inscriptionum Iudaeae/Palaestinae.* Vol. III: *South Coast (2161–2648)*. Berlin: De Gruyter, 2014.

Boeckhio, Augusto, and Joannes Franzius, eds. *Corpus Inscriptionum Graecarum* Vol. 2–3. Berlin: Officina Academica, 1843–1853.

Bormann, Eugenius, and Henzen Guilelmus, eds. *Corpus Inscriptionum Latinarum*. Vol. 6/1. Berlin: Georgium Reimerum, 1876.

Cagnat, René, and Georges Lafaye, eds. *Inscriptiones Graecae ad Res Romanas Pertinentes Tomus I; IV*. Ernest Leroux, Paris, 1901–1927.

Comfort, Philip Wesley. *The Text of the Earliest New Testament Manuscripts.* Vol. 2: *Papyri 75–139 and Uncials.* Gran Rapids: Kregel Academic, 2019.

Comfort, Philip Wesley, and David P. Barrett. *The Text of the Earliest New Testament Manuscripts.* Vol. 1: *Papyri 1–72.* Gran Rapids: Kregel Academic, 2019.

Cotton, Hannah M., Leah Di Segni, Werner Eck, et al., eds. *Corpus Inscriptionum Iudaeae/Palaestinae.* Vol. 1: *Jerusalem. Part 1 (1–704).* Berlin: De Gruyter, 2010.

Cowley, A. *Aramaic Papyri of the Fifth Century BC.* Oxford: Clarendon, 1923.

Dessau, Hermannus, ed. *Inscriptiones Latinae Selectae.* Vol. 3/2. Berlin: Weidmannsche Buchhandlung, 1916.

Hartman, Dorota. *Archivio di Babatha.* Vol. 1: *Testi Greci e Ketubbah.* Brescia: Paideia, 2016.

Kenyon, Frederic G. *The Chester Beatty Biblical Papyri: Descriptions and Texts of Twelve Manuscripts on Papyrus of the Greek Bible. Fasciculus I: General Introduction; II: The Gospels and Acts.* London: Emery Walker, 1933–1934.

Kraeling, Emil G. *The Brooklyn Museum Aramaic Papyri: New Documents of the Fifth Century B.C. from the Jewish Colony of Elephantine.* New Haven, CT: Yale University Press, 1953.

Lehmann, Clayton Miles, and Kenneth G Holum. *The Joint Expedition to Caesarea Maritima Excavation Reports: The Greek and Latin Inscriptions of Caesarea Maritima.* Boston: American Schools of Oriental Research, 2000.

Milne, J. G. "Greek Inscriptions from Egypt." *JHS* 21 (1901) 275–92.

Mommsen, Theodorus, ed. *Corpus Inscriptionum Latinarum.* Vol. 3: *Pars Prior.* Berlin: Georgium Reimerum, 1873.

Mouterde, René. *Monuments et Inscriptions de Syrie et du Liban.* Beyrouth: Imprimerie Catholique, 1942.

Reisch, Emil, ed. *Forschungen in Ephesos.* Vol. 3. Wien: Österreichischen Akademie der Wissenshaften, 1923.

Other Authors

Abbott, T. K. *A Critical and Exegetical Commentary on the Epistles to the Ephesians and to the Colossians.* Edinburgh: T. & T. Clarck, 1974.

Achtemeier, Paul J. *1 Peter.* Minneapolis: Augsburg Fortress, 1996.

Adam, James Noel. *Bilingualism and the Latin Language.* Cambridge: Cambridge University Press, 2008.

Álvarez, David. "The Centurion's Statement (Mark 15:39): A Restitutio Memoriae." In *Jesus-Gestalt und Gestaltungen Band 100: Rezeptionen des Galiläers in Wissenschaft, Kirche und Gesellschaft,* edited by Petra von Gemünden, David G. Horrell, and Max Küchler, 146–61. Göttingen: Vandenhoeck & Ruprecht, 2013.

Andrews, D.K. "The Translation of the Aramaic *dî* in the Greek Bibles." *JBL* 66/1 (1947) 15–51.

Avi Yonah, Michael, and Shimon Gibson. "Caesarea." In *EncJud* 4:333–34.

Barag, Dan. "Brick Stamp-Impressions of the Legio X Fretensis." In *Bonner Jahrbücher,* vol. 167, 244–67. Darmstadt: Verlag Philipp Von Zabern, 1967.

Basso, Michele. *Eschatological Symbolism in the Vatican Necropolis.* Vatican City: Tipografia Poliglotta Vaticana, 1982.

Bauckham, Richard. "Papias and Polycrates on the Origin of the Fourth Gospel." *JTS* 44/1 (1993) 24–69.

Baum, Armin D. "Mark's Paratactic *Καί* as a Secondary Syntactic Semitism." *NovT* 58/1 (2016) 1–26.

Beatrice, Pier Franco. "The Gospel according to the Hebrews in the Apostolic Fathers." *NovT* 48/2 (2006) 147–95.

Beauvery, Robert. "La Route Romaine de Jérusalem a Jéricho." *RB* 64/1 (1957) 72–101.

Beaven, James. *An Account of the Life and Writings of S. Irenaeus, Bishop of Lyon and Martyr: Intended to Illustrate the Doctrine, Discipline, Practices, and History of the Church*. London: J. G. F. & J. Rivington, 1841.

Bellinzoni, Arthur J. "The Gospel of Luke in the Apostolic Fathers: An Overview." In *Trajectories through the New Testament and the Apostolic Fathers*, edited by Andrew Gregory and Christopher Tuckett, 45–68. Oxford: Oxford University Press, 2005.

Benovitz, Moshe. *Kol Nidre: Studies in the Development of Rabbinic Votive Institutions*. Atlanta: Scholars, 2020.

Berdowski, Piotr. "Garum of Herod the Great (Latin Greek Inscription on the Amphora from Masada)." *TQC* 16/3–4 (2008) 107–22.

Berlin, Andrea M. "Jewish Life before the Revolt: The Archaeological Evidence." *JSJ* 36/4 (2005) 417–70.

Black, C. Clifton. *Mark: Images of an Apostolic Interpreter*. Minneapolis: Fortress, 2001.

Black, Matthew. *An Aramaic Approach to the Gospels and Acts*. Eugene, OR: Wipf & Stock, 2020.

Blakely, Jeffrey A. "Ceramics and Commerce: Amphorae from Caesarea Maritima." *BASOR* 271 (1988) 31–50.

Boring, Eugene. *Mark: A Commentary*. Louisville: Westminster John Knox, 2012.

Bradley, Keith R. "Remarriage and the Structure of the Upper-Class Roman Family." In *Marriage, Divorce and Children in Ancient Rome*, edited by Beryl Rawson, 79–98. Oxford: Clarendon Press, 1992.

Broughton, T. Robert S. *The Beginning of Christianity*. Vol. 5. London: Macmillan, 1933.

———. *The Magistrates of the Roman Republic*. Vol. 2. New York: American Philological Association, 1952.

Brown, Raymond E., and John P. Meier. *Antioch and Rome: New Testament Cradles of Catholic Christianity*. London: Geoffrey Chapman, 1983.

Burkett, Delbert. *Rethinking the Gospel Sources: From Proto-Mark to Mark*. New York: T. & T. Clark, 2004.

Casey, Maurice. *An Aramaic Approach to Q: Sources for the Gospels of Matthew and Luke*. Cambridge: Cambridge University Press, 2002.

———. *Aramaic Sources of Mark's Gospel*. Cambridge: Cambridge University Press, 1998.

Charlesworth, Scott D. "T.C. Skeat, P^{64+67} and P^4,and the Problem of Fibre Orientation in Codological Reconstruction." *NTS* 53/4 (2007) 582–604.

Conzelmann, Hans. "El Lugar de Lucas en el Desarrollo del Cristianismo Primitivo." Translated by Antonio Rodríguez. In *La Investigación de los Evangelios Sinópticos y los Hechos de los Apóstoles en el Siglo XX*, edited by Rafael Aguirre and Antonio Rodríguez, 375–97. Estella: Verbo Divino, 1996.

Corbo, Virgilio. *The House of Saint Peter at Capharnaum: A Preliminary Report of the Two Campaigns of Excavations, April 16–June 19, Sept. 12–Nov. 26, 1968*. Jerusalem: Franciscan, 1969.

Cortés, Juan B., and Florence M. Gatti. "The Son of Man or the Son of Adam." *Bib* 49/4 (1968) 457–502.

Cosgrove, Charles H. "Justin Martyr and the Emerging Christian Canon: Observations on the Purpose and Destination of the Dialogue with Trypho". *VC* 36/3 (1982) 209–34.

Cotter, Wendy. "Women's Authority Roles in Paul's Churches: Countercultural or Conventional?" *NovT* 36/4 (1994) 350–72.

Couchoud, Paul-Louis. "L'Evangile de Marc a été Écrit en Latin?" *RHR* 94 (1926) 161–92.

Cranfield, C. E. B. *The Gospel according to Saint Mark*. Cambridge: Cambridge University Press, 2000.

Dąbrowa, Edward. "Legio X Fretensis." In *Les Légions de Rome sous le Haut-Empire*, vol. 1, edited by Yann Le Bohec and Catherine Wolff, 317–25. Paris: De Boccard, 2000.

Dalman, Gustaf. *Sacred Sites and Ways: Studies in the Topography of the Gospels*. New York: Macmillan, 1935.

D'Andria, Francesco. *Hierapolis of Phrygia (Pamukkale): An Archaeological Guide*. Istanbul: Ege Yayinlari, 2010.

Davidson, Benjamin. *A Concordance of the Hebrew and Chaldee Scriptures*. 1876. Reprint, Seattle: Scholar Select, 2016.

De Vaux, Roland. "Fouilles de Khirbet Qumrân: Rapport préliminaire sur les 3e, 4e et 5e Campagnes." *RB* 63/4 (1956) 533–77.

Donahue, John R. "Windows and Mirrors: The Setting of Mark's Gospel." *CBQ* 57/1 (1995) 1–26.

Donfried, Karl Paul. *The Setting of Second Clement in Early Christianity*. Leiden: Brill, 1974.

———. "The Theology of Second Clement". *HTR* 66/4 (1973) 487–501.

Dormandy, Richard. "The Expulsion of Legion: A Political Reading of Mark 5:1–20." *ExpTim* 111/10 (2000) 335–37.

Doudna, John Charles. *The Greek of the Gospel of Mark*. Philadelphia: Society of Biblical Literature and Exegesis, 1963.

Dupont, Jacques. *Études sur les Actes des Apotres*. Paris: Du Cerf, 1967.

Elliott, James Keith. "Greek New Testament Papyri and Their Text in the Second-Third Centuries". In *Gospels and Gospel Traditions in the Second Century*, edited by Jens Schröter, Tobias Nicklas, and Joseph Verheyden, 1–26. Berlin: De Gruyter, 2020.

Ember, Aaron. "The Pluralis Intensivus in Hebrew." *AJSLL* 21 (1905) 195–231.

Evans, Jane DeRose. *The Joint Expedition to Caesarea Maritima Excavation Reports: The Coins and the Hellenistic, Roman and Byzantine Economy of Palestine*. Boston (Mass.): American Schools of Oriental Research, 2006.

Ferguson, Everett. "Canon Muratori: Date and Provenance." StPatr 17/2 (1982) 677–83.

———. "Factors Leading to the Selection and Closure of the New Testament Canon." In *The Canon Debate*, edited by Lee Martin McDonald and James A. Sanders, 295–320. Grand Rapids: Baker Academic, 2019.

Fialová, Radka. "Scripture and the Memoirs of the Apostles." In *The Process of Authority: The Dynamics in Transmission and Reception of Canonical Texts*, edited by Jan Dušek and Jan Roskovec, 165–78. Berlin: De Gruyter.

Foster, Paul. "Ignatius and the Gospels." In *Gospels and Gospel Traditions in the Second Century*, edited by Jens Schröter, Tobias Nicklas, and Joseph Verheyden, 81–106. Berlin: De Gruyter, 2020.

Frend, William H.C. *The Archaeology of Early Christianity*. Minneapolis: Augsburg Fortress, 1996.

Friedman, Mordechai A. "Termination of the Marriage upon the Wife's Request: A Palestinian Ketubba Stipulation." *PAAJR* 37 (1969) 29–55.

Garroway, Joshua. "The Invasion of a Mustard Seed: A Reading of Mark 5.1–20." *JSNT* 32/1 (2009) 57–75.

Gathercole, Simon. "The Earliest Manuscript Title of Matthew's Gospel (BnF Suppl. gr. 1120 ii 3/P4)." *NovT* 54/3 (2012) 209–35.

Gibson, Shimon. "The Trial of Jesus at the Jerusalem Praetorium: New Archaeological Evidence." In *The World of Jesus and the Early Church*, edited by Craig A. Evans, 97–118. Peabody: Hendrickson, 2011.

Govaars, Marylinda, Spiro, Marie, and L. Michael. White. *The Joint Expedition to Caesarea Maritima Excavation Reports: Field O: The "Synagogue" Site*. Boston: American Schools of Oriental Research, 2009.

Grant, Robert M. *Irenaeus of Lyon*. London: Routledge, 1997.

Grenfell, Bernard P., and Arthur S. Hunt, eds. *The Oxyrhynchus Papyri Parts III–IV*. London: Egypt Exploration Fund, 1903–1904.

Guarducci, Margherita. *La Tomba di San Pietro: Una Straordinaria Vicenda*. Milano: Rusconi, 1989.

Habermas, Gary R. *The Historical Jesus: Ancient Evidence for the Life of Christ*. Joplin: College Press, 1996.

Haenchen, Ernst. *Acts of the Apostles: A Commentary*. Philadelphia: Westminster, 1971.

Haensch, Rudolf. "The Contribution of Inscriptions to our Knowledge of the Herodian Dynasty." *SCI* 33 (2014) 99–116.

Hahneman, Geoffrey Mark. "The Muratorian Fragment and the Origins of the New Testament Canon." In *The Canon Debate*, edited by Lee Martin McDonald and James A. Sanders, 405–15. Grand Rapids: Baker Academic, 2019.

Hall, Robert G. "The Ascension of Isaiah: Community Situation, Date, and Place in Early Christianity." *JBL* 109/2 (1990) 289–306.

Hare, Douglas R. A. *The Theme of Jewish Persecution of Christians in the Gospel According to St Matthew*. London: Cambridge University Press, 1967.

Harnack, Adolf von. *The Acts of the Apostles*. London: William & Norgate/Putnam, 1909.

Head, Peter M. "The Date of the Magdalen Papyrus of Matthew (P.Magd. Gr.17= P64): A Response to C.P. Thiede." *TB* 46/2 (1995) 251–85.

———. "Is P4, P64 and P67 the Oldest Manuscript of the Four Gospels?: A Response to T.C. Skeat." *NTS* 51/3 (2005) 450–57.

Heard, Richard. "The ΑΠΟΜΝΗΜΟΝΕΥΜΑΤΑ in Papias, Justin, and Irenaeus." *NTS* 1/2 (1954) 122–29.

Hendin, David. *Guide to Biblical Coins*. New York: American Numismatic Society, 2021.

———. "The Metrology of Judaean Small Bronze Coins." *AJN* 21 (2009) 105–21.

Hengel, Martin. *Studies in the Gospel of Mark*. Translated by John Bowden. Philadelphia: Fortress, 1985.

Hertling, Ludwig, and Engelbert Kirschbaum. *The Roman Catacombs and their Martyrs*. London: Darton, Longman & Todd, 1975.

Hill, Charles E. "Ignatius, the Gospel, and the Gospels." In *Trajectories through the New Testament and the Apostolic Fathers*, edited by Andrew Gregory and Christopher Tuckett, 267–85. Oxford: Oxford University Press, 2005.

Hostetter, Edwin C. *An Elementary Grammar of Biblical Hebrew*. Sheffield: Sheffield Academic, 2000.

Hurtado, Larry W. *The Earliest Christian Artifacts: Manuscripts and Christian Origins*. Grand Rapids: Eerdmans, 2006.

Incigneri, Brian J. *The Gospel to the Romans: The Setting and Rhetoric of Mark's Gospel*. Leiden: Brill, 2003.

Iverson, Kelly R. "A Centurion's Confession: A Performance-Critical Analysis of Mark 15:39." *JBL* 130/2 (2011) 329–50.

Jacobson, David M. "Coins of the First Century Roman Governors of Judaea and Their Motifs." *Elec* 26 (2019) 73–96.

Jensen, Morten Hørning. "Message and Minting: The Coins of Herod Antipas in their Second Temple Context as Source for Understanding the Religio-Political and Socio-Economic Dynamics of Early First Century Galilee." In *Religion, Ethnicity, and Identity in Ancient Galilee: A Region in Transition*, edited by Jürgen Zangenberg, Harold W. Attride, and Dale B. Martin, 277–313. Tübingen: Mohr Siebeck, 2007.

Jidejian, Nina. *Beirut through the Ages*. Beirut: Librairie Orientale, 1997.

Johns, Alger F. *A Short Grammar of Biblical Aramaic*. Berrien Springs: Andrews University Press, 1972.

Jones, Linda. *Roman Berytus: Beirut in Late Antiquity*. London: Routledge, 2004.

Jöris, Stephen. "More than Family Dispute: Mk 13:12–13a and Isa 66:5". *RB* 121/3 (2014) 359–74.

Kadman, Leo. "Temple Dues and Currency in Ancient Palestine in the Light of Recent Discovered Coin-Hoards." In *Congresso Internazionale di Numismatica: Roma 11–16 Settembre 1961 Vol. II: Atti*, 69–76. Roma: Istituto Italiano di Numismatica, 1965.

Kalin, Everett R., "The New Testament Canon of Eusebius." In *The Canon Debate*, edited by Lee Martin McDonald and James A. Sanders, 386–404. Grand Rapids: Baker Academic, 2019.

Kelhoffer, James A. "The Ecclesiology of 2 Clement 14: Ephesians, Pauline Reception, and the Church's Preexistence". In *Receptions of Paul in Early Christianity: The Person of Paul and his Writings through the Eyes of His Early Interpreters*, edited by Simon Butticaz, Andreas Dettwiler, and Jens Schröter, 377–409. Berlin: De Gruyter, 2018.

King, Cathy E. "Quadrantes from the River Tiber." *NumC* 15 (1975) 56–90.

Kloppenborg, John S. "Dating Theodotos (CIJ II 1404)." *JJS* LI/2 (2000) 243–80.

———."Evocatio Deorum and the Date of Mark." *JBL* 124/3 (2005) 419–50.

Lampe, Peter. *From Paul to Valentinus: Christians at Rome in the First Two Centuries*. Minneapolis: Fortress, 2003.

Lernau, Omri, Hannah Cotton, and Yuval Goren. "Salted Fish and Fish Sauces from Masada: A Preliminary Report." *Archaeo* 5 (1996) 35–41.

Lindsay, W. M. *Syntax of Plautus*. Oxford: James Parker, 1907.

Loffreda, Stanislao. *Cafarnao II: La Ceramica*. Jerusalem: Franciscan, 1974.

———. *Recovering Capharnaum*. Jerusalem: Franciscan, 2001.

Löhr, Winrich Alfried. "Gnostic Determinism Reconsidered." *VC* 46/4 (1992) 381–90.

Lönnqvist, Kenneth. *The Report of the Amman Lots of the Qumran Silver Coin Hoards: New Chronological Aspects of the Silver Coin Hoard Evidence from Khirbet Qumran at the Dead Sea*. Amman: Jordan, 2007.

Mack, Burton L. "The Spyglass and the Kaleidoscope: From a Levantine Coign of Vantage." In *Redescribing the Gospel of Mark*, edited by Barry S. Crawford and Merrill P. Miller, 181–205. Atlanta: SBL, 2017.

Maloney, Elliott C. *Semitic Interference in Marcan Syntax*. Atlanta: SBL, 1981.

Mann, Christopher Stephen. *Mark: A New Translation with Introduction and Commentary*. New York: Doubleday, 1986.

Marcus, Joel. "The Jewish War and the Sitz im Leben of Mark." *JBL* 111/3 (1992) 441–62.

Marguerat, Daniel. *The First Christian Historian: Writing the "Acts of the Apostles"*. Cambridge: Cambridge University Press, 2004.

Martin, Raymond A. *Syntactical Evidence of Semitic Sources in Greek Documents*. Cambridge (Mass.): Society of Biblical Literature, 1974.

Martin, Troy W. "Watch During the Watches (Mark 13:35)." *JBL* 120/4 (2001) 685–701.

Mason, Hugh J. *Greek Terms for Roman Institutions: A Lexicon and Analysis*. Toronto: A.M. Hakkert, 1974.

Mattila, Sharon Lea. "Capernaum, Village of Nahum, from Hellenistic to Byzantine Times." In *Galilee in the Late Second Temple and Mishnaic Periods: The Archaeological Record from Cities, Towns and Villages*, edited by David A. Fiensy and James Riley Strange, 217–57. Minneapolis: Fortress, 2015.

———. "Revisiting Jesus' Capernaum: A Village of Only Subsistence-Level Fishers and Farmers?" In *The Galilean Economy in the Time of Jesus*, edited by David A. Fiensy and Ralph K. Hawkins, 75–138. Atlanta: SBL, 2013.

Meade, David G. *Pseudonymity and Canon*. Tübingen: Mohr (Paul Siebeck), 1986.

Metzger, Bruce M. *A Textual Commentary on the Greek New Testament*. London: United Bible Societies, 1971.

Metzger, Bruce M., and Bart D. Ehrman. *The Text of the New Testament: Its Transmission, Corruption, and Restoration*. New York: Oxford University Press, 2005.

Millar, Fergus. *Rome, The Greek World and the East*. Vol. 3: *The Greek World, the Jews and the East*. Chapel Hill: University of North Carolina Press, 2006.

Miller, Stuart S. "Some Observations on Stone Vessel Finds and Ritual Purity in Light of Talmudic Sources". In *Zeichen aus Text und Stein. Studien auf Weg zu einer Archäologie des Neuen Testaments*, edited by Stefan Alkier and Jürgen Zangenberg, 402–19. Tübingen: Francke, 2003.

Moulton, J. H., and W. F. Howard. *A Grammar of New Testament Greek*. Vol. 2: *Accidence and Word-Formation with an Appendix on Semitisms in the New Testament*. London: T. & T. Clark, 2004.

Naudé, J.A. "A Syntactic Analysis of Dislocation in Biblical Hebrew." *JNSL* XVI (1990) 115–30.

Norelli, Enrico. "Χριστιανισμός e Χριστιανός in Ignazio di Antiochia e la Cronologia delle sue Lettere." In *Gesù e la Storía: Percorsi sulle Origini del Cristianesimo*, edited by M. Beatrice Durante, Marco Vitelli, and Dario Garribba, 171–89. Trapani: Il Pozzo di Giacobbe, 2015.

O'Callaghan, José. *Los Papiros Griegos de la Cueva 7 de Qumrân*. Madrid: BAC, 1974.

———. "¿Papiros Neotestamentarios en la Cueva 7 de Qumrân?" *Bib* 53/1 (1972) 91–100.

O'Callaghan, Roger T. "Recent Excavations underneath the Vatican Crypts." *BA* 16/4 (1953) 70–87.

Osborn, Eric. *Clement of Alexandria*. Cambridge: Cambridge University Press, 2005.

Patterson, L. G. "The Divine Became Human: Irenaean Themes in Clement Alexandrine." StPatr 31 (1997) 497–516.

Peleg-Barkat, Orit. "Herod's Western Palace in Jerusalem: Some New Insights." *Elec* 26 (2019) 53–72.

Piper, Otto A. "The Nature of the Gospel according to Justin Martyr." *JR* 41/3 (1961) 155–68.

Pryke, E. J. *Redactional Style in the Marcan Gospel.* Cambridge: Cambridge University Press, 1978.

Rathbone, Dominic. "Egypt, Augustus and Roman Taxation." *CCGG* 4 (1993) 81–112.

Ray, Stephen K. *Upon This Rock: St. Peter and the Primacy of Rome in Scripture and the Early Church.* San Francisco: Ignatius, 1999.

Reed, Jonathan L. *Archaeology and the Galilean Jesus: A Re-Examination of the Evidence.* Harrisburg, PA: Trinity, 2000.

———. "Stone Vessels and Gospel Texts. Purity and Socio-Economics in John 2." In *Zeichen aus Text und Stein. Studien auf Weg zu einer Archäologie des Neuen Testaments*, edited by Stefan Alkier and Jürgen Zangenberg, 381–401. Tübingen: Francke, 2003.

Re'em, Amit. "First and Second Temple Period Fortifications and Herod's Palace in the Jerusalem Kisleh Compound." In *Ancient Jerusalem Revealed*, edited by Hillel Geva, 136–44. Jerusalem: Israel Exploration Society, 2019.

Rook, John T. "Boanerges, Sons of the Thunder (Mark 3:17)." *JBL* 100/1 (1981) 94–95.

Roskam, H.N. *The Purpose of the Gospel of Mark in its Historical and Social Context.* Leiden: Brill, 2004.

Rothschild, Clare K. "The Muratorian Fragment as Roman Fake." *NT* 60/1 (2018) 55–82.

Safrai, Shmuel, and Michael Avi Yonah. "Temple." In *EncJud* 19:611–16.

Sánchez Bosch, Jordi. *Escritos Paulinos.* Estella: Verbo Divino, 1998.

Schnabel, Eckhard J. "The Muratorian Fragment: The State of Research." *JETS* 57/2 (2014) 231–64.

Schweitzer, Albert. *The Quest of the Historical Jesus: A Critical Study of Its Progress from Reimarus to Wrede.* Translated by W. Montgomery. 1906. Reprint, Greenwood: Suzeteo, 2011.

Schweizer, Eduard. "The Son of Man." *JBL* 79/2 (1960) 119–29.

Sellew, Philip. "Eusebius and the Gospels." In *Eusebius, Christianity, and Judaism*, edited by Harold W. Attridge and Gohei Hata, 110–38. Leiden: Brill, 1992.

Senior, Donald. "With Swords and Clubs . . . : The Setting of Mark's Community and His Critique to Abusive Power." *BTB* 17/1 (1987) 10–20.

Skeat, T. C. "The Oldest Manuscript of the Four Gospels?" *NTS* 43/1 (1997) 1–34.

Smit, J. "Ignatius and Matthew." *NovT* 8/2 (1966) 263–83.

Sokoloff, Michael. *A Dictionary of Jewish Palestinian Aramaic of the Byzantine Period.* Ramat-Gan: Bar Ilan University Press, 1992.

Speidel, Michael P. "The Roman Army in Judaea under the Procurators: The Italian and the Augustan Cohort in the Acts of the Apostles." *Ancient Society* 13–14 (1982) 233–40.

Stanton, Graham N. "The Fourfold Gospel." *NTS* 43/3 (1997) 317–46.

Stern, Ephraim, ed. *The New Encyclopedia of Archaeological Excavations in the Holy Land V.* New York: Israel Exploration Society & Carta, 2008.

Struthers, Elizabeth. "The Jesus of Mark and the Sea of Galilee." *JBL* 103/3 (1984) 363–77.

Sutherland, C. H. V. *The Roman Imperial Coinage I: From 31 BC to AD 69*. London: Spink, 1984.

Taylor, Vincent. *The Gospel according to St. Mark: The Greek Text with Introduction, Notes, and Indexes*. Houndmills, Hampshire, UK: Macmillan, 1984.

Thayer, John Henry. *Greek-English Lexicon of the New Testament*. 1887. Reprint, London: Forgotten Books, 2018.

Tollinton, R. B. *Clement of Alexandria: A Study in Christian Liberalism*. Vol. 2. London: Williams and Norgate, 1914.

Toynbee, J. M. C. "The Shrine of St. Peter and its Setting." *JRS* 43/1 (1953) 1–26.

Treggiari, Susan. "Divorce Roman Style: How Easy and How Frequent Was It?" In *Marriage, Divorce and Children in Ancient Rome*, edited by Beryl Rawson, 31–46. Oxford: Clarendon, 1992.

Tuñí, Josep-Oriol, and Xavier Alegre. *Escritos Joánicos y Cartas Católicas*. Estella: Verbo Divino, 1995.

Turner, N. "The Style of Mark." In *The Language and Style of the Gospel of Mark: An Edition of C.H. Turner's "Notes on Marcan Usage" together with Other Comparable Studies*, edited by James Keith Elliott, 215–37. Leiden: Brill, 1993.

Udoh, Fabian E. *To Caesar What Is Caesar's: Tribute, Taxes, and Imperial Administration in Early Roman Palestine*. Providence, RI: Brown Judaic Studies, 2020.

Van Tine, R. Jarrett. "Castration for the Kingdom and Avoiding the αἰτία of Adultery (Matthew 19:10–12)." *JBL* 137/2 (2018) 399–418.

Varner, William. *Second Clement: An Introductory Commentary*. Eugene: Cascade, 2020.

Vermes, Geza. "The Use of שנ רב/אשנ רב in Jewish Aramaic." In *An Aramaic Approach to the Gospels and Acts*, by Michael Black, 310–30. Eugene, OR: Wipf & Stock, 2020.

Wacks, Mel. *The Handbook of Biblical Numismatics: 45th Anniversary Edition*. Woodland Hills: Mel Wacks, 2021.

Walsh, John Evangelist. *The Bones of Saint Peter: The Fascinating Account of the Search for the Apostle's Body*. Glasgow: Collins, 1984.

Wasserman, Tommy. "Papyrus 72 and the Bodmer Miscellaneous Codex." *NTS* 51/1 (2005) 137–54.

Westbury, Josh. "A Functional Profile of Left Dislocation in Biblical Hebrew." *SPLP* 50 (2016) 65–90.

Wilkinson, John. "The Way from Jerusalem to Jericho." *BA* 38/1 (1975) 10–24.

Wilson, C. W., and C. Warren. *The Recovery of Jerusalem: A Narrative of Exploration and Discovery in the City and the Holy Land*. 1871. Reprint, Seattle: Scholar Select, 2018.

Yarbro, Adela. "Mark and His Readers: The Son of God among Greeks and Romans." *HTR* 93/2 (2000) 85–100.

Yarbrough, Robert W. "The Date of Papias: A Reassessment." *JETS* 26/2 (1983) 181–91.

Zeichmann, Christopher B. "Loanwords or Code-Switching?: Latin Transliteration and the Setting of Mark's Composition." *JJMJS* 4 (2017) 42–64.

———. "Military Forces in Judaea 6–130 CE: The Status Quaestionis and Relevance for New Testament Studies." *CurBR* 17/1 (2018) 86–120.

Zetterholm, Marcus. *The Formation of Christianity in Antioch: A Social-Scientific Approach to the Separation Between Judaism and Christianity*. Abingdon: Routledge, 2003.

Analytical Index

In issues related to the New Testament, especially Mark, the information opened by the index can be used in substitution of a concordance. A sustained reading will also offer the reader further utility of the index with a detailed second assimilation of the monograph's subjects.

Entries to notes are preceded by number of chapter.

www.ingramcontent.com/pod-product-compliance
Lightning Source LLC
LaVergne TN
LVHW050639100826
845148LV00011B/1912

* 9 7 8 1 6 6 6 7 6 7 1 8 6 *